English law

By George D. James LLB, FCII

1983

STUDY COURSE 020

THE CII TUITION SERVICE

This is a coursebook of the CII Tuition Service
of 31 Hillcrest Road, London, E18 2JP
a division of the Education & Training Trust
of the Chartered Insurance Institute
of 20 Aldermanbury, London EC2V 7HY

ISBN 0 907323 07 3

THE AUTHOR

George James began his career in insurance with the Guardian Assurance Co. Ltd
(now part of the Guardian Royal Exchange Group), at its Preston branch in 1952, and
was resident Inspector at its Burnley office from 1956 to 1958.
From 1958 to 1978 he was employed by the Chartered Insurance Institute in various
capacities, being Principal of the Institute's College of Insurance from 1966 to 1970.
In 1978 he was appointed Director of the Chartered Institute of Loss Adjusters.
Mr James is a Bachelor of Laws of the University of London and a Fellow of the
Chartered Insurance Institute.
For over twenty years he has lectured and written on legal and insurance matters, and
he is a frequent contributor to the insurance press.

Cover illustration: Crown Copyright – reproduced with permission of the Controller of
Her Majesty's Stationery Office

Produced for the CII by Book Production Consultants,
47 Norfolk Street, Cambridge
and printed in England by
The Burlington Press (Cambridge) Limited,
Foxton, Cambridge

Contents

It is intended that books in this series will be reissued in new editions as necessary. In order to keep this process as economical as possible the system has been adopted of numbering the pages in each chapter in a separate sequence. Thus each page bears a composite number, in which the number before the stroke indicates the chapter, and the number after the stroke indicates the page within that chapter.

Introduction

1. Sources of English Law, 1/1

    1A.   The nature of English law, 1/1
    1B.   Sources of English law, 1/3
    1C.   Common law, 1/3
    1D.   Equity, 1/4
    1E.   Custom, 1/6
    1F.   The law merchant, 1/6
    1G.   Statute law, 1/7
    1H.   Delegated legislation, 1/9
    1I.   Statutory interpretation, 1/11
    1J.   EEC legislation, 1/13
    1K.   Judicial precedent and case law, 1/15
    1L.   Law reports, 1/19
    1M.   Examples of statute and case law, 1/19

2. The administration of justice – 1, 2/1

    2A.   Terminology, 2/1
    2B.   Civil courts, 2/1
    2C.   Criminal courts, 2/7
    2D.   European Court, 2/9
    2E.   Other courts, 2/9
    2F.   Administrative tribunals, 2/11
    2G.   Domestic tribunals, 2/13
    2H.   Arbitration, 2/14

3. The administration of justice – 2, 3/1

    3A.   Function and status of judges, 3/1
    3B.   The European Court, 3/3
    3C.   Magistrates, 3/3
    3D.   Other persons exercising judicial functions, 3/4
    3E.   Judicial independence and immunity, 3/5
    3F.   The jury system, 3/6
    3G.   The legal profession, 3/8
    3H.   Legal aid and advice, 3/11

4. Legal status and personality, 4/1

    4A.   Status, 4/1
    4B.   Legal personality, 4/4

5. Classification of English law, 5/1

    5A.   Distinction between civil and criminal law, 5/1
    5B.   General principles of criminal liability, 5/4
    5C.   Qualifications to criminal liability, 5/6
    5D.   Civil and criminal remedies, 5/6

Contents

6. Contract – 1, 6/1

    6A.   Privity of contract, 6/4
    6B.   Types of contract, 6/4
    6C.   Offer and acceptance, 6/6
    6D.   Consideration, 6/10
    6E.   Estoppel, 6/11
    6F.   Capacity to contract, 6/12
    6G.   Legality, 6/14
    6H.   Void, voidable and unenforceable contracts, 6/14
    6I.   Consensus ad idem, 6/15
    6J.   Assignment, 6/19

7. Contract – 2, 7/1

    7A.   Discharge of contract, 7/1
    7B.   Remedies, 7/5
    7C.   Limitation, 7/10
    7D.   Interpretation of contracts, 7/10

8. Agency, 8/1

    8A.   Creation of agency, 8/2
    8B.   Duties of an agent, 8/3
    8C.   Rights of an agent, 8/4
    8D.   Authority of an agent, 8/5
    8E.   Relationship between principal and third party, 8/6
    8F.   Relationship between agent and third party, 8/8
    8G.   Termination of agency, 8/8

9. Torts – 1, 9/1

    9A.   The nature of tortious liability, 9/1
    9B.   General conditions of tortious liability, 9/1
    9C.   General defences in tort, 9/2
    9D.   Parties to an action, 9/7
    9E.   Joint torts, 9/9
    9F.   Vicarious liability, 9/10
    9G.   Survival of actions, 9/12
    9H.   Remedies in tort, 9/12

10. Torts – 2, 10/1

    10A.   Negligence, 10/1
    10B.   Breach of statutory duty, 10/4
    10C.   Nuisance, 10/6
    10D.   Strict liability, 10/8
    10E.   Trespass to land, 10/11
    10F.   Wrongful interference with goods, 10/12
    10G.   Trespass to the person, 10/13
    10H.   False imprisonment, 10/13
    10I.   Defamation, 10/14
    10J.   Malicious falsehood, 10/16

Appendix A

Appendix B

Cases cited

List of statutes

Index

Introduction

To everyone some knowledge of the law is essential, and to lay a sound foundation it is wise to begin with general principles. It is then easier to understand any particular branch of the law that it may be necessary to study in later years.

People sometimes believe that law is a 'dry' subject to study. As a rule this is because their approach is wrong. Law is essentially a human study. With the right method law can hardly fail to be interesting, indeed it is absorbing, if only because it governs the large majority of personal relationships. Law in democratic countries provides a set of rules designed to ensure justice between every man and his fellows in all kinds of situations. A good legal system is the basis of civilised life.

A grasp of legal principles is especially valuable in insurance because a contract of insurance is first and foremost a legal document creating rights and liabilities. It is not necessary to study law to the same depth as the professional lawyer, but benefit will be gained from a knowledge of the law on which insurance must be based.

The purpose of this book *inter alia* is to give an outline of the English legal system, and a description of the main branches of English law. It begins, therefore, with an account of the sources of English law and how it has developed. This is followed by chapters on the development and present functions of the various courts, and the status and functions of those persons who are concerned with the administration of the law — judges, magistrates, juries, barristers and solicitors. The division of English law into its various main branches is then considered.

An occasional visit to a court of law will enable one to see the legal process at work. The greatest value is probably gained from a visit to a Crown Court, where within a day or perhaps less it may be possible to see and hear the whole of a trial, from the swearing of the jury to acquittal or sentence. All courts of law have public galleries, and there is no need to make advance arrangements for the visit.

Recommended reading

There are a number of books on the principles of English law. Perhaps the best is:
James, P. S., *Introduction to English Law*. Butterworth.
Also recommended is: Newton, C. R., *General principles of law*. Sweet and Maxwell.
Edition numbers are not given, because they tend very quickly to become out of date; the latest editions should be obtained.

1. Sources of English law

1A.The nature of English law
1B.Sources of English law
1C.Common law
  1C1.History of common law
1D.Equity
1E.Custom
1F.The law merchant
1G.Statute law
  1G1.The nature of statute law
  1G2.Types of legislation
  1G3.Special types of Acts
1H.Delegated legislation
1I.Statutory interpretation
1J.EEC legislation
1K.Judicial precedent and case law

1K1.History of precedent
1K2.Rules of precedent
  1K2A.Civil courts
  1K2B.Criminal courts
  1K2C.Judicial Committee
    of the Privy Council
1K3.Ratio decidendi and obiter
  dictum
1K4.Reversing, overruling,
  disapproving and distinguishing
1K5.Advantages and disadvantages
  of precedent
1L.Law reports
1M.Examples of statute and case law

A legal system is the framework within which everyone lives. Whenever people live in communities they have to find rules which are generally recognised as binding, to regulate their lives. They must also have adequate machinery to enforce those rules, for otherwise they may be ignored and a state of anarchy may develop.

Some of the rules which are given the force of law are developed from custom; others are enacted in some formal way, for example at the meeting of an assembly or parliament. The body of these rules in England is known as English law. In fact it applies to England and Wales, and also, generally, to Northern Ireland. Although Parliament can and does also enact legislation which applies to Scotland, the basic system of law in Scotland is quite different from that which applies in England, and is more akin to the legal systems of some of the Continental countries.

Public law governs the relationships between the state and individual members of the community, and between one state and another. It includes:

— constitutional law, which is concerned with such matters as the structure of the legislature, the executive and the judiciary within the state, and their relationships with one another;
— administrative law, which is concerned with ministerial and local government agencies within the state and their relationships with individuals;
— criminal law, which is dealt with in detail later.

Private law governs relationships between individuals rather than the state and individuals. It has many branches, of which the following are the most important:

— the law of contract;
— the law of torts;
— the law of trusts;
— the law of property;
— family law.

This book is concerned only with the section of public law called criminal law and, within private law, only with the law of contract and the law of torts which, for the purposes of this book, are called civil law.

1A.The nature of English law

The most important feature of any system of law is its binding force. It must be as certain as can be that a breach of the law will incur some sanction, that is, a penalty, and it is therefore necessary that there be adequate machinery for the detection of breaches of the law and the enforcement of justice. Generally, it is necessary that law should reflect the feelings of the community as to what is right and what is wrong, and to this extent it is true that law is based on morality. This argument must not be taken too far, however, because there may be many different viewpoints as to what is right and what is wrong, for example in divorce law; in such circumstances the law must try to reflect the majority view, and the minority must accept the law in the interests of good order. Nevertheless, in a democratic society any law which is not broadly in accord with public opinion can be modified or annulled by the legislative body and, to some degree, by the courts. Even in a totalitarian society the ultimate possibility of revolution ensures that the rulers do not altogether disregard the feelings of the community which they govern.

Whether or not a legal system reflects public opinion, it is essential that the system aims at certainty, so that men and women can order their affairs in the knowledge that they are acting within the law, and without the possibility that they will be held in breach of the law because a particular judge or tribunal takes a different view of what is 'just' from that which the community in general holds. This element of certainty is achieved in two ways:

— there is a strict system of binding precedent, fully discussed later in this chapter, which aims to ensure that any case which comes before a court will be treated in the same way as any earlier similar case;

— with very few exceptions, legislation operates only for the future, and is not applied to past transactions. Retroactive (or retrospective) legislation, by which Parliament makes illegal something which when it was done at some earlier time was not illegal, is looked upon with great disfavour in England, and is enacted only on the rarest occasions.

The characteristics of English law which distinguish it from other systems are:

Antiquity and continuity. English law has a long and continuous history, unlike many Continental systems.

Absence of codification. In many countries a great deal of the law has been reduced to the form of written codes which contain the whole of the law on a particular subject, but with minor exceptions, (such as the Marine Insurance Act 1906, which, when it was enacted, contained the whole of the law relating to marine insurance) this is not so in England.

Importance of the judiciary. The decisions of judges of the superior courts have had, and still have, a profound effect on the development of English law, whereas in many other countries the most important function of the judges is merely to interpret and apply statutory codes of law.

Concurrent development of the systems of common law and equity. It will be seen later that a fairly rigid set of rules of law, known as the common law, grew up, and side by side with this a supplementary set of rules, known as equity, the purpose of which was to alleviate the harshness of, and remedy defects in, the common law. At one time equity was administered only in one court, the Court of Chancery, but now, although the systems of common law and equity remain distinct, they are administered in all courts.

Absence of influence of Roman law. Many systems of law are based on Roman law, for example the modern Roman-Dutch law of South Africa, but except in Admiralty, ecclesiastical, and mercantile law, English law owes little to the Roman system. In English law a large number of Latin words and phrases are used, but this does not indicate any association with Roman law.

Widespread influence. English law is the basis of the legal systems of many parts of the world, notably the USA and many Commonwealth countries.

Independence of the judges and the legal profession. Although judges are appointed by or on the advice of the Lord Chancellor or the Prime Minister, both of whom are members of Her Majesty's Government, judges are in practice free from control by the government, as they cannot be removed before their retirement age of seventy-five without an address moved in each House of Parliament or for misconduct, something which has never happened. Judges do not hesitate in appropriate cases to give a judgment against the Crown. Similarly, barristers and solicitors are not state officials and must, in accordance with the traditions of their profession, give advice or assistance to any client, whether he be popular or not.

Contentious procedure. In English law, even in criminal cases, the court remains neutral, treating both parties as litigants with success dependent on establishing the case on law and facts. In criminal cases the prosecutor is usually the Crown, which, far from receiving any preferential treatment from the court, must establish its case beyond reasonable doubt. Contentious procedure is to be distinguished from inquisitorial procedure, under which the court does not remain neutral but plays an active part in discovering the truth. Exceptionally, the inquisitorial process is used in England in coroners' courts.

These characteristics will be dealt with in greater detail later in the book.

'English' law in general applies to England and Wales. Many Acts of the United Kingdom Parliament extend also to include Northern Ireland and/or Scotland, but in some cases Acts are passed which apply only to Northern Ireland or to Scotland. The common law of England is in many respects fundamentally different from Scots law, but some branches are largely identical, and the position of the House of Lords as the final court of appeal in civil matters assists in ensuring that in these branches English and Scots law are kept in step. Even where the principles of law are identical, the English and Scottish courts use differing terminology, but as this book is concerned only with English law, English terminology only will be used.

English law differs from many other systems in that it does not specifically give to citizens any fundamental, unchangeable, rights. It is, however, generally accepted that what has become known as the Rule of Law must always apply. This involves the following concepts:

— No man shall be punished unless he is convicted in an ordinary court of law for a definite breach of the law. (This was illustrated by an incident in 1982 when an intruder made his way into the Queen's bedroom: however reprehensible his conduct may have been considered, he was not prosecuted, as he had not committed a breach of the criminal law.)

— All men are equal before the law, and are subject to the ordinary laws and procedures of the courts. The only exception to this is the Queen in her personal capacity.

— If there has been a breach of the law, it is certain that justice will be enforced (assuming, of course, that the law-breaker is detected).

— Every person has the right to appear before the courts, which will defend his liberties and freedoms.

1B. Sources of English law

The term 'sources of English law' is used to denote several kinds of source:

Legal sources: that is, those sources recognised as such by the law itself. These include legislation, judicial precedent, custom, and EEC law, and are the subject of the bulk of this chapter.

Historical sources: that is, factors which have influenced the development of the law but which, although sources of law in fact, are not now recognised as such by the law. Examples are religious beliefs, ideas of natural justice and public policy, the opinions of eminent lawyers, and borrowings from Roman law.

Literary sources. These may be either authoritative, such as Acts of Parliament, law reports, and certain textbooks which are relied upon by judges and cited by counsel, or unauthoritative, that is, other books which may be unofficially employed to assist towards a judgment. It used to be the rule, for which it is difficult to see any justification, that no textbook by a living author could be considered to be authoritative. This rule has now been abandoned, and various modern textbooks, such as Cheshire and Fifoot on the Law of Contract, are now accepted by the courts as authoritative.

Formal sources: namely, that which gives the law its validity, which for example can be the Sovereign, the state, or the will of the people, depending on the theory of politics and law in force in any country at any particular time. In England the supreme source of law is the Queen in Parliament, that is, the House of Commons, the House of Lords, and the Queen. In practice the House of Lords has very restricted powers, and the Queen plays only a nominal part in the enactment of legislation.

There is considerable overlap between these various categories. To take one example, Acts of Parliament are both legal and literary sources.

1C. Common law

The main source of English law is the common law of England, that is, the underlying, unwritten law and general legal customs of the country. The expression common law is also used in contrast to:

— statute law, that is, Acts of Parliament;

— equity, that is, the special system of law administered only in the Court of Chancery before 1875 but now administered by all courts;

— the whole body of English law, in comparison with the systems in force in other countries.

The common law consists of the ancient customs and usages of the land, which have been recognised by the courts and given the force of law. It is in itself a complex system of law, both civil and criminal, although it is greatly modified and extended by statute law and equity. It is unwritten law, and has come down in the recorded judgments of judges who for hundreds of years have interpreted it. The judgments are reported in various authoritative records, reports, and textbooks.

Despite the existence of records, common law is still known as unwritten law, mainly to distinguish it from legislation, which is embodied in a statute or code. Common law consists of numerous more or less well-defined principles sufficiently flexible to be adapted to the cause of doing justice between the parties to a suit. It is the common law principle, rather than precise words, which is applied in deciding a case at common law, whereas if a matter is governed by statute, it is the exact words of the statute which have to be applied in arriving at a decision. The records of proceedings at common law are evidence of the principles involved, and are not applied literally to later cases.

1C1. History of common law

Although this book is not concerned with the history of law, a short digression into history is essential to show how common law developed, and how its shortcomings and weaknesses were remedied by legislation and by equity.

Although there were laws and courts in England before the Norman Conquest, it is to the period following the accession of Henry II (1154–1189) that English law as it is known today can be traced. The sending out of royal commissioners to determine lawsuits during the latter part of the twelfth century and thereafter led to the growth of a law common to the whole country. Whereas previously laws had differed widely in various parts of the country, a judge would now determine a case on the same principles in all parts of the country.

Under Edward I (1272–1307) the judges of assize began to travel round the country regularly, rather than in the uncertain and sporadic manner they had adopted during previous reigns. Although the term assize has now been dropped, the system of itinerant justices continues to this day, with courts held several times every year in regional centres throughout the country.

In order to begin proceedings in the common law courts it was necessary for a plaintiff — the party who sought a remedy or relief — to obtain an original writ, which had to be bought from the main royal office, the Chancery. The writ served two main purposes:

— it ordered the sheriff of the county, who was the chief officer of the Crown in the county, to ensure the attendance at the trial of the defendant — the person against whom the remedy or relief was sought; and

— it outlined the cause of action, that is, the legal wrong of which the plaintiff complained.

For every cause of action there was a separate writ, and these writs together formed what was known as the Register of Writs. Unless a plaintiff could bring his claim within one of the recognised writs he could not proceed with his action in the common-law courts. The Chancery officials, whose livelihood depended in part on the sale of writs, were willing enough to sell new writs to cover new causes of action, but the wealthy landowners took a different view: every new writ meant an extension of the authority of the royal courts and a corresponding diminution of the powers of the landowners themselves, who still exercised some jurisdiction in their own courts. During the reign of Henry III the landowners, under the leadership of Simon de Montfort, became sufficiently influential to secure the enactment of the Provisions of Oxford 1258, which provided that recognised writs were to be issued only by the Chancery. New writs could only be issued by the authority of the Great Council, which the barons themselves controlled. The expansion of the common law was thus effectively impeded.

In 1285 the Statute of Westminster II modified the strictness of the law laid down by the Provisions of Oxford. It empowered the clerks in Chancery to issue a new writ when the circumstances of the plaintiff were similar (*in consimili casu*) to those covered by an existing writ. The new actions which were developed as a result were known as 'actions on the case'. How far the statute assisted in the development of the common law is a matter of dispute among legal historians, but it is clear that despite the statute the common law tended to become rigid and incapable of development. This led to the growth in the system of equity.

To summarise, the deficiencies of the common law were as follows:

— The plaintiff had either to fit his action into the framework of an existing writ, or to show that it was similar to such a writ. If he could do neither he had no remedy.

— The only remedy which the common law courts could give was an award of damages. They could not order a defendant to carry out definite obligations (the remedy now known as specific performance) or require him to refrain from a particular course of conduct (the remedy now known as injunction).

— There were elaborate rules governing the procedure which had to be followed in bringing a case, and any slight breach of the rules might have left without redress a plaintiff who substantially had a good case.

— In the earlier days of the common law the courts had some discretion to use the tests of what was just and reasonable, but the law was unable to develop in this way because of the Provisions of Oxford.

1D. Equity For a time it was the practice for those who could not obtain satisfaction from the common-law courts to bring their cases before the General Eyre, which consisted of a group of royal officials representing the King who used to travel round the country at infrequent intervals to enquiry into local government matters and to see that justice was being properly administered. These officials did not consider themselves bound by the rigid rules of the common law and gave relief where appropriate to persons who had no, or inadequate, remedy at common law. They often dealt with cases of oppression or fraud where, for example, a person complained that he had been induced to enter into an agreement by fraud, a matter with which the common-law courts could not deal, as they were bound to enforce the letter of the agreement. However, the General Eyre was disliked on account of its habit of imposing heavy fines on districts because of alleged defects in administration. From about 1300 its power declined and by the reign of Richard II (1377–1399) it had disappeared.

As the Eyre declined the need for some system to remedy the defects of the common law became more apparent. It was in these circumstances that the system of equity developed.

The object of equity was to ensure something like natural justice, or a remedy for grievances for which the common law supplied no remedy. The system owes its origin to the doctrine that the King himself was not bound by the law — a doctrine which still exists — and that, as the fountain of justice, he could deal with petitions presented to him by his subjects and ensure that justice was done. Persons dissatisfied with the common law therefore began to petition the King for relief.

In practice, the King passed these petitions on to the Lord Chancellor, who was his chief minister and head of the secretarial establishment. In early days the Lord Chancellor was always an ecclesiastic ('the keeper of the King's conscience'), and as such he was more concerned with ensuring that persons carried out their moral obligations than with applying the strict letter of the law. It was on this basis that petitions were decided.

At first when the Chancellor had considered a petition he reported to the King's Council and gave his decision with the consent of the Council. Later the theory that the Chancellor was only exercising a delegated function was dropped; petitions were addressed direct to the Chancellor and dealt with solely by him. In 1474 a Court of Chancery distinct from the King's Council was formally established and was presided over by the Lord Chancellor.

The types of case with which the Court of Chancery dealt increased in the course of time and its jurisdiction became wider. It allowed the remedies of specific performance and injunction and gave relief where contracts had been entered into by mistake or induced by fraud. The whole of the law of trusts was a product of equity, and the Court of Chancery also supervised the administration of the estates of deceased persons. These are only a few of the more important matters which came within the sphere of equity.

Until the reign of Henry VIII (1509–1547) all the Chancellors were ecclesiastics, but in that reign an important innovation was made when Sir Thomas More, an eminent lawyer, was appointed Chancellor. By this time the influence of the Court of Chancery was widespread and its jurisdiction was a considerable threat to that of the common-law courts. More himself avoided conflict with the common-law judges, but in the chancellorship of Lord Ellesmere there was open conflict between the two system. The immediate cause was the result of a case heard in 1616 by Chief Justice Coke, in which the plaintiff obtained a verdict by a gross fraud. The defendant petitioned the Chancellor and obtained an injunction preventing the plaintiff from executing judgment. Coke decided that this practice of the Chancery issuing common injunctions, as they were called, had gone too far and proceedings were begun to punish the people at whose instance the injunction had been obtained. The matter was referred to the King, James I, who decided in favour of the Chancellor, and thenceforth the right of the Court of Chancery to issue injunctions was never seriously challenged.

Despite this victory for the Chancellor, equity still suffered from many defects. There was always a degree of uncertainty whether the desired relief would be granted, so that at one time it was said that 'equity varies with the length of the Chancellor's foot'. This was because equity was based primarily on conscience and was therefore too flexible and uncertain to be satisfactory.

In 1673 Lord Nottingham was appointed Chancellor, and he did much to remove the defects of equity. In particular he established the principle that the Court of Chancery was bound to follow its own precedents and that discretion was only to be used where there was no accepted existing principle on which a case could be determined. The work of Lord Nottingham was followed by that of Lord Hardwicke in the eighteenth century and by successive Lord Chancellors into the nineteenth century, so that eventually equity became a defined system administered on a settled basis.

Even in the nineteenth century, however, a great defect still remained, namely the lengthy delays which occurred in actions in Chancery, so that it was sometimes said that a person beginning an action in Chancery could not expect to live to hear the result of it. Legislation was passed with the object of reducing these delays, notably the Chancery Regulation Act 1833 and the Chancery Amendment Act 1858, the latter of which empowered the Court of Chancery to make an award of damages in lieu of an injunction or specific performance.

Finally, the Judicature Act 1873 made widespread changes in the administration of common law and equity. It provided that the principles and remedies of both could be administered in all courts concurrently instead of in separate courts as previously. It also provided that if there should be any conflict between the principles of common law and equity, the latter should prevail. This principle is now embodied in the Supreme Court Act 1981. Thus the principles of common law and equity remain distinct, but their administration by the courts has been merged. In practice, however, many of the matters which were dealt with in the old Court of Chancery have, for convenience, been allotted to the present Chancery Division of the High Court.

Equity, unlike common law, cannot stand alone. Common law is in theory a complete system of law, but equity is merely a gloss or supplement which modifies or improves the common law.

It must be emphasised that, despite its origins, equity is now a fixed body of rules in the same way as is common law, and is no more dependent on ideas of 'justice' than is common law. For example, the whole of the law of trusts was developed in the Court of Chancery, but it is no more 'equitable' (in the normal sense of the term) than is, say, the law of contract. Indeed, the main source of equity, in the non-legal sense of the term, is statute, as Parliament can always amend law which it considers to be unjust, whereas the courts are bound by the doctrine of precedent.

1E. Custom It has been noted that common law was based on customs which were applied generally throughout the country. There are, however, certain customs (sometimes rather misleadingly referred to as local customs) which by their nature can apply only to particular groups of people or in particular areas, and the term custom as a source of law is used to refer only to such customs.

A good example of a very ancient custom being recognised as having the force of law occurred as recently as 1975. In *New Windsor Corporation* v. *Mellor* a lady successfully established the right of local inhabitants to engage in sports and pastimes in an area in the centre of New Windsor. There was some evidence to show that this custom dated back to 900 A.D.

The following conditions must be fulfilled before a custom will be recognised by the courts as legally binding:

Immemorial existence. The custom must have existed since the beginning of 'legal memory', which is arbitrarily fixed as the year 1189. It will be presumed that a custom has been in existence since that year unless there is evidence to prove the contrary. In *Mercer* v. *Denne* (1905) the defendant owned part of a beach on which he wished to erect buildings. Local fishermen objected on the ground that they had a customary right to dry their nets on the land. They could prove that their right went back seventy years and probably more, and as the defendant could bring no evidence to show that the right had not been in existence since 1189 it was held that the fishermen were entitled to succeed.

Continuity. It must be proved that the custom has been observed continuously. This does not mean that the custom has been exercised continuously, merely that the right to exercise it has existed without interruption.

Reasonableness. It is a matter for the court in any particular case to decide whether a custom is reasonable.

Certainty. The right claimed must be proved to affect a defined group of people or a defined area, and the subject-matter of the custom must be definite. As was said in one case, 'If a custom is not certain it cannot be proved to have been in existence since time out of mind, for how can anything be said to have existed since time out of mind when it is not certain what it is?'

Peaceful user. The custom must have been exercised *nec per vim, nec clam, nec precario* — that is, peaceably, openly, and as of right.

Compulsion. It must be shown that the custom has been recognised by the persons concerned as binding upon all of them. For this reason, if two customs are inconsistent, neither can be recognised.

Not contrary to statute. Since statute law is supreme, it overrules any custom which is inconsistent with it.

Custom as just described is sometimes called legal custom in contradistinction from conventional custom or usage. A usage is an implied term in a contract, that is, a term which although not written into the contract is nevertheless binding. For example, in *Hutton* v. *Warren* (1836) the defendant landlord gave the plaintiff, who was the tenant of his farm, six months' notice to quit, and during the six months the plaintiff continued to work the farm in accordance with usual practice. He then sued for work and materials expended during the six months and it was held that, although there was no express agreement between the parties, he was entitled to be paid. Parke, B. said: 'It has long been settled that, in commercial transactions, extrinsic evidence of custom and usage is admissible to annex incidents to written contracts in matters with respect to which they are silent . . . this has been done upon the principle of presumption that, in such transactions, the parties did not mean to express in writing the whole of the contract by which they intended to be bound, but to contract with reference to those known usages.'

1F. The law merchant Another important source of law, although not treated as a distinct type of law, was the law merchant, from which originated, for example, much of the law relating to insurance. The law merchant was based upon mercantile customs and usages, was largely international in character, and was administered in the courts of fairs and boroughs, some known as courts of Pie Powder and some as Staple Courts, with a jury composed of merchants. As the disputes with which these courts were concerned often involved foreign merchants, they tended to be ignored by the common law courts.

From the seventeenth century onwards, however, with the development of the Court of Admiralty, the common law courts began to be more concerned with mercantile cases, and much mercantile law was incorporated into the common law. Lord Mansfield and Lord Holt, two Lord Chancellors, did much to further this development, so that in due course the law merchant became merged with common law and some parts of it were enacted as statutory codes, including, for example, the Bills of Exchange Act 1882, the Sale of Goods Act 1893 and the Marine Insurance Act 1906.

Although there is now no separate law merchant, there are two courts within the Queen's Bench Division of the High Court, the Admiralty Court and the Commercial Court, which deal largely with the types of cases which have their origins in the law merchant.

1G. Statute law

By far the most important source of law at present is statute law, otherwise known as Acts of Parliament.

1G1. The nature of statute law

Parliament is the supreme law-making body, and at least in legal theory there are no limits whatsoever to its law-making powers. In this it is different from the parliaments of many other countries, whose powers are often defined and restricted. In the USA, for example, Congress is not supreme, for two reasons. First, the American Constitution divides powers between the federal authority, which is Congress, and the individual states, and Congress has no power to interfere in matters which are within the competence of the individual states. And second, the US Supreme Court can, in appropriate circumstances, rule that legislation passed by Congress is unconstitutional, that is, outside the powers bestowed on Congress by the (written) Constitution. This could not happen in the UK, which has no written constitution. There are certain constitutional conventions to which Parliament invariably conforms, but if in passing legislation it chose to ignore a convention the courts would have no power to declare the legislation void.

Thus there are no legal limits to what Parliament can do. Acts of Parliament may create entirely new law, overrule, modify, or extend existing principles of common law and equity, and repeal or modify existing statute law.

Parliament, in anything like its present form, was unknown in the early stages of English legal history, but in the reign of Edward I a law-making authority began to develop. It consisted of the King, the feudal tenants-in-chief (forerunners of the present House of Lords), and the representatives of the shires (forerunners of the present House of Commons). Over a long period the supreme authority of Acts of Parliament was established. It became recognised that, although in the fields of common law and equity the judges had (and indeed still have) considerable powers to develop the law, in relation to Acts of Parliament their task was (and is) merely to interpret the Acts, and not to question their authority.

Parliament consists of the Monarch, the House of Lords, and the House of Commons, and, in general, legislation must be approved by both Houses of Parliament and receive the Royal Assent. In practice the Royal Assent is a mere formality — it has not been refused since the days of Queen Anne. The power of the House of Lords is very much restricted; it has virtually no powers over 'money bills', that is, legislation concerned with taxation, and its effective power over other legislation is restricted to delaying its passage for a period of one year. Real power therefore lies with the House of Commons, and particularly with the government, provided that it can command a majority in the House. It is this situation which in practice, as distinct from legal theory, sets limits on what can be done by way of legislation. The House of Commons is elected by popular vote at intervals of not more than five years, and the government consists mainly of members of the Commons. It is therefore always aware that if its legislation is not broadly acceptable to the electorate it faces defeat at the next general election.

Although statute law is supreme, it has only become of major importance within the past two hundred years, and it still forms only a small part of the total body of law.

1G2. Types of legislation

Before it becomes law an Act of Parliament is known as a Bill. Bills may be of two types, public or private, and if they pass into law become known as public or private Acts respectively.

A public Act is one which affects the whole community, whereas a private Act is passed for the benefit of an individual or group of individuals. For example, before companies could be formed under the Companies Acts a common method of forming companies (among them some of the older insurance companies) was by private Act of Parliament.

Private Bills are not to be confused with private members' Bills, which are Bills introduced by individual members rather than by the government, and which, if passed, become public Acts. Unless it has government support, a private member's Bill has virtually no chance of becoming law, because the government largely controls the timetable of the House and the subjects for debate and legislation. For all practical purposes, therefore, it is for the government to decide what legislation is to be introduced.

The normal process by which a public Bill becomes an Act is as follows below (it is here assumed that the Bill is introduced first in the House of Commons, but some Bills, simply as a matter of time-tabling convenience, go first to the House of Lords):

— There is a first reading, which is a mere formality.
— The second reading is a debate involving the whole of the House. At the end of the second reading there may be a vote, and if the Bill is rejected that is the end of the matter. Very often there is no vote at all at this stage, as a vote is not required unless at least 20 members of the House object to the Bill.
— The next stage is known as the committee stage. The Bill is examined clause by clause, perhaps word by word, by a standing committee of the House. At any given time there are a number of standing committees, each dealing with different Bills.
— The Bill as amended by the committee is 'reported' to the House as a whole.
— The final stage is the third reading, which offers a further opportunity for general debate.
— Assuming that the Bill survives all these stages in the House of Commons, it then goes through a similar procedure in the House of Lords, and if successful there, receives the Royal Assent and thus becomes an Act.
— Unless otherwise stated in the Act itself, an Act comes into force immediately it receives the Royal Assent.

If a public Bill has not completed all its stages during a particular session of Parliament, or when Parliament is dissolved, it lapses, and must start its passage anew during the next session or be dropped entirely. This does not apply to private Bills, the passage of which may straddle two or even more sessions. A notable example of this was the Lloyd's Act 1982, which was introduced in October 1980 and was not completed until July 1982.

1G3. Special types of Acts

Codifying Acts

A codifying Act involves the enactment of the whole of the law on a particular subject, including all existing statute and case law, with or without amendment. There is no legal reason why virtually the whole of English law should not be codified. The Sale of Goods Act 1979 and the Marine Insurance Act 1906 are examples of codifying Acts, which mean that it is necessary to look no further back than 1979 and 1906 to discover the whole of the existing law relating to the sale of goods and marine insurance respectively.

Although it may appear useful to have all the law on a particular subject encapsulated into a single Act, some areas of law are by their nature extremely complex, and codification in itself does not make them easier to understand. Further, the methods of legal interpretation employed in English courts involve the accretion of a body, sometimes a very large body, of decided cases which must be consulted to discover the interpretation put on an Act, codifying or otherwise, by the courts. And, of course, Parliament may pass further legislation supplementing or modifying the code.

The existence of a permanent Law Commission, which was established by the Law Commission Act 1965 to consider and suggest amendments to particular areas of law which might be referred to it from time to time, may result in a greater degree of codification in the future. There is a possibility, for example, that in the not-too-distant future the Commission will present detailed proposals for the codification of the law of contract. One difficulty here, however, is that so much of the time of Parliament is occupied with current political, social, economic, and fiscal matters that governments are never very keen to allocate sufficient time to deal with what is sometimes referred to as 'lawyers' law'.

Consolidating Acts

A consolidating Act is one which draws together and re-enacts all the statute law on a subject, including, where appropriate, statutory regulations. Two examples of such Acts are the Factories Act 1961, which re-enacted the Factories Acts 1937–1959 and various other Acts affecting factories, and the National Insurance Act 1965, which re-enacted the law relating to national insurance, including certain statutory instruments.

A consolidating Act differs from a codifying Act in that it applies only to statute law, whereas a codifying Act applies to all the law on a particular subject. Furthermore, a consolidating Act as such creates no change in the law; it merely makes it easier to find. A consolidating Act, however, is similar to a codifying Act in that it is by no means the last word on the subject, for it may be subject to extension, modification or repeal. For example, a number of Acts relating to the supervision of insurance, the first dating from 1909, were eventually absorbed into a consolidating Act, the Insurance Companies Act 1958, which at the time it was passed included all the legislation relating to insurance supervision. However, since that date so much new legislation on the subject was passed that the 1958 Act became obsolete and has now been replaced by a new consolidating Act, the Insurance Companies Act 1982.

Retroactive (or retrospective) legislation

It has been mentioned that the normal rule is that, unless otherwise specifically stated, an Act comes into force immediately it receives the Royal Assent. Retroactive, sometimes called retrospective, legislation is legislation which affects acts done, or rights acquired, before it came into effect. As a general rule Parliament, and public opinion, dislike retroactive legislation as it offends against the principle that it is unjust that a person who orders his affairs in a way which is within the law should later find that what he has done is deemed to be contrary to law. There are, however, two sets of circumstances in which retroactive legislation is considered to be justified:

Firstly, sometimes, particularly in time of war or national emergency, a person may do something which is strictly illegal but which, in the special circumstances, is seen to have been done in the best interests of the community. In such circumstances Parliament may pass an Indemnity Act, legalising the action which, at the time it was taken, was illegal.

Secondly, there are occasions where people, in full knowledge of what the law is, exploit loopholes in it, knowing that they are acting against the spirit, although perhaps not the letter, of the law. The most typical cases are those involving tax-avoidance. Here Parliament may either change the law to plug the loopholes for the future, or if the avoidance has been blatant, change the law with retrospective effect. It should perhaps be added that there are those who consider that even in these circumstances retroactive legislation is unjust, on the ground that Parliament is wholly responsible for passing legislation, and that if the legislation is defective it ought not to complain if people turn the defects to their own advantage.

1H. Delegated legislation

It has become a common practice for Acts of Parliament to confer on persons or bodies, particularly Ministers of the Crown in charge of government departments, power to make rules and regulations for specified purposes. Acts which confer such power are called parent or enabling Acts, and rules made under the authority of such Acts are known as delegated or subordinate legislation. Delegated legislation has the same legal force as the enabling Act. The most important types of delegated legislation are as follows:

Orders in Council. An Order in Council is drafted by a Minister, but cannot come into force until it has been approved by a meeting of the Queen in Council, that is, a meeting at which at least three Privy Councillors are present. The meeting is a formality.

Rules and regulations. Rules and regulations are made by Ministers of the Crown and government departments acting in accordance with the provisions of enabling Acts.

Bye-laws. Statutory authority may be given to certain bodies, particularly local authorities, to make bye-laws which are of local application.

Statutory instruments. These comprise several types of delegated legislation. It is not necessary for the purpose of this book to list them.

In quantitative terms, a Parliamentary session now produces far more delegated legislation than Acts of Parliament, and the use of delegated legislation is growing. The main reasons are that:

—the enabling statutes very often deal with highly complex technical matters. An example is the Insurance Companies Act 1982, under which a mass of detailed regulations must be made, requiring technical skills and knowledge which few, if any, members of Parliament possess;

—even if members of Parliament had the necessary expertise, Parliament does not have the time to deal with the precise details of all legislation;

—delegated legislation is more flexible than primary legislation. If an Act of Parliament is found to be defective it can be altered only by the passing of an amendment Act which has to go through the full Parliamentary process. A statutory instrument which proves to be unsuitable can be amended or repealed by another statutory instrument.

—delegated legislation can be put into force more speedily. The Parliamentary procedure for enacting Bills is slow (although there are occasions on which, in times of emergency, Parliament is able to pass legislation very quickly);

—Parliament, at the time of passing an Act, may not be able to foresee all the problems which may arise in connection with it. Delegated legislation can deal with such problems as and when they arise.

There are, however a number of disadvantages of delegated legislation as follows:

—Parliamentary control over legislation is reduced, despite the powers of control which are mentioned below;

—arguably, there is far too much delegated legislation, so that it is difficult to know what the law is at any particular time. Most Acts of Parliament are readily brought to the notice of lawyers, and even to the notice of the public if they are of general importance, whereas very little publicity is given to delegated legislation;

—despite the assumption, mentioned below, that delegated legislation does not confer powers of sub-delegation, in some cases sub-delegation is allowed. In an extreme case, there may be an enabling Act under which regulations may be made; orders made pursuant to the regulations; and directions made under the orders. In such circumstances the only legislation which is under the control of Parliament is the enabling Act and the regulations directly made under it.

Since delegated legislation gives wide powers to a variety of people and bodies, it is important that both the courts and Parliament take every reasonable step to ensure that there is no abuse of the powers conferred.

So far as the courts are concerned, their most important weapon of control is the *ultra vires* (beyond the powers of) rule. The person or body with power to make delegated legislation must ensure that the rules and regulations made are strictly within the powers conferred by the enabling Act. If they are not, the courts will declare them void. There are certain general rules which the courts apply to determine whether or not delegated legislation is *ultra vires*. It is assumed that the enabling Act, unless it contains clear words to the contrary:

—does not confer power to make unreasonable or uncertain rules;

—does not confer any power of sub-delegation. For example, it is assumed that where powers are conferred on a Minister he cannot delegate them to anyone else;

—does not confer power to make retroactive rules;

—does not confer power to infringe fundamental rights, such as the right of personal liberty;

—does not confer power to make rules levying taxes.

The courts can also declare delegated legislation to be *ultra vires* if the person on whom a power has been bestowed has failed to carry out a prescribed procedure, for example, if he has not consulted interested parties before putting the legislation into force.

Parliament also exercises control over delegated legislation:

—The enabling legislation is passed by Parliament, which therefore can determine the desirability or otherwise of delegating any particular power.

—All delegated legislation is subject to one or other of certain Parliamentary procedures. The enabling Act may provide that the delegated legislation must be laid before Parliament for forty days before it comes into effect, and during this period either House may pass a resolution to annul it. In practice, such power is not so strong as it may appear, because the sheer weight of delegated legislation makes it difficult for members of Parliament to scrutinise it in the way they would wish, and the government is under no obligation to debate it. In other cases, an instrument must first be laid before Parliament, which therefore knows of its existence, but has no power to change it. Yet another possibility is that each House of Parliament must pass a resolution approving the instrument, in which case the government must find time for it to be debated, otherwise it will not become law. Often there is no apparent reason why a particular procedure is prescribed.

—Some statutory instruments cannot continue in force unless both Houses of Parliament pass a resolution allowing them to continue to exist.

—Some enabling Acts provide that the person to whom power is delegated must consult interested parties before making delegated legislation. In practice, consultation is common whether or not the enabling Act provides for it. For example, there is close consultation between the Department of Trade and such bodies as the British Insurance Association before regulations are made under Insurance Companies Acts.

—There is a Joint Committee of the House of Lords and the House of Commons which considers:

(*a*) every instrument which is laid before each House of Parliament, being:

(i)   a statutory instrument or a draft thereof or scheme requiring approval by statutory instrument;

(ii)   any other instrument where the proceedings in pursuance of an Act of Parliament are proceedings by way of an affirmative resolution; or

(iii)   An order subject to special Parliamentary procedure.

(*b*) every general statutory instrument not within the above classes and not required to be laid before or to be subject to proceedings in the House of Commons only, with a view to determining whether the special attention of the Houses should be drawn to the legislation on various grounds. The grounds are that the legislation:

(i)   imposes a tax on the public;

(ii)   is made in pursuance of an enactment containing special provisions excluding it from challenge in the courts;

(iii)   purports to have retrospective effect where there is no express authority in the enabling statute;

(iv)   has been unduly delayed in publication or in laying before Parliament;

(v)   has come into operation before being laid before Parliament and there has been unjustifiable delay in informing the Speaker of the delay;

(vi)   it is of doubtful validity or makes some unusual or unexpected use of the powers conferred by the enabling statute;

(vii)   calls for any special reason for elucidation;

(viii)   is defective in its drafting.

—There is a House of Commons Select Committee on statutory instruments which considers legislation which is to be laid before and subject to proceedings in the House of Commons only.

—There is a Standing Committee of the House of Commons which considers the merits of statutory instruments and draft statutory instruments which are referred to them.

1I. Statutory interpretation

The function of the courts, in relation to both primary and subordinate legislation, is to interpret and apply it; they have no discretion to refuse to apply it even if they feel that it is unjust or causes hardship in any particular case. When legislation is drafted by Parliamentary draftsmen great care is taken to ensure that there is no room for doubt as to the meaning of the legislation, and that it contains no ambiguity. To assist those who may be affected by them, and also to assist the courts, Acts of Parliament often contain an 'interpretation' section in which words and phrases used in the Acts are defined. In addition, all Acts are governed by the Interpretation Act 1889, which lays down certain rules of interpretation which apply generally. For example, it provides that 'words in the singular shall include the plural and words in the plural shall include the singular'. Such general rules may, however, be excluded by the express provisions of a particular Act.

In *Hutton* v. *Esher Urban District Council* (1973) the council had power to construct a public sewer 'in, on or over any land . . .' and proposed to demolish the plaintiff's house so that it could build a sewer. The plaintiff argued that the word 'land' did not include a house. His argument was, however, unsuccessful, as the Interpretation Act 1889 provides that the term 'land' includes 'messuages, tenements and hereditaments, houses and buildings of any tenure.'

The final statute or statutory instrument should be absolutely clear, so that the task of the judges in applying it should present no problem. This is, however, a counsel of perfection, and in practice ambiguities do creep in, so that it has become necessary for the courts in such circumstances to devise rules of interpretation. There are three rules: the 'literal' rule; the 'golden' rule; and the 'mischief' rule.

The literal rule

The literal rule is the primary rule which takes precedence over the others. Words and phrases should be construed by the courts in their ordinary sense, and the ordinary rules of grammar and punctuation should be applied. If, applying this rule, a clear meaning appears, then this must be applied, and the courts will not inquire whether what the statute says represents the intention of the legislature: 'The intention of Parliament is not to be judged by what is in its mind, but by the expression of that mind in the statute itself.'

The literal rule is strongly criticised by many lawyers. It has been said to be '. . . a rule against using intelligence in understanding language. Anyone who in ordinary life interpreted words literally, being indifferent to what the speaker or writer meant, would be regarded as a pedant, a mischief-maker or an idiot.' Such criticism, it is submitted, is misguided. For example, the Hotel Proprietors Act 1956 provides that in certain circumstances an hotel proprietor is liable for loss of or damage to guests' property, but that this liability does not usually extend to guests' motor vehicles or property left 'therein'. The question arises — is the hotel proprietor liable for property left *on*, rather than *in*, a vehicle, for example, on a roofrack. On a literal interpretation, the hotel proprietor is liable, because if Parliament had intended to exclude property left on a vehicle, the Act would have said 'therein or thereon'. The 'commonsense' school would say that it is ridiculous to make a distinction between property left in or on a vehicle. That may be so in the admittedly trivial example given, but if this line of argument is accepted, it means that the courts would have power to rewrite Acts of Parliament, which many people would consider to be highly dangerous, particularly where it takes the form of assuming that Parliament 'intended' something, when in truth it is more than likely that Parliament never gave the matter a moment's thought. It is better that the courts interpret statutes strictly, and if this leads to unsatisfactory or inequitable results, then Parliament should pass amending legislation to indicate clearly what its intention was.

The full force of the literal rule was demonstrated in the case of *Whitely* v. *Chappell* (1869). The defendant had voted in the name of a person who had died, but was found not guilty of the offence of personating 'any person entitled to vote': a dead person is not entitled to vote.

The literal rule involves two subsidiary rules. The first is the *noscitur a sociis* rule, a high-sounding rule which simply means that the meaning of a word must be determined by its context. For example, the word 'ring' has no specific meaning in isolation, but its meaning becomes clear in a context such as 'ring the bell', or 'he bought her an engagement ring'.

The second subsidiary rule is the *ejusdem generis* rule, which is that the meaning of any general term is dependent on any specific terms which precede it. A good example is the Betting Act 1853, which prohibited the keeping of a 'house, office, room or other place' for the purposes of betting. How wide is the term 'or other place' in this context? The term is so vague that it is impossible to say, but in *Powell* v. *Kempton Park Racecourse Co.* (1899) it was held that it did not include Tattersall's ring at a racecourse; the specific places mentioned in the Act — house, office, room — are all indoors, whereas Tattersall's ring is not.

The golden rule

Where the meaning of words in a statute, if strictly applied, would lead to an absurdity, the golden rule is that the courts are entitled to assume that Parliament did not intend such absurdity, and they will construe the Act to give it the meaning which Parliament intended. So, for example, the Offences Against the Person Act 1861 provided that 'whosoever being married *shall marry another person* during the life of the *former* husband or wife' is guilty of bigamy. Interpreted literally, this definition is absurd on two counts. First, the phrase 'shall marry another person' is meaningless in the context, as the essence of bigamy is that a married person cannot marry again while his first marriage subsists. Secondly, the reference to a 'former' husband or wife is quite inappropriate. The word 'former' suggests that the original marriage no longer exists, but if that were the case the person marrying again would not be guilty of bigamy. Despite the slipshod draftsmanship of the Act, however, the intention was clear, and the courts have interpreted the relevant section as meaning that a person who purports to marry another while his or wife or husband is still alive is guilty of bigamy.

The mischief rule

When it is not clear whether an act falls within what is prohibited by a particular piece of legislation, the judges can apply the mischief rule. This means that the courts can take into account the reasons why the legislation was passed; what 'mischief' the legislation was designed to cure, and whether the act in question fell within the 'mischief'. For example, the Street Offences Act 1959 made it an offence for a prostitute to solicit men 'in a street or public place'. In *Smith* v. *Hughes* the question was whether a woman who had tapped on a balcony and hissed at men passing by was guilty of an offence under the Act. Parker, L.C.J., found her guilty: 'I approach the matter by considering what is the mischief aimed at by this Act. Everybody (*sic*) knows that this was an Act intended to clean up the streets, to enable people to walk along the streets without being molested or solicited by common prostitutes. Viewed in that way, it can matter little whether the prostitute is soliciting while in the street or standing in a doorway or on a balcony'.

In the case mentioned, it was comparatively easy to apply the mischief rule as the circumstances which caused the passing of the Act were well known. The rule does, however, have limitations as it is by no means always easy to discover the 'mischief' at which a particular Act was aimed.

The rules of interpretation discussed above do not apply to the interpretation of EEC legislation. The European Communities Act 1972 provides that questions of interpretation of EEC law must be decided in accordance with the principles laid down by any relevant decision of the European Court. Therefore, although EEC legislation has the force of law in England and thus becomes part of English law, the courts cannot interpret it by the methods which they apply to the main body of English law.

In interpreting statutes, the courts make certain presumptions:

(a)   that the statute is not intended to have retrospective effect;

(b)   that it applies only to the United Kingdom;

(c)   that it is not intended to interfere with existing vested rights;

(d)   that the property of any person will not be confiscated without compensation;

(e)   that there is no intention to interfere with existing contractual rights;

(f)   that there is no intention to interfere with personal liberty;

(g)   that any person to whom judicial or quasi-judicial power is given will exercise such power in accordance with the rules of natural justice;

(h)   that the statute is not intended to derogate from the requirements of international law.

Any of these presumptions may be overruled by the precise words of the statute.

Private Acts (but not public Acts) always have a preamble which sets out the objects of the legislation. Preambles can on occasion be of considerable assistance to the courts in interpreting the Acts.

1J. EEC legislation

It is necessary to deal with EEC legislation at some length, not only because it is now an important source of English law, but also because it is surrounded by misunderstandings and misconceptions. It is also necessary to state the obvious: that this section, indeed this whole book, is concerned solely with law, and not at all with politics. A great deal of discussion regarding the EEC is conducted on a political level, but this section is concerned only with the legal consequences of UK membership of the EEC.

At the outset it must be stated that the term 'EEC legislation' is a misnomer. There are in fact three European Communities: the European Economic Community (the EEC), the European Coal & Steel Community (the ECSC), and the European Community of Atomic Energy (Euratom). In Brussels in 1972 the UK was one of the prospective members who signed a Treaty of Accession agreeing to join the three communities and accepting all their rules.

However, despite the existence of the three communities, all of them share four common institutions: the Assembly (now called the European Parliament), the Commission, the Council, and the Court of Justice.

In practice, therefore, it is possible for the purposes of this book to treat the Communities as one, and in deference to popular usage the singular term Community and the expression EEC legislation will here be used.

Following the signature of the Treaty of Accession in 1972, the European Communities Act 1972 was passed and the UK became a member of the EEC as from 1 January 1973. This involved acceptance of the facts:

—that certain legislation not passed by the UK Parliament would become part of the law of the UK;

—that the UK Parliament would be obliged to enact as English law some decisions made by Community institutions, without being at liberty to alter them in substance or to reject them; and

—that this legislation must be interpreted in accordance with Community rules rather than in accordance with traditional English principles.

Article 89 of the European Economic Community Treaty, better known as the Treaty of Rome, provides that in order that the Council and the Commission can carry out their tasks they shall:

—make regulations which shall have general application. Such regulations are binding in their entirety and are directly applicable to all member states;

—issue directives which are binding on the member states to which they are addressed as regards the results to be achieved. The choice of form or method, however, is left to the member state;

—issue decisions which are binding upon those to whom they are addressed;

—offer recommendations and opinions which have no binding force.

Section 2 of the European Communities Act 1972 provides that:

—all rights, powers, liabilities, obligations, and restrictions created under the Treaties and all remedies and procedures which from time to time are provided shall, without further enactment, be given legal effect in the UK;

—Her Majesty by Order in Council and a designated Minister of the Crown or Government department may, by regulations, make provisions for:
—implementing any Community obligation of the UK; or
—enabling to be implemented any rights to be enjoyed by the UK. The person exercising this power shall have regard to the objects of the Communities;
—the amounts required to meet Community obligations or to make payments to any member state are to be met out of the consolidated fund (all revenue collected for the national exchequer) or, if the Treasury so determines, the national loan fund. Sums received by virtue of the treaty arrangements are paid into the consolidated fund or, if the Treasury so directs, into the national loan fund, save for any sums required for disbursements under any other enactment. Expenses incurred by a Minister of the Crown or Government department by virtue of the treaties are met out of money provided by Parliament.

Section 3 of the Act provides as follows:
—any question arising in litigation as to the meaning or effect of the treaties, or of a Community instrument, if not being answered in a European Court, shall be determined in accordance with European Court principles;
—judicial notice shall be taken of the treaties. This means simply that judges in UK courts shall recognise the treaty enactments as though they were statutes created by the UK Parliament;
—if a document or instrument issued by a Community institution is required for litigation in the UK courts a copy of such a document or instrument certified by an official of the Council or Commission must be accepted in evidence;
—evidence may also be by way of production of a Queen's printer's copy of a document or instrument or by a copy held by a Government department.

Where a question of the interpretation of some provision of a European treaty arises in a case being dealt with by an English court and there is no appeal from that court (as in the case with, say, the House of Lords), the court must refer the question to the European Court of Justice for a ruling. The decision of the European Court must be accepted by the English court.

Where there is a clear conflict between English law and Community law, the courts must apply Community law. For example, in *Schorsch Meier Gmbh* v. *Hennin* (1975) the question arose whether the English courts could give judgment in a foreign currency. In an earlier case the House of Lords had ruled that they could not, but Article 106 of the EEC Treaty requires the English courts to give judgment in favour of a creditor who is a subject of a member state in the currency of that state. The Court of Appeal ruled that Article 106 overruled the House of Lords decision so far as cases involving EEC countries are concerned.

It is sometimes said that, because the UK is now part of the EEC, and because therefore the UK is bound by Community regulations and directives irrespective of the will of the UK Parliament, Parliament has surrendered some degree of its sovereignty. This assertion requires close examination, and the five following points should be considered:
—The bulk (some 90 per cent) of Community law is concerned with the administration of the Common Agricultural Policy, and is trivial in the extreme. It therefore does not justify close scrutiny, and such scrutiny as may be necessary can be carried out by the European Parliament.
—The EEC has a directly elected Parliament in which the UK itself is fully represented. The EEC Parliament is not a law-making body, but it has supervisory powers over the Commission, including the ultimate power of calling for the resignation of the entire Commission.
—The Commission consists of fourteen Commissioners, two of whom are British.
—The Council is composed of one representative of each member state. All major proposals for Community legislation must be unanimously approved by the Council, and in an extreme case the UK member could use his right of veto to prevent proposals from becoming law.
—The UK Parliament has devised a system whereby all proposals for major Community legislation are debated in the UK Parliament before they come before the Council of Ministers. The British representative on the Council is therefore well aware of the attitude of the UK towards the proposed legislation and it is inconceivable that he would ignore the wishes of Parliament in his negotiations with the other members of the Council. This consideration, together with the power of veto, ensures that legislation is not passed against the expressed wish of the UK Parliament.

These are the practical considerations, but in addition the strictly legal position must be considered. As mentioned earlier in this chapter, Parliament has 'the right to make or unmake any law whatever', and this position has been in no way altered by Britain's membership of the EEC. The reasons for this are:

— The only reason why Community law has become enforceable in the UK is that the sovereign Parliament, by the European Communities Act 1972, decreed that it should do so.

— As has been said by an eminent judge, 'If the Queen in Parliament were to make laws which were in conflict with this country's obligations under the Treaty of Rome, those laws, and not the conflicting provisions of the Treaty, would be given effect to as the domestic law of the UK.'

— The power of Parliament to repeal the European Communities Act 1972 remains unfettered. It is this factor which establishes beyond question that the sovereignty of Parliament remains unimpaired. If the 1972 Act were repealed the UK would leave the EEC and in so doing would commit breaches of treaties by which it has agreed to be bound. The possibility that this might happen lies in the realms of politics rather than law, and so requires no further discussion here.

1K. Judicial precedent and case law

In order fully to understand the effect of judicial precedent and case law as sources of law, it is necessary to anticipate a topic which will be dealt with fully in later chapters, namely the hierarchy of civil and criminal courts.

Civil courts

The majority of minor civil cases are dealt with by the County Courts. More serious cases are heard in the first instance by one or other of the three divisions of the High Court. Appeals from both the County Court and the High Court are dealt with by the Court of Appeal – Civil Division, and subject to certain stringent conditions there may be a further appeal to the House of Lords, which is the final court of appeal.

Criminal courts

Minor offences are dealt with by magistrates' courts, from which there may be an appeal to the Crown Court or High Court. More serious offences are dealt with at first instance, after a preliminary enquiry in the magistrates' court, by the Crown Court, from which there may be an appeal to the Court of Appeal – Criminal Division. As with civil cases, but subject to even more stringent conditions, there may be a further appeal to the House of Lords.

1K1. History of precedent

Precedents, that is, decisions in previous similar cases, have for many hundreds of years been important in the development of English law, but until the latter part of the nineteenth century were only persuasive; that is, a judge would be influenced by the decision in a previous case, but did not consider himself bound by it. The modern doctrine of precedent, under which a judge is bound by the decision in a previous case, even if he considers it to be unjust or illogical, is of comparatively modern origin.

In the early days of common law, judges considered that their judgments were merely declaratory; common law was based on general custom, and they were merely enunciating what that custom was. This attitude left no room for the development of a doctrine of precedent. In any event, there was no method of recording judgments fully and accurately.

The development of printing and the improvement in the standards of reporting meant that from the sixteenth century onwards more attention was paid to decisions in previous cases. By the early nineteenth century it had been accepted that regard must be paid to previous decisions and that it was not for the courts 'to reject them and abandon all analogy to them'. Later in the nineteenth century two events occurred which laid the groundwork for the establishment of the system of binding precedent:

— in 1865 the Council of Law Reporting was created, and this ensured that for the future there would be a consistent and reliable system of reporting cases. There had been many earlier series of reports, but their reliability varied considerably;

— the whole system of courts was reorganised by the Judicature Acts 1873–1875 and the Appellate Jurisdiction Act 1876, and this made easier the task of recognising the hierarchy of courts.

1K2. Rules of precedent

The present rules relating to judicial precedent are as follows:

1K2A. Civil courts

House of Lords

In *London Street Tramways Co.* v. *L.C.C.* (1898) the House of Lords ruled that it was bound by its own decisions. This meant that a decision of the House could be overruled only by legislation. In 1966, however, a statement was issued by the Lord Chancellor on behalf of the House of Lords. It is worth quoting in full, as it indicates both the importance and the limitations of precedent as a source of law:

Their Lordships regard the use of precedent as an indispensable foundation upon which to decide what is the law and its application to individual cases. It provides at least some degree of certainty upon which individuals can rely in the conduct of their affairs, as well as a basis for orderly development of legal rules. Their Lordships nevertheless recognise that too rigid adherence to precedent may lead to injustice in a particular case and also unduly restrict the proper development of the law. They propose, therefore, to modify their present practice and, while treating former decisions of this House as normally binding, to depart from a previous decision when it appears right to do so. In this connection they will bear in mind the danger of disturbing retrospectively the basis on which contracts, settlements of property and fiscal arrangements have been entered into and also the especial need for certainty as to the criminal law . . . This announcement is not intended to affect the use of precedent elsewhere than in this House.

The House of Lords is therefore not bound by its own decisions, but its decisions are binding on all lower courts.

The House of Lords hears appeals in civil cases from both the English and the Scottish courts. Where the principles of English and Scots law are the same (as they are, for example, in the law of torts (called delict in Scotland) but not generally in the law of contract) a decision in an English case is binding on the Scottish courts and *vice versa*. A number of very important principles of English law are in fact derived from appeals to the House of Lords in Scottish cases.

Court of Appeal – Civil Division

A decision of the Court of Appeal – Civil Division is binding on all inferior courts and on itself. The court is bound by decisions of the House of Lords.

The rule that the Court of Appeal is bound by its own previous decisions was fully discussed in *Young* v. *Bristol Aeroplane Co. Ltd* (1944), in which it was laid down that the general rule is subject to the following qualifications:

— Where there are previous inconsistent decisions of the Court of Appeal, the court may follow either of the previous decisions, in which case the other is overruled.

— Where a previous decision of the Court of Appeal has been overruled by the House of Lords, it must follow the decision of the House of Lords rather than its own previous decision.

— The Court of Appeal need not follow its own previous decision where it was reached *per incuriam*, that is, as a result of some error. For example, in arriving at the previous decision the court may have overlooked the existence of some statutory provision.

A decision of the Court of Appeal – Criminal Division is not binding on the Civil Division.

High Court

A decision of the High Court is binding on inferior courts, but does not bind the High Court itself: it is of persuasive influence only. It is therefore possible for there to exist two or more conflicting High Court decisions. The only way to solve the problem thus created is to take a case to the Court of Appeal. The High Court is itself bound by decisions of the House of Lords and of the Court of Appeal.

County Court

The County Court is bound by all decisions of the higher courts, but its own decisions never create precedents.

1K2B.Criminal courts

House of Lords

As in civil cases, the House of Lords is not bound by its own previous decisions, but its decisions are binding on all lower courts.

Court of Appeal – Criminal Division

A decision of the Court of Appeal – Criminal Division is binding on all lower courts. In general it can overrule its own previous decision given against a defendant, but not in his favour. However, a 'full court' (of five judges) can overrule a previous decision of an ordinary court. The court is not bound by decisions of the Court of Appeal – Civil Division, but it is bound by decisions of the House of Lords.

In *R* v. *Gould* (1968) the defendant was convicted of bigamy when he went through a ceremony of marriage in the mistaken belief that a decree *nisi* of divorce in respect of his former marriage had been made absolute. Although in an earlier case the Court of Criminal Appeal had held that a reasonable belief in the dissolution of a previous marriage was no defence, his appeal against conviction was allowed. In giving judgment Diplock, L.J. said that in its criminal jurisdiction the Court of Appeal does not apply the doctrine of precedent as rigidly as in its civil jurisdiction, and if it is of the opinion that the law has been misapplied or misunderstood it will depart from a previous decision.

Where, in a criminal matter, an appeal lies direct from the Divisional Court of the Queen's Bench Division of the High Court to the House of Lords, the Divisional Court is not bound by the decisions of the Court of Appeal – Criminal Division.

Crown Court

A decision of the Crown Court is not binding, but is of persuasive influence. The court is bound by decisions of the House of Lords and of the Court of Appeal – Criminal Division.

Magistrates' courts

Magistrates' courts are bound by the decisions of higher courts, except that they are not bound by the decisions of the Crown Court hearing appeals from magistrates' courts. Cases heard in the magistrates' courts never create precedents.

1K2C. Judicial Committee of the Privy Council

The Judicial Committee of the Privy Council is the final court of appeal from some Commonwealth countries and colonies, from ecclesiastical and prize courts, and from the Channel Islands and the Isle of Man. Strictly it is not within the system of English courts, but the majority of the members who hear appeals are the Lords of Appeal who perform the appellate functions of the House of Lords. It is for this reason that judgments of the Privy Council receive so much respect in English courts and are regarded as persuasive precedents which will be followed unless there is some cogent reason for departing from them. The importance of the Privy Council has been eroded in recent years as some countries have left the Commonwealth and others, while remaining in the Commonwealth, have decided to establish their own supreme courts from which there is no appeal. The Privy Council is not bound by its own previous decisions.

1K3. Ratio decidendi and obiter dictum

So far as the parties to any particular case are concerned, all that matters is the judge's decision; he gives judgment either for the plaintiff or for the defendant and that, subject to any right of appeal which may exist, is an end of the matter. In delivering judgment, however, the judge gives reasons for his decisions, and it is these reasons which may be important as precedents in future cases. No two cases which come before the courts are exactly alike, and to discover whether there is a binding precedent it is necessary to establish the *ratio decidendi*, that is, the exact reason or reasons for the decision. It is the *ratio decidendi* alone which is binding for the future.

There are various views as to the precise meaning of the phrase *ratio decidendi*, but for present purposes it is enough to say that it means the legal principle on which the decision rests. Any statement made by the judge which is not essential to his decision is not part of the *ratio decidendi* and therefore not binding for the future. It is known as *obiter dictum,* which may or may not have persuasive influence in future cases.

A good example of both *ratio decidendi* and *obiter dictum* is to be found in the judgment in the most famous of all insurance law cases, *Castellain* v. *Preston* (1883) which was concerned with the principle of indemnity in relation to a policy of fire insurance. A passage from the judgment reads:

> The very foundation, in my opinion, of every rule which has been applied to insurance law is this, namely, that the contract of insurance contained in a marine or fire policy is a contract of indemnity, and of indemnity only, and that this contract means that the insured, in case of a loss against which the policy has been made, shall be fully indemnified, but shall never be more than fully indemnified.

The only principle which this case laid down was that a policy of fire insurance is a policy of indemnity. That was all that was in issue, and the words 'a marine or' were *obiter dicta.* In fact the reference to marine insurance in this particular case would not have to be relied upon even as a persuasive precedent in future cases relating to marine insurance, as the proposition that a policy of marine insurance is a policy of indemnity was settled law well before *Castellain.* On the other hand, it is a persuasive precedent so far as newer classes of property insurance, such as theft, are concerned.

In cases heard in the House of Lords and in the Court of Appeal, there may be more than one *ratio decidendi* given. For example, three judges of the Court of Appeal may come to the same result, that is, they may all be agreed that the appeal should be allowed or dismissed, but each judge may give different reasons. This is even more likely to happen in the House of Lords, where there are usually five judges. In such circumstances, it cannot be said that any particular precedent has been created, and the law thus remains in a state of uncertainty.

1K4. Reversing, overruling, disapproving and distinguishing

Once a legal principle has been stated as the *ratio decidendi* of a case it stands until it is reversed or overruled. Alternatively, although not reversed or overruled, it may be disapproved or distinguished.

Reversing. A case is reversed when it is taken on appeal to a higher court, say from the High Court to the Court of Appeal, and the higher court allows the appeal, in which case the original judgment is of no legal effect whatever.

Overruling. A case is overruled when, in a later case, a higher court decides a similar matter on a different principle, thus nullifying the *ratio decidendi* in the earlier case. It is to be noted that overruling does not in any way affect the decision in the earlier case as between the parties to it. A person cannot ask that his case be reopened because it has been overruled by a later case; if any such procedure were allowed, people would never be sure that a particular piece of litigation had ended.

Disapproving. If the *ratio decidendi* of a later case is not wide enough to cover an earlier case, the earlier case cannot be overruled. However, the court may say that in its opinion the earlier case was wrongly decided, and if it does so then the earlier case is said to be disapproved. Such an opinion is *obiter dictum,* but it may help to lead to the overruling of the case if a suitable opportunity arises later.

Distinguishing. Distinguishing occurs when in a later case the court finds some material distinction which justifies its not following the *ratio decidendi* of an earlier case. It is commonly used as a device for not following an earlier case which is thought to have been wrongly decided, but which cannot be overruled except by an appeal to the House of Lords (with no certainty that the House of Lords will in fact overrule it). Distinguishing may in many cases be justified, but it does tend to make the law more complicated, and sometimes cases (of which examples will be found in the section of chapter 7 relating to frustration of contracts) are so finely distinguished that the dividing line between one and another is almost invisible.

1K5. Advantages and disadvantages of precedent

There are advantages and disadvantages of the system of judicial precedent as it has developed in English law.

The advantages are as follows:

Certainty. Scrutton, L.J. in *Hill* v. *Aldershot Corporation* (1933) expressed this point admirably: 'In my view, liberty to decide each case as you think right without any regard to principles laid down in previous similar cases would only result in a completely uncertain law in which no citizen would know his rights or liabilities until he knew before what judge his case would come and could guess what view that judge would take on a consideration of the matter without any regard to previous decisions'. However, it is necessary for any system of law to have a degree of flexibility, and to the extent that law is flexible it cannot be certain, and *vice versa.* The courts, particularly the House of Lords, must therefore always balance the need for certainty against the need for flexibility in any particular case.

Possibility of growth. The system allows for new rules to be established and old rules to be adapted to meet new circumstances and the changing needs of society. Where a precedent is considered to be particularly valuable its scope can be extended in later cases: conversely, where a precedent is felt to be defective, its scope can be restricted by the process of distinguishing mentioned above.

Wealth of detailed rules. No code of law could be devised which would provide the wealth of detail to be found in English case-law.

Practicality. The rules of English case-law do not derive from a particular theory of law, and do not attempt to deal with hypothetical circumstances. They are the result of the consideration of real situations which have come before the courts.

The disadvantages of the system of judicial precedent are:

Rigidity. Once a rule has been laid down it is binding even if the decision is thought to be wrong, and alteration, other than by distinguishing, which is less than wholly satisfactory, is difficult. This disadvantage is modified to the extent that the House of Lords is not bound by its own previous decisions, but people are reluctant to bring appeals before the House of Lords because of the enormous expense involved, particularly bearing in mind that the House will not overrule its own previous decision except in the most compelling circumstances. The possibility that case-law will be abrogated or modified by legislation alleviates the disadvantage of rigidity to some degree, but in practice it is rare for the legislature to interfere with case-law.

Bulk and complexity. There is so much law that no one can learn all of it. There is a danger that even an experienced lawyer may overlook some important rule in any given case. This is particularly so with those branches of law which have been developed mainly by case-law, as, for example, the law of torts.

Slowness of growth. The system depends on litigation for rules to emerge. As litigation tends to be slow and expensive the body of case-law cannot grow quickly enough to meet modern demands.

Where it is felt that a particular case which has long been a precedent operates unfairly, or where the law on an important point is unclear, it is argued by some that appeals to the House of Lords should be financed at public expense, as it is inequitable that the law should be developed or clarified at the expense of private litigants. (It is worth noting, however, that many cases heard in the House of Lords are in effect financed by public funds, where the parties are either legally aided or are bodies, such as the Commissioners of Customs and Excise, who are financed entirely out of public funds.)

1L. Law reports

It was mentioned earlier that the system of precedent relies for its efficiency on an effective system of law reporting, and since many law cases are referred to throughout this book, it is appropriate here to say something about the main series of law reports and how they are cited.

The Incorporated Council of Law Reporting was established in 1870, and publishes the semi-official Law Reports. Separate volumes are published each year in respect of cases heard in the Queen's Bench, Family and Chancery Divisions of the High Court and appeals from those courts to the Court of Appeal. Thus a case may be cited:

Carlill v. *Carbolic Smoke Ball Co.* [1893] 1 Q.B. 256

This means that the case is reported in the first volume of the Queen's Bench Division reports for 1893, and the report of the case commences at page 256. It is to be noted that in official citations, such as in the index to this book, the date is shown in square brackets, rather than round brackets, as it is an essential part of the citation: it means that the case was reported in 1893, but it might well have been heard the previous year.

There is a separate series of reports relating to appeals heard by the House of Lords, which can easily be identified by the letters A.C. in the citation. Thus a case may be cited:

Adam v. *Ward* [1917] A.C. 309

This means that the appeal was heard by the House of Lords, and can be found in the 1917 volume, the report of the case starting at page 309.

Another important series of law reports commonly used at the present day is the All England Reports, which started in 1936. This is a private series of reports which is highly respected. The series includes reports of cases heard in various courts. Thus a case is cited:

Beach v. *Reed Corrugated Cases Ltd* [1956] 2 All E.R. 652

This means that the report of the case is to be found in the second volume of the All England Reports for 1956, the report starting on page 652. The reference does not indicate the court in which the case was heard, but the report itself makes this clear.

There are various other current series of reports, the most important of which, from the point of view of the insurance student, is Lloyd's Reports, which specialise in reporting commercial cases. Before 1870 there were a large number of series of private reports, as a glance at the table of cases cited at the end of this book will show. It is unnecessary here to give any detail about these, if only because few if any of these reports would be available for consultation by readers of this book.

An easy way to keep abreast of new case law is to read the brief reports of cases which appear daily in *The Times* newspaper while the courts are in session. On the other hand, the reports of 'newsworthy' cases which appear in the popular press are, from the point of view of the law student, of minimal value and are often misleading.

1M. Examples of statute and case law

A study of an Act of Parliament and of a judgment given by the courts is extremely helpful to emphasise a number of the points made earlier in this chapter, and for this purpose the Hotel Proprietors' Act 1956 and the judgment of the House of Lords in the case of *A.C.T. Construction Ltd* v. *Commissioners of Customs and Excise* (1981) form Appendices A and B to this book. In neither instance is the substance important for the purpose of this course (although most students will find that as their studies advance they will require to know the provisions of the Hotel Proprietors' Act in detail), and both the Act and the case have been chosen mainly because of their brevity. They should be studied in conjunction with the following notes:

Hotel Proprietors' Act 1956
— 'Chapter 62' means simply that this was the 62nd Act passed in the 1956–1957 session of Parliament. At one time there was a fiction that only one piece of legislation was passed in each session of Parliament, and so each individual Act of the session was a 'chapter' of the sessional legislation as a whole. The word 'chapter' has been retained, but it simply means 'number'.
— The preamble (beginning with the words 'Be it enacted . . .' and ending '. . . as follows'), is the same in every Act. It indicates that the Act has been passed by the House of Commons, the House of Lords (the Lords Spiritual are the arch-bishop and bishops of the Church of England who are entitled to sit in the House

of Lords, and the Lords Temporal are all the other members of the House) and has received the Royal Assent.

—The Act received the Royal Assent on 2 August 1956, but it will be noted from section 3 (4) that it did not come into force until 1 January 1957. It is common for there to be a delay, sometimes much greater than the period involved in this case, between the Royal Assent and the coming into force of an Act.

—The Act contains only three sections. Sections 1 and 2 each have three sub-sections and section 3 has four sub-sections.

—Since the Act is concerned with inns and innkeepers, it is made clear what these terms mean for the purpose of the Act, and this necessarily involves a precise definition of the expression 'hotel'.

—Section 1 (2) is a good example of legislation which clarifies a point on which, under previous legislation or case law, there has been doubt or dispute. In this particular case, it had always been accepted that under certain circumstances an hotel proprietor was liable to make good loss to property of guests in certain circumstances but whether he was liable for damage, as distinct from loss, was a matter of doubt. The sub-section resolves this doubt.

—The sidenote to section 2 (sidenotes, incidentally, are not strictly part of an Act) makes it clear that the Act modifies the liabilities and rights of innkeepers rather than creating substantial new rights and liabilities or abolishing substantial existing rights and liabilities.

—Section 3 is a typical final section of any Act, and is self-explanatory.

—Schedules to Acts are commonly found. It is convenient to place them at the end of an Act rather than in the sections of the Act (in this case section 2) to which they relate.

It is often said that Acts of Parliament are written in 'legalistic jargon' but this criticism is not entirely fair. Some Acts deal with matters which are of extreme complexity (an example is the Finance Act 1972, with which the *A.C.T. Construction* case discussed below was concerned), and can create difficulties even for experienced lawyers, but an Act such as the Hotel Proprietors' Act is capable of being understood by any intelligent reader, although several readings and a good deal of concentration are required.

A.C.T. Construction Ltd v. *Commissioners of Customs and Excise*
The point at issue in this case was fairly simple. Builders had carried out work of underpinning, that is, constructing new foundations under existing buildings which had been damaged by subsidence, the original foundations having been found to be inadequate. If this work came within the meaning of 'construction, alteration or demolition of any building', it was zero-rated for purposes of value added tax. If it was 'work of maintenance or repair', it was subject to value added tax at the standard rate. The question was simply into what category did it fall.

—From the judgment it will be seen that A.C.T. Construction had been assessed to value added tax in the sum of £1,072.44 and had appealed to a value added tax tribunal which had dismissed their case. A.C.T. then appealed to the High Court, which reversed the decision of the tribunal. From the High Court, Customs and Excise appealed to the Court of Appeal, which upheld the decision of the High Court, and from the report of the House of Lords decision it will be seen that Customs and Excise were also unsuccessful there.

   It is generally accepted that there should be a right of appeal to the ordinary courts from such bodies as value added tax tribunals, but many lawyers doubt whether justice demands that there should ever, in cases like this, be as many as three appeals, especially in view of the delays and costs involved. (The dispute arose on 9 January 1978, and the House of Lords judgment was delivered on 11 November 1981.) It should be noted, however, that the case was considerably more important than at first sight appears. Although the amount in dispute in this case was small, it was in fact a 'test case', in the sense that it was known that the final decision would affect many hundreds of other cases in which similar work had been done. (As the necessity for the work arose out of subsidence, against which many people are insured, the outcome of the case was of considerable interest to insurers also.)

—Although the appeal in the House of Lords was brought by Customs and Excise, the case is cited as *A.C.T. Construction Ltd* v. *Commissioners of Customs and Excise* (rather than the reverse) as A.C.T. Construction were the original appellants and once the citation of a case is fixed it remains the same, whichever party may be the appellant in any particular court.

—All the judges begin their judgments with the words 'My Lords', and Lord Roskill uses these words at the beginning of every paragraph. This is a survival from the days when House of Lords judgments were delivered in the form of speeches to the House of Lords as a whole; nowadays, of course, the judgment is directed mainly to the parties to the case.

— It will be noted that, in accordance with the usual practice, the case was heard before five Law Lords but, unusually, only one judgment, by Lord Roskill, was delivered, the other judges simply expressing their agreement. In this case clearly all the judges were agreed, not only as to the decision, but also as to the reason for the decision, so that more than one judgment would have been superfluous. In more important or disputable cases, it is common for each judge to deliver judgment, even if they all agree, as they may agree as to the decision but not necessarily as to the reasons for it, or the judges individually may wish to place emphasis on particular points. In addition, dissenting judgments are by no means uncommon, in which event a majority decision is reached.

— The point at issue was whether the underpinning work was work of 'maintenance or repair'. There was no precedent on which the House of Lords could rely, and it will be noted that Lord Roskill did not consider that previous cases relating to obligations of landlords and tenants to repair or maintain buildings were of great help in the present case. He thus based his judgment on that of Brandon L.J. in the Court of Appeal. Underpinning was 'entirely new work'. It was 'not capable of coming within the expression "maintenance" in the ordinary and natural meaning of the word' (and it was common ground that it was certainly not 'repair'). The *ratio decidendi* of the case can therefore be summarised as laying down the rule that underpinning involving the extension of a building is not work of maintenance, but rather of alteration to a building, and as such is zero-rated for value added tax purposes.

— Finally, it follows from what has been written that the *ratio decidendi* of this case is very narrow, The legislation which was being considered refers to 'construction', 'alteration', 'demolition', 'repair' and 'maintenance', but no attempt was made (because it was not necessary) to define or distinguish between any of these terms. The Court did go so far as to express the view that the term 'alteration' involves structural alteration, but even this was *obiter*. Although, therefore, the case is interesting as an illustration of how the courts operate, it is in itself of little importance of an indication of how the courts on occasion interpret difficult wordings of statutes.

2. The administration of justice – 1

2A.Terminology
2B.Civil Courts
  2B1.Magistrates' Courts
  2B2.The County Court
  2B3.The High Court
    2B3A.Chancery Division
    2B3B.Family Division
    2B3C.Queen's Bench Division
  2B4.The Court of Appeal – Civil Division
  2B5.The House of Lords
2C.Criminal Courts
  2C1.Magistrates' Courts
  2C2.The Crown Court
  2C3.The Court of Appeal – Criminal Division
  2C4.The House of Lords

2D.European Court
2E.Other Courts
  2E1.Courts-Martial
  2E2.Ecclesiastical Courts
  2E3.Coroners' Courts
  2E4.The Restrictive Practices Court
2F.Administrative Tribunals
  2F1.Social Security Tribunals
  2F2.Lands Tribunal and Rent Tribunals
  2F3.Conciliation and Industrial Tribunals
  2F4.The Employment Appeal Tribunal
  2F5.Advantages and Disadvantages
2G.Domestic Tribunals
2H.Arbitration

2A.Terminology

Before considering the system of civil and criminal courts, it is useful to consider the terminology used in those courts.

In a civil case, the person who brings the action is known as the plaintiff, and the person against whom it is brought is known as the defendant, so that if Jones brings a case against Brown, it will be cited as *Jones* v. *Brown*, Jones being the plaintiff and Brown the defendant. At the end of the case it is said that judgment is given, either for the plaintiff or for the defendant. If the losing party (who may be either the plaintiff or the defendant) decides to appeal against the judgment he becomes known as the appellant in any appeal court, the other party being known as the respondent. Thus if the plaintiff loses his case in the court in which it is originally heard (known as the court of first instance) and appeals, say, to the Court of Appeal, he is the appellant in the Court of Appeal and the defendant becomes the respondent.

A person found to be responsible in civil proceedings is said to be liable, rather than guilty. So, for example, one talks of a person being 'liable in negligence,' not 'guilty of negligence,' and damages (or some other civil remedy) are awarded against him.

In criminal law, a person who brings a prosecution (criminal prosecutions are usually brought in the name of the monarch, that is, R. – Rex (King) or Regina (Queen) – although in summary cases they are brought in the name of the actual prosecutor, who is usually a police officer) is called the prosecutor, and the person against whom the proceedings are brought is known as the defendant, or the accused, or sometimes the prisoner, although the latter term should be avoided as it is misleading. If the case against the defendant is proved, he is said to be guilty, or to have been convicted, and the penalty imposed upon him, such as a fine or imprisonment, is known as a punishment. This terminology applies irrespective of the magnitude of the offence, so that both the speeding driver and the murderer have committed criminal offences, and will be found guilty and punished, although the punishments will be vastly different. The notion common amongst many laymen that certain minor offences, particularly traffic offences, are 'technical' offences and not criminal offences at all, is quite wrong.

Various courts have been well established since the reign of Henry II, but from time to time they have been re-organised, most recently by the Administration of Justice Act 1970 and the Courts Act 1970.

Before enumerating the main courts, it is necessary to note that courts are referred to as either superior or inferior courts, and that unfortunately the terms superior and inferior are used in two different senses.

In a non-technical sense, a court is said to be inferior if it ranks below another. For example, the Court of Appeal is the second highest court in England, but it is inferior to the House of Lords, which ranks above it, and thus is called superior. In this sense, all courts except the lowest (magistrates' courts and the County Court) are in some contexts superior and all except the House of Lords are in some contexts inferior.

In a legally recognised sense, an inferior court is one which is subject to control by the Queen's Bench Division of the High Court, whereas a superior court is not. The supervisory jurisdiction of the Queen's Bench Division over inferior courts is explained in detail later in this chapter.

2B.Civil courts

The main civil courts comprise, in ascending order of importance:

—in some matters, magistrates' courts, although these courts deal mainly with criminal matters;

—the County Court;

—the High Court of Justice, which has three divisions – Queen's Bench, Family, and Chancery – and which, together with the Court of Appeal and the Crown Court (a purely criminal court) is known somewhat misleadingly as the Supreme Court of Judicature (misleading because for practical purposes the House of Lords is the supreme court);

—the Court of Appeal – Civil Division;

—the House of Lords.

2B1. Magistrates' Courts

As mentioned above, magistrates' courts are primarily criminal courts, but magistrates have power to make separation and maintenance orders on grounds such as desertion, ill-treatment, or habitual drunkenness. They also have power to issue licences for the sale of alcoholic drinks and the running of betting shops, and they can deal with the recovery of small civil debts, such as outstanding bills for gas and electricity.

2B2. The County Court

The term County Court is a misnomer to the extent that there is no connection between County Courts and geographical counties. There are in fact over four hundred County Courts distributed over the country on the basis of need.

Proceedings begun in County Courts total some two million a year, but only about 5% of cases actually come to trial, the remainder being settled by the parties between the date of issue of the writ, which is the first step in commencing proceedings, and the date when the case is due to be heard.

The County Court is a court of first instance only. This means that it deals only with original disputes rather than appeals from other courts (a court which hears appeals is called an appellate court). The types of cases which are heard by County Courts are as follows:

—actions for breach of contract, where the amount claimed does not exceed £5000;

—actions in tort, with the exception of actions for defamation, where the amount claimed does not exceed £5000;

—actions in equity, such as those concerning trusts, dissolution of partnerships, and mortgages, where the amount involved does not exceed £30,000;

—actions concerning title to land, and actions for the recovery of possession of land, where the net annual value of land for rating purposes does not exceed £1000;

—disputes regarding the grant of probate or letters of administration, that is, authority to deal with a deceased person's estate, where the estate is valued at less than £15,000;

—actions which could be heard by the High Court but are remitted by the High Court to the County Court;

—jurisdiction regarding the adoption of children. Both the High Court and the magistrates' courts also have jurisdiction in this field;

—in some County Courts, jurisdiction in bankruptcy, unlimited in amount. In London, however, all bankruptcy cases are dealt with by the Bankruptcy Court, which is a section of the High Court;

—in some County Courts, jurisdiction to wind up companies with a share capital not exceeding £750,000;

—in some County Courts, jurisdiction to deal with proceedings brought by the Race Relations Board in respect of racial discrimination;

—in some County Courts, jurisdiction to deal with maritime cases up to £5000 and disputes in connection with salvage up to £15,000;

—undefended matrimonal cases, including actions for divorce, judicial separation, or nullity of marriage. If a case is defended, however, it must be heard in the High Court;

—in County Courts with divorce jurisdiction, claims for ancillary relief and for the protection of children, wilful neglect to maintain dependants, and the variation of maintenance agreements;

—actions involving 'extortionate' credit agreements, where the amount involved does not exceed £5000;

—various social matters, such as disputes regarding housing and the welfare of children;

—in some matters, particularly breach of contract and tort, the County Courts have unlimited jurisdiction if both parties agree that the case shall be heard in the County Court rather than the High Court. On the other hand, on giving security for costs, a defendant may ask for a case which would normally be heard in the County Court to be transferred to the High Court if the claim exceeds £150 and some important point of law or fact is likely to arise.

The monetary limits mentioned under the various headings above are subject to fairly frequent change as inflation erodes real values, and it is therefore not of great importance that precise amounts should be remembered.

Where the parties have a choice of tribunal, there are advantages if the case is heard in the County Court rather than the High Court. The proceedings are speedier and less formal, and as a result costs are less.

The jurisdiction of the County Courts is limited to the geographical area which they cover, and an action must normally be brought in the court for the district in which the defendant resides or carries on business, or in the court for the district in which the cause of action arose.

There is provision for any action to be transferred from the County Court to the High Court where the sum involved is over £600 and the defendant objects to the case being tried in the County Court, provided that the County Court judge certifies that in his opinion some important question of law or fact is likely to arise and the defendant gives security for the amount claimed and the costs of the trial in the High Court. If an action is brought in the High Court for a sum of not more than £5000, the defendant may apply to have the case transferred to the County Court, and it will be transferred if the judge or master who hears the case thinks fit. If in an action brought in the High Court the amount recovered is less than £600, the plaintiff is not entitled to costs. If he recovers less than £3000 he will be awarded costs only on the County Court scale unless it appears to the judge or master that there were reasonable grounds to suppose that he would have recovered more than he could have claimed in the County Court, or if they are satisfied that there were reasonable grounds for bringing the case in the High Court, or if the defendant objected to the case being transferred to the County Court.

Another important function of the County Court is the enforcement of judgments, whether County Court or High Court judgments, where a party against whom an award has been made fails to comply with the order of the court. Where an award of money has been made, but it has not been paid, a number of options are open to the County Court.

Attachment of earnings. An order for attachment of earnings is an instruction to the employer of the debtor, ordering him to make periodical deductions from the earnings of the debtor, and to pay them to the collecting officer of the court. An order of this sort is often made in respect of arrears of maintenance.

Execution. A judgment creditor may seek a warrant of execution against the personal property of the debtor. If such a warrant is granted, it is executed by a bailiff who is entitled to seize as much of the debtor's personal property as is necessary to satisfy the debt. The debtor must, however, be left with clothes, bedding, and the tools of his trade to the value of £50.

Garnishee proceedings. The judgment creditor may institute garnishee proceedings. Garnishee proceedings involve three parties: the judgment creditor (A), the judgment debtor (B), and a third party (C), very often a bank with whom B has an account in credit, who owes money to B. Under garnishee proceedings the court orders C to pay direct to A so much of the amount it owes to B as will satisfy the judgment debt, or the whole of the amount it owes if this is less than the judgment debt.

Charging order. The judgment creditor may obtain from the court a charging order. This enables the creditor, if the debt remains unpaid, to sell the property subject to the charge in order to recover the debt.

Appointment of a receiver. The court may, at the request of the judgment creditor, appoint a receiver to whom income which would normally go to the judgment debtor will be paid, and the receiver will pay it to the judgment creditor until the debt is repaid.

Bankruptcy proceedings. The judgment creditor may serve upon the judgment debtor a notice to pay the amount due within seven days, and if the debtor does not pay within that time, the creditor may institute bankruptcy proceedings. Such proceedings should not be instituted lightly, however, because unless the debtor is able to pay in full, the creditor will receive only a fraction of the amount due to him, and then will have no further recourse against the debtor.

Judgment summons. A judgment summons involves an investigation by the court into a judgment debtor's means, and generally involves an order by the court to the debtor to pay the debt by instalments. Until 1970, the advantage of a judgment summons from the point of view of a judgment creditor was that the judgment debtor could be imprisoned if he failed to comply with it. In general, this is not now the case, so that attachment of earnings is sought much more frequently than judgment summons.

Sometimes a judgment involves something other than an award of money, and the court's powers of enforcement are different from those mentioned:
—where a successful plaintiff is entitled to receive or recover possession of land, a warrant of possession may be executed by a bailiff;

—where there is a judgment for possession of specific goods, a warrant of delivery may be executed by a bailiff.

In these cases the bailiff is entitled to seize the land or goods and hand over possession to the plaintiff.

When the court has awarded an injunction against a defendant, failure to comply with its terms constitutes contempt of court. In these circumstances the court may punish the defendant by making a committal order. The effect of this is that if the defendant continues to refuse to comply with the injunction he may be imprisoned.

2B3. The High Court

The High Court can, and does, sit anywhere in the country as business requires, although a great deal of its business is done in the Royal Courts of Justice in the Strand in London. There are three divisions of the High Court: the Chancery Division, the Family Division, and the Queen's Bench Division. Within each division there is what may be called an ordinary court, in which cases are heard at first instance, and what is confusingly known as a Divisional Court (so that one talks, for example, of the Divisional Court of the Chancery Division) which deals with certain appeals from lower courts.

Each division deals with specified matters as detailed below, and will not hear cases which are within the jurisdiction of another division. If, however, a plaintiff brings an action in the wrong division he will not necessarily lose his case: it will instead be transferred to the correct division.

2B3A. Chancery Division

The Chancery Division deals with the following matters:
—company law;
—the administration of trusts;
—partnership actions;
—mortgages;
—taxation;
—bankruptcy;
—conveyancing and certain aspects of land law;
—rectification and cancellation of deeds;
—specific performance of contracts;
—contentious probate business, that is, disputes as to the validity of a will, disputes as to the meaning of a will, and cases concerning disputes arising where the deceased made no will.

Within the Chancery Division there are four special courts:
—the Companies Court, which deals with such matters as the winding-up of companies; cases are heard by judges who specialise in such matters;
—the Bankruptcy Court, which deals with bankruptcy cases arising in the London area;
—the Court of Protection which deals with the affairs of minors and of people who have been found to be of unsound mind;
—the Patents Court.

The Divisional Court of the Chancery Division deals with certain appeals, particularly those from the County Court in bankruptcy matters.

Appeals from the decisions of the Commissioners of Inland Revenue are heard by a single judge of the Chancery Division.

2B3B. Family Division

The Family Division deals with the following matters:
—non-contentious or common form probate business, that is, the granting of probate where there is no dispute as to the grant;
—proceedings relating to the presumption of death;
—proceedings relating to the dissolution of marriages (divorce);
—matters relating to legitimacy, validity of a marriage, nationality, and matrimonial status;
—proceedings in connection with the wardship of minors, adoption, guardianship of minors, and other matters in connection with the care, custody, and control of minors, including proceedings to obtain the court's consent to the marriage of a minor;
—disputes between spouses as to their respective rights to property, including disputes as to entry to and occupation of the matrimonial home;
—the enforcement of maintenance orders.

The Divisional Court of the Family Division is concerned with appeals from the County Court and from magistrates' courts on a number of matters connected with matrimonial disputes and the affairs of minors.

2B3C. Queen's Bench Division

The Queen's Bench Division deals with all civil matters which do not fall within the jurisdiction of the other divisions. They include civil actions arising out of common-law liability, mainly actions in contract and tort, for example negligence, nuisance, and defamation.

There are two special courts within the Queen's Bench Division:

—The Admiralty Court, which deals with such matters as disputes arising out of collisions at sea and salvage claims:

—the Commercial Court, which specialises in dealing with commercial cases. For example, cases arising out of disputes in connection with insurance contracts are dealt with in this court by judges who have a specialised knowledge of commercial matters.

An ordinary court of the division has power to deal with appeals from certain tribunals such as VAT tribunals which deal with disputes as to whether, in given circumstances, value added tax is payable.

The Divisional Court of the Queen's Bench Division deals with appeals from magistrates' courts by way of case stated. This is criminal rather than civil jurisdiction, and so will be dealt with more fully later. It also deals with appeals from some of the more important tribunals, appeals from the less important tribunals being dealt with by the ordinary court, as already indicated.

The Divisional Court has important supervisory jurisdiction which has no parallel in either of the other two divisions. This jurisdiction is given to the division to enable it to prevent abuse of power by inferior courts, government departments, administrative and domestic tribunals, other organisations, and individuals, and is probably the most important safeguard which a person can invoke to protect himself against injustice. The court has authority to issue the prerogative writ of *habeas corpus*, and the prerogative orders of *mandamus*, prohibition, and *certiorari*.

> *Habeas corpus.* The purpose of the writ of *habeas corpus* is to secure the release of a person who has been unlawfully detained. The proceedings may relate to either a criminal or a civil matter. In a criminal matter a single judge can issue the writ or refer the case to a Divisional Court of three judges. The Divisional Court can issue or refuse the writ, and if it refuses there may be an appeal to the House of Lords. In a civil case in which, for example, it is alleged that a husband or father is unlawfully detaining a wife or child, a single judge may grant or refuse the application. If he refuses, appeal lies to the Court of Appeal – Civil Division, and thence to the House of Lords.

> *Mandamus.* A person seeking an order of *mandamus* must show that the person or body against whom he is seeking the order is failing to carry out a statutory duty. For example, a local authority has a statutory duty to produce accounts and to make them available for public inspection, and if it failed to do so any ratepayer could apply for an order of *mandamus*. Such an order is a command by the court to the person or body concerned to carry out its duty. *Mandamus* may also be used to compel an inferior court or tribunal to try a case if it wrongfully refuses to do so. The order of *mandamus* is a discretionary remedy, and it is not used if there is a satisfactory alternative.

> *Certiorari.* The order of *certiorari* is a device to bring before the Queen's Bench Division a case heard by, or in the process of being heard by, an inferior court or a body, such as an administrative tribunal, which is not a court but which is under a duty to act judicially, where it is alleged that the inferior court or other body has either acted outside its jurisdiction or has not had proper regard to the principles of natural justice. What constitutes natural justice is something which has exercised the minds of lawyers, philosophers, and theologians for at least three thousand years, but 'for present purposes the rules of natural justice are as follows:

> —No man may be a judge in his own cause. This means that if a judge or magistrate has any personal interest in the outcome of a case, he must play no part in hearing it. So strictly is this rule applied that in *Dimes* v. *Grand Junction Canal Proprietors* (1852), for example, a decision of the Lord Chancellor was set aside because it was discovered that he held shares in the canal company.

> —The *audi alteram partem* rule must be observed. This means that both parties to a case have a right to be heard, but does not mean that both parties must in fact be heard. In criminal cases, for example, it is for the prosecution to prove beyond reasonable doubt that the defendant is guilty, and there is no requirement on the defendant to prove his innocence. The defendant is therefore at liberty to refrain from saying anything if that is what he wishes, and his 'right of silence' is equally as important as his right to be heard. There is not necessarily a right to an oral hearing: written evidence may be acceptable. A person has a right to notice of the case which is to be brought against him

and a right to cross-examine witnesses. There is no inherent right to legal representation, but if a case involves difficult points of law it should be heard before the ordinary courts, rather than, for example, an administrative or domestic tribunal, and legal representation should be allowed.

In *Ridge* v. *Baldwin* (1963), the plaintiff, a chief constable, was acquitted on a criminal charge, but the Watch Committee subsequently dismissed him under a power which they had to dismiss 'any constable whom they think negligent in the discharge of his duty or otherwise unfit for the same.' It was held that the dismissal was void, as the plaintiff had not been given the opportunity to answer the charges brought against him or to appear before the Watch Committee.

—In arriving at a decision, a court or tribunal must not act in bad faith or from some wrong motive. It must be strictly impartial. In *R.* v. *Bingham Justices, ex parte Jowitt* (1974) the chairman of the justices, in finding a person guilty of a speeding offence, said: 'Quite the most unpleasant cases which we have to decide are those where the evidence is a direct conflict between a police officer and a member of the public. My principle in such cases has always been to believe the evidence of the police officer. . . .' On an appeal to the Divisional Court for *certiorari* it was held that the attitude of the chairman was clearly biased and the conviction was quashed.

Prohibition. As the name suggests, prohibition is an order to prevent something being done, and thus is the converse of *mandamus*. It is, however, significantly different from *mandamus* in that it can be used only against inferior courts and bodies with quasi-judicial functions. Thus it can be used to prevent courts, tribunals, and other bodies exceeding their judicial powers.

If the Queen's Bench Division finds that the inferior court or tribunal has acted outside its jurisdiction, or has not observed the principles of natural justice, the decision will be quashed or, where a case is still being heard, the proceedings will be discontinued.

2B4. The Court of Appeal – Civil Division

Appeals from the County Court and from any of the three divisions of the High Court are heard by the Court of Appeal – Civil Division. An appeal is said to be by way of re-hearing, but it is only in the most rare circumstances that witnesses are heard in the Court of Appeal. Almost invariably the court relies on a transcript of the evidence given in the lower court and the reasoned judgment; in practice, therefore, re-hearing means that every aspect of law and fact is reviewed by the Court of Appeal.

A problem can arise in connection with an appeal to the Court of Appeal because of the fact that the court is bound by its own previous decisions. Suppose, for example, that in case A the Court of Appeal has established a precedent; for the future both the Court of Appeal and the High Court are bound by that precedent, but it may be felt that the case was wrongly decided. Whether it was or not is something which can be decided only by the House of Lords. If later there is a similar case B which comes before the High Court, that court is bound by the decision in case A. There is little point, however, in appealing to the Court of Appeal, because it is known in advance that the Court of Appeal is also bound, and so the appeal would be a fruitless formality.

To deal with this situation, the Administration of Justice Act 1969 provides that in certain circumstances an appeal may be made from the High Court direct to the House of Lords, by-passing the Court of Appeal. Where this is done the trial judge must certify that the case is a suitable one for direct appeal, both parties to the case must agree to the procedure, and the case must involve a point of general public importance relating wholly or mainly to a statute or statutory instrument. This 'leapfrog' procedure, as it is somewhat inelegantly known, makes it worth while for the parties to consider an appeal, because the House of Lords, not being bound by precedent, or perhaps never having heard a similar case before, may, depending on the circumstances, overrule the previous Court of Appeal decision.

2B5. The House of Lords

From a decision of the Court of Appeal – Civil Division (or from the High Court in the special circumstances just outlined) appeal lies to the House of Lords, which is the highest court of appeal in the UK. An appeal can only be brought before the House of Lords, however, if leave is granted by the Court of Appeal, or by the trial judge in 'leapfrog' cases, or by the House of Lords itself.

Although the House of Lords is the supreme court of appeal, it is not part of the Supreme Court of Judicature, which consists of the Court of Appeal and the High Court (in civil cases) and the Crown Court (in criminal cases) only.

When an appellant in effect intends to invite the House of Lords to overrule its own previous decision, he must give advance notice to this effect to the House of Lords.

Ignoring magistrates' courts, which are of little importance in civil law, the system of the main civil courts may be shown diagrammatically as follows:

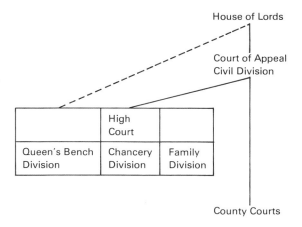

2C. Criminal courts   The most important criminal courts, in ascending order of importance, are:
  —magistrates' courts;
  —the Crown Court;
  —the Queen's Bench Division of the High Court;
  —the Court of Appeal – Criminal Division;
  —the House of Lords

2C1. Magistrates' Courts   It has already been noted that in certain minor matters magistrates' courts have civil jurisdiction, but their main function is to deal with criminal cases. Although from a strictly legal point of view magistrates' courts are of comparatively little importance, from a practical viewpoint they have enormous importance, as they hear and dispose of well over 90% of criminal cases. There are over 700 magistrates' courts throughout the country, staffed by some 24,000 lay magistrates and 52 stipendiary magistrates (see chapter 3).

Magistrates' courts are also known as 'petty sessions' or 'courts of summary jurisdiction', and also, colloquially and very wrongly, as 'police courts'. It is unfortunate that different names are used, because they signify no distinction, and can lead to confusion.

Magistrates' courts can themselves deal with summary cases, that is, comparatively minor offences. At the other extreme there are offences triable only on indictment, the more serious crimes such as murder and rape, which can be tried only in the Crown Court. In between, there are certain crimes, for example, theft, which are triable 'either way', that is, they can be dealt with by a magistrates' court if the defendant agrees, but otherwise they are tries by the Crown Court. With offences triable either way, the defendant can always insist on trial by jury at the Crown Court, but he cannot always insist on summary trial. If the magistrates feel that the trial would be better heard by the Crown Court, they may transfer it to that court, although they must first consider any representations made by the defendant. Magistrates have power to impose a fine up to £1000 and/or a sentence of imprisonment of up to six months, but if they consider that these penalties are inadequate, perhaps because the defendant already has a bad criminal record, they can commit the defendant to the Crown Court with a view to a heavier sentence being imposed.

Children under fourteen years of age must always be tried by magistrates for any offence other than homicide (murder or manslaughter), and young people aged between fourteen and seventeen may, if they consent, always be tried by magistrates, again with the exception of homicide.

From a magistrates' court the defendant (but not the prosecutor) may appeal to the Crown Court against either conviction or sentence. The Crown Court may allow the appeal, but if it does not, it may pass any sentence which the magistrates' court could have passed, that is, a fine of £1000 and/or sentence of imprisonment of not more than six months, which means that in some circumstances the sentence may be increased. For example, a fine of £250 imposed by the magistrates may be increased to £500, or a sentence of imprisonment of three months may be increased to six months. There is therefore a certain danger to the defendant if he appeals to the Crown Court.

An appeal from a magistrates' court may also be made, by either the defendant or the prosecutor, to the Queen's Bench Division of the High Court by way of case stated. The magistrates set out in writing the reasons for their decision, and the appeal must involve a matter of law only. A further appeal to the House of Lords in possible, but only if the appeal raises a matter of law of public importance and leave to appeal is granted either by the Divisional Court or by the House of Lords.

Juvenile courts

When trying people under the age of seventeen the magistrates sit as a Juvenile Court. In such a court there must be magistrates of both sexes, and the proceedings must be held at a different place, or at a different time, from the normal proceedings of the court. Generally, the hearing is less formal, and it is conducted in provate. The normal requirement is that the parents of the defendant must be present.

The juvenile court also deals with care proceedings, where a child is brought before the courts at the instance of a local authority, the police, or such people as officials of the National Society for the Prevention of Cruelty to Children on the grounds that the child is being beglected, or is beyond the control of, his parent or parents, irrespective of whether he has committed a crime. The parent or parents of the child are expected to attend the hearing and persons who can give evidence as to the child's conduct or condition, such as the headmaster of his school, also attend. Both the child and the parents are invited to make statements. If it is shown that the child is in need of care, the magistrates will make a care order which may, but does not always, involve putting the child into the care of the local authority; this means that he will live in a community home until he is eighteen or until the care order is revoked.

The second main function of magistrates' courts is to hold a preliminary examination when a person is accused of an indictable offence. In exercising this function the magistrates are not concerned with establishing a defendant's guilt – although they may dismiss the charge if the case against him is so weak as not to justify a trial – but with determining whether the facts are such as to warrant a trial in the Crown Court. If they are, the defendant is committed for trial, but this does not imply any presumption of guilt; the defendant may have a good defence which he chooses not to disclose until the Crown Court hearing.

The value of this preliminary hearing is open to grave doubt. The legal theory is that is saves the time of the Crown Court, but in practice this is true only to an infinitesimal degree; 997 out of every thousand preliminary hearings result in the defendant being sent for trial. On the other hand, the hearings occupy a great deal of time of hard-pressed magistrates, and all the evidence given at the preliminary hearing must be given again at the trial, at a greater expenditure of time and money. It is worthy of note that Scotland has always managed without the preliminary hearing.

2C2. The Crown Court

The main criminal court of first instance is the Crown Court, which deals with all criminal proceedings on indictment, except for some comparatively minor indictable offences where the defendant exercises his option to be tried instead by a magistrates' court. In all cases which come before the Crown Court there will of course have been a preliminary hearing before magistrates or, in very rare cases, a finding by a coroner's court that death resulted from criminal action on the part of named persons.

Cases heard by the Crown Court are divided into four categories:

—Class One. These include murder, treason, and genocide.
—Class Two. These include manslaughter, rape and other serious sexual offences, sedition, mutiny, piracy, and offences under the Geneva Conventions Act, which is mainly concerned with securing the humane treatment of prisoners of war.
—Class Three. These include all indictable offences not included in classes One, Two, or Four.
—Class Four. These include the comparatively minor indictable offences where the defendant has the option to have them dealt with by either the magistrates' court or by the Crown Court, and also certain common but serious offences, among which are causing death by reckless or dangerous driving and burglary.

The main significance of this classification is that different degrees of offences are dealt with by different ranks of judges. Details will be found in chapter 3.

The Crown Court for the City of London is known officially as the Central Criminal Court, and colloquially as the Old Bailey, from the street in which it is situated. Its official status is the same as that of any other Crown Court.

2C3. The Court of Appeal – Criminal Division

The main appellate court in criminal matters is the Court of Appeal – Criminal Division, which hears appeals from the Crown Court. An appeal may be against conviction, or sentence, or both. A person has an unrestricted right of appeal against conviction on a question of law, but the agreement of the Court of Appeal is necessary to an appeal against sentence. Where a sentence is fixed by law, for example life imprisonment for murder, there can be no appeal against sentence as such.

If the Court of Appeal refuses leave to appeal against sentence, a defendant may petition the Home Secretary, and if his petition is successful, the Home Secretary will refer the matter to the Court of Appeal for determination.

The Court of Appeal may, depending on the circumstances, dismiss an appeal, allow it, or reduce the sentence, but it may not increase the sentence. In some cases it has power to order a new trial.

It is possible for a person to appeal against a finding of insanity or unfitness to pleas by a lower court. Where a person charged with a crime would, were he sane, have been found guilty and sentences, he is, if insane, found 'not guilty on the grounds of insanity'. This is of course an acquittal, and rightly so, as a person cannot be held responsible if he did not know the nature of his acts, and therefore did not know that they were wrong. But in such a case the usual order of the court is that the defendant be confined in a mental hospital. He thus loses his freedom, and it is therefore only equitable that he be allowed to appeal. In order to regain his freedom he would of course have to satisfy the court both that he was sane, and given that, that he was not guilty of the crime with which he had been charged.

Most of the work of the Court of Appeal – Criminal Division is done in London, but it also sits in some of the larger provincial cities.

2C4.The House of Lords

From the decision of the Court of Appeal – Criminal Division, a final appeal lies to the House of Lords, as in civil cases. Appeal to the House of Lords in criminal cases, however, lies only if the lower court provides a certificate (which is not required in civil cases) to the effect that a point of law of general public importance is involved and that the point ought to be considered by the House of Lords. It sometimes happens that the Court of Appeal indicated that a point of law of general public importance is involved, but nevertheless refuses leave to appeal to the House of Lords. In such circumstances, it is for the House of Lords itself to decide whether the appeal will be heard. In addition to the defendant having an appeal to the House of Lords, subject to the conditions just mentioned, the prosecution also has a right of appeal, although it has no right of appeal from the Crown Court to the Court of Appeal.

The system of the main criminal courts may be shown diagrammatically as follows:

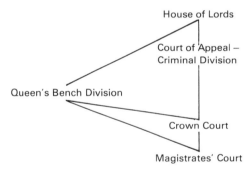

Cities and towns, known as court centres, in which the High Court (for civil cases) and the Crown Court (for criminal cases) sit are divided into three tiers:
—There are 24 first tier centres in which civil and criminal cases are dealt with by High Court judges and circuit judges.
—There are 19 second tier centres where criminal cases only are dealt with by High Court judges and circuit judges.
—There are 46 third tier centres where the (comparatively) less serious criminal cases are dealt with by circuit judges.
The functions of the different types of judges are dealt with in detail in chapter 3.

2D.European Court

Although the system of courts so far described is considered to constitute the mainstream of English courts (though there are a number of others which will be considered later), special consideration must be given to the Court of Justice of the European Communities (the European Court), because its judgments become part of English law, and in the sphere in which it operates it is superior even to the House of Lords.

The Treaty of Rome provides that any court in a member state from which there is no right of appeal – which in the UK is the House of Lords – and which has before it a case concerned with the meaning of any of the European treaties must suspend the case and remit it to the European Court for a preliminary ruling on the meaning of the treaty, unless the matter has already been decided by the European Court.

2E.Other courts

As well as the main system of English courts so far described, there are a number of other courts which dispense justice in England, some of them of considerable importance, others less so. They cannot be ranked or classified in any particular way, as they are so dissimilar, and the order in which they are dealt with below is to a large extent arbitrary.

2E1. Courts-Martial

Members of the armed services are subject to military law as well as to the ordinary law of the land, and may be tried by court-martial for any offence committed abroad, and for all except the most serious offences, for example treason and murder, committed in the UK. There are two types of court-martial:

—district courts-martial, consisting of at least three officers, which deal with lesser offences committed by 'other ranks'; and

—general courts-martial, consisting of at least five officers, which deal with the more serious offences committed by 'other ranks' and with all offences committed by officers.

From the decision of a court-martial appeal lies to the Courts-Martial Appeal Court, which is the Court of Appeal – Criminal Division by another name with the addition of some Scottish judges, and thence to the House of Lords in appropriate cases.

2E2. Ecclesiastical courts

For ecclesiastical purposes the country is divided into the Provinces of Canterbury and York, presided over by the Archbishops of Canterbury and York respectively, with the provinces being further divided into dioceses, each diocese having its own bishop.

Each diocese has a consistory court which deals with allegations of misconduct and breach of duty, the court being presided over by a Chancellor. An exception is the diocese of Canterbury, which has instead a Commissary Court presided over by a Commissary General.

Each province has a provincial court, that for Canterbury being known as the Arches Court of Canterbury, which is presided over by the Dean of Arches, and that for York being known as the Chancery of York, which is presided over by the Auditor. From a consistory court appeal lies to the provincial court, and from the provincial courts to the Judicial Committee of the Privy Council.

Jurisdiction over bishops and archbishops is exercised by Commissions of Convocation. There is also a Court of Ecclesiastical Causes Reserved, which is responsible for any dispute relating to doctrine, ritual, or ceremonial. From these two courts appeal lies to a Commission of Review consisting of two Law Lords and two Lords Spiritual, that is, archbishops and bishops who have seats in the House of Lords.

The foregoing applies to the Church of England only. English law does not recognise any bodies which have jurisdiction over other Christian denominations or religions other than Christianity.

2E3. Coroners' Courts

The office of coroner can be traced back to the twelfth century. From the earliest times one of his most important duties was to enquire into unnatural deaths or deaths in unusual or perhaps suspicious circumstances, and this has become his chief function in the present day. The coroner also conducts enquiries into treasure trove, which consists of objects of gold and silver and coins of any metal once hidden and now found, and which have become the property of the Crown because the original owner cannot be traced. At present treasure trove is handed over to the Treasury, but it is customary for the Treasury to reward the finder and the owner of the land on which it is found.

The coroner sits with a jury of between seven and eleven people in cases of suspected murder, manslaughter, infanticide, suicide, poisoning, and road accidents. He can summon and examine on oath any person who is believed to have knowledge of the circumstances of the death. Interested parties may be represented at the inquest by counsel or solicitors, who do not make speeches but who may, with the permission of the coroner, put questions to the witnesses.

A verdict as to the cause of death is returned by the jury, or by the coroner himself if he is sitting without a jury. If the cause of death cannot be fully established, an 'open' verdict is returned. If the verdict is murder or manslaughter by some known person a warrant for his arrest is issued and he is tried by the Crown Court. This rarely happens, however, because the coroner must adjourn the inquest if, before its conclusion:

—he is told by a clerk of a magistrates' court that some person has been charged with murder, manslaughter or infanticide of the deceased, or of causing death by reckless driving, or of aiding, abetting, counselling or procuring the death of the deceased; or

—he is informed by the Director of Public Prosecutions that some person has been charged with an offence committed in circumstances connected with the death of the deceased.

After the conclusion of the relevant criminal proceedings the coroner may resume the adjourned inquest if he thinks that there is sufficient reason to do so, but this is very much a formality, as his findings must not be inconsistent with the outcome of the criminal proceedings.

The coroner's court is the only English court in which the inquisitorial process is used. The coroner is charged with the function of discovering the cause of death, and is not merely an impartial judge. Thus he himself is responsible for questioning witnesses, and he does not allow speeches by persons acting on behalf of interested parties. As mentioned above, solicitors and barristers may question witnesses, but only with the permission of the coroner.

2E4. The Restrictive Practices Court

The Restrictive Practices Court was established by the Restrictive Trade Practices Act 1956. It is staffed by three judges of the High Court, one judge of the Court of Session of Scotland and one judge of the Supreme Court of Northern Ireland. The judges are assisted by laymen who have knowledge of, or experience in, industry, commerce or public affairs. A court consists of one judge and two laymen. The judge decides all questions of law, but matters of fact are decided by a majority of the members of the court.

It has two main areas of jurisdiction. In the first it deals with restrictive trading agreements registered with the Director General of Fair Trading. The Restrictive Trade Practices Act 1976 assumes that collective agreements between two or more persons under which restrictions are accepted in respect of prices, quantities, or descriptions of goods to be produced, are contrary to the public interest. In any case which comes before the court it is for the parties to show that their agreement is not contrary to the public interest; this they may be able to do by showing that it comes within any of eight categories set out in the Act. If the parties can establish their case the agreement will be held to be valid; if not, the court will decide that the restriction is against the public interest and so is void.

In the court's second area of jurisdiction it hears cases relating to resale price maintenance. The Resale Prices Act 1976 provides that in general any contract between a supplier and a dealer for the sale of goods which provides for a minimum resale price is void. However, such an agreement is valid if the parties can satisfy the court by showing that any one of five grounds exist. In general, these grounds provide reasons for holding that the restrictive agreement is in the public interest.

From a decision of the Restrictive Practices Court, appeal lies on a point of law to the Court of Appeal – Civil Division.

From the Court of Appeal there may be a further appeal to the House of Lords.

2F. Administrative tribunals

The growth of state control in recent years has involved the setting up of many bodies known as administrative tribunals. Some of these have solely administrative functions, that is, they are concerned with the carrying out of government policy, and as such are outside the scope of this book. Most of them, however, have judicial functions as well, in that they deal with disputes between individuals and government departments or between one individual and another.

The powers of an administrative tribunal and control of its activities are laid down in the legislation by which it is created. The only factor common to all administrative tribunals is that they do not operate in the same way as does an ordinary court. In fact the majority of them are not courts of law in the proper sense but, rather, are concerned with the administration of government policy, and are therefore not alternatives to the ordinary courts. The powers and procedures of different tribunals vary greatly, but an insight into them can be gained by considering the working of some of the more important types of tribunal.

2F1. Social security tribunals

Where a person makes a claim for a particular social security benefit, such as unemployment benefit, a local insurance officer may in certain circumstances refuse payment or refer the claim to a local tribunal if there is a doubt whether it should be paid. Where benefit is refused, the claimant has a right to appeal to the tribunal.

The tribunal is composed of three persons, the first a qualified lawyer, the second a person representing employers and the third a person representing employees. The tribunal will decide the appeal in favour of either the insurance officer or the claimant, but the unsuccessful party may then appeal further to a National Insurance Commissioner. A Commissioner is either a barrister or a solicitor of at least ten years' standing and his decision is usually binding. It is possible, however, for a person to appeal to the High Court from the decision of a Commissioner on a matter of law, and if the record discloses an error of law, *certioriari* (see earlier) lies to quash it.

2F2. Lands Tribunal and rent tribunals

The Lands Tribunal settles the amount of compensation to be paid when disputes arise following the compulsory acquisition of land by government departments and local authorities. It also hears appeals concerning the valuation of premises for rating purposes.

The Tribunal has a President who is a person who has held high judicial office or is a barrister of at least seven years' standing, and other members who are either senior barristers or solicitors or persons experienced in the valuation of land. Any one member of the Tribunal may exercise its jurisdiction.

The Tribunal normally sits in public, and there is a right of audience and legal representation. The Tribunal gives reasoned decisions, and either party may state a case for consideration by the Court of Appeal. Legal aid is available in respect of proceedings in the Lands Tribunal.

Rent tribunals were established by the Furnished Houses (Rent Control) Act 1946 to determine fair rents as between landlord and tenant for furnished accommodation. Their procedure is now governed by the Rent Act 1977. The members are appointed by the Secretary of State for the Environment and the proceedings are less formal than those in an ordinary court. Oral evidence is given by the parties, who may be represented by solicitor or counsel, and the tribunal, after hearing the evidence, may reduce a rent which it considers to be excessive. It also has power to give tenants security of tenure for a limited period.

Until 1958 rent tribunals did not give reasons for their decisions, and there was no right of appeal. Now, however, an appeal on a point of law lies in some cases to the High Court, and the High Court has a right to intervene in any case where the tribunal exceeds its jurisdiction or does not act in accordance with the rules of natural justice.

The county courts administer the Rent Restriction Acts which govern the rents of unfurnished accommodation.

2F3. Conciliation and industrial tribunals

When an industrial dispute arises, the main aim of the Advisory, Conciliation and Arbitration Service (ACAS) is to settle a complaint or claim without the necessity for it to go before an industrial tribunal. Complaints relating to such matters as equal pay or sex discrimination are sent by the industrial tribunal to a Conciliation Officer, who will attempt to settle the dispute, if the complainant asks him to or if he thinks that there is a good chance of a settlement, without the need for a full hearing before the industrial tribunal. The procedure before the Conciliation Officer is completely informal, and any statement made to him is not admissible in later proceedings before an industrial tribunal unless the person making the statement agrees.

If conciliation fails, the dispute will be heard by an industrial tribunal, which is concerned with such matters as disputes arising out of contracts of employment, unfair dismissal, redundancy, equal pay and sex discrimination. The chairman of the tribunal is a barrister or solicitor of at least seven years' standing, who sits with two other persons who have knowledge or experience of employment problems in industry and commerce. The tribunal has power to make or refuse a monetary award, the amount depending on the circumstances of the particular case. Hearings before the industrial tribunal are usually in public, although in exceptional circumstances they may be in private. Decisions are either unanimous or by a majority, and are recorded in a document which gives the reasons for the decision.

2F4. The Employment Appeal Tribunal

The Employment Appeal Tribunal was established by the Employment Protection Act 1978, and consists of both judges and laymen who have special knowledge or experience of industrial relations, either as representatives of employers or as representatives of workers. Its main function is to hear appeals on points of law from decisions of industrial tribunals. Parties may appear in person before the Tribunal, or may be represented by another person, such as a trade union official.

The Employment Appeal Tribunal has the same status as the High Court (the judge being either a High Court judge, or a judge of the Court of Appeal) and may sit at any time and in any place in Great Britain. Its hearings are normally in public and legal aid is available for appellants.

From decisions of the Tribunal there is a right of appeal on a point of law to the Court of Appeal-Civil Division, with the leave either of the Tribunal or of the Court of Appeal, with a further possible appeal to the House of Lords.

2F5. Advantages and disadvantages

The main advantages and disadvantages of administrative tribunals are as follows:

Advantages

—The ordinary courts as at present constituted could not cope with the enormous number of cases now dealt with by administrative tribunals, and any attempt by them to do so would cause inordinate delays. Tribunals, therefore, help prevent delays, and their proceedings do not last so long.

—As a result, the cost of bringing a case before a tribunal is much less than the cost of proceedings in the ordinary courts.

—The tribunals are usually composed of experts in the matters with which they deal.

—Tribunals are not bound so rigidly by precedent as the ordinary courts, although they do aim to secure consistency in their decisions.

—The tribunals assist the efficient conduct of public administration and promote a policy of social improvement.

—Tribunals are usually local by nature, and can therefore acquaint themselves with local conditions and carry out inspections of property and sites (particularly in the case of the Lands Tribunal) where this will assist them in their decisions.

Disadvantages

—The lack of publicity where hearings are in private and no reasons are given for decisions.

—The poor quality of investigation of facts where the rules of evidence are not observed.

—The possibility of political interference by the government preventing the tribunal from giving an impartial decision. There is, however, little or no evidence of this having ever occurred.

—The danger that important judicial functions may be exercised by unqualified persons.

—With the exception of the Lands Tribunal and the Employment Appeal Tribunal, legal aid is not available for persons appearing before tribunals, and they may therefore not be properly represented. This applies particularly to bodies such as mental health review tribunals.

In November 1955 a Committee on Administrative Tribunals and Enquiries was established to consider the constitution and working of tribunals. The Committee reported as follows:

—The principles of openness, fairness, and impartiality had not always been manifest, but in general the tribunal system worked well.

—Proceedings should be given publicity, steps should be taken to ensure that people knew their rights and were able to present their cases properly, and tribunals should be free from outside influences, especially government influence.

—Tribunals are essential in modern society, but they should not be used simply as convenient alternatives to courts of law. There should be demonstrably good reasons for setting up a tribunal, and in any case ultimate control should be excercised by the ordinary courts.

The position has been improved by the passing of the Tribunals and Inquiries Acts 1958 and 1966, now consolidated in the Tribunals and Inquiries Act 1971. These Acts provide for a Council on Tribunals, which keeps under review the working of certain tribunals, and reports to the Lord Chancellor on matters relevant to administrative tribunals which they may refer to him. The Lord Chancellor nominates the members of the Council, and the dismissal of members of certain tribunals can take place only with his approval, which gives the tribunals a great measure of independence. As has been seen from the examples of tribunals given above, there is very often a right of appeal from the decision of a tribunal to the High Court and in some cases even to higher courts, and all tribunals are subject to the supervisory jurisdiction of the High Court by means of the prerogative orders of *certiorari*, prohibition and *mandamus* (see earlier).

All tribunals are also subject to the *ultra vires* doctrine, that is, any decision which they make or any action which they take must be within the powers conferred on them, or at least must be reasonably incidental to such powers. A person who is aggrieved by an *ultra vires* decision or action of a tribunal may appeal to the High Court for a declaration that the decision or activity is void.

It is now much more common than it used to be for tribunals to have public hearings and to allow people appearing before them to be legally represented, and the reports of inspectors who have conducted inquiries are very often made public.

2G. Domestic tribunals

Somewhat akin to administrative tribunals are the domestic tribunals associated with many professions and trades. These tribunals exercise judicial or quasi-judicial functions over their members. Some such tribunals, varying from the Disciplinary Committee of the Law Society to the Milk Marketing Board, are established by statute, others by contract between members of a particular body; for example, if a person joins the Chartered Insurance Institute he agrees to be bound by its Charter and Bye-Laws including provisions which may in certain circumstances result in disciplinary action being taken against him.

The precise circumstances in which a person may be disciplined and the procedure to be followed are laid down by the statute, charter or other relevant document, but certain general principles usually apply. If, for example, a body operating under a Royal Charter proposed to take action against one of its members for unprofessional conduct the Charter would usually provide that:

—a special meeting of the disciplinary committee of the governing body must be called to hear the complaint;

—the person against whom accusation of misconduct is made must be given a reasonable opportunity of attending the meeting either himself or by his representative (usually a lawyer);

—he has a right to call witnesses on his own behalf and to cross-examine witnesses called against him;

—if he is found guilty, he has a right of appeal.

The Charter will also provide what penalties may be imposed, for example, a reprimand or suspension or expulsion from membership.

In the case of bodies established by statute, there may be provision for an appeal from the disciplinary body to the ordinary courts.

Like administrative tribunals, all domestic tribunals are governed by the *ultra vires* doctrine, and an aggrieved person may appeal to the ordinary courts on the grounds that the tribunal acted *ultra vires* or has not observed the principles of natural justice. If the court is satisfied that the allegation is well-founded it can grant an injunction to prevent the tribunal from implementing the decision which it has made, or give a declaratory judgment indicating the legal position of the parties.

2H. Arbitration

Disputes are sometimes referred not to the ordinary courts or to tribunals, but to arbitration. This may arise from the fact that certain statutes provide that disputes are to be referred to arbitration rather than to the ordinary courts; but it is more usual for arbitrations to arise from disputes under commercial contracts, such as many insurance contracts, where the parties have agreed that disputes shall be referred to arbitration rather than normal litigation.

Typical of an arbitration clause in a contract is that in the standard fire policy issued by insurance companies, namely:

> If any difference shall arise as to the amount to be paid under this Policy (liability being otherwise admitted) such difference shall be referred to an Arbitrator to be appointed by the parties in accordance with the statutory provisions in that behalf for the time being in force. Where any difference is by this condition to be referred to arbitration the making of an award shall be a condition precedent to any right of action against the Company.

The statutory provisions referred to in the clause are the Arbitration Acts 1950–79. Before dealing with these, however, it must be emphasised that the fact that the making of an award by an arbitrator is a condition precedent to any right of action does not mean that a person dissatisfied with an award can recommence proceedings in the ordinary courts. All it means is that if the person against whom the award is made does not comply with the arbitrator's ruling, legal proceedings can be brought to enforce the award. It is only in the most rare circumstances, which need not be enumerated here, that an arbitrator's award can be overruled by the courts. However, an arbitration clause which prohibits the parties completely from having access to the courts is invalid.

There are several reasons, apart from the fact that a statute may so require, why people may prefer to refer disputes to arbitration rather than to the ordinary courts:

Firstly, arbitration proceedings are comparatively private. It is said, for example, that the publicity of an open court is not liked by insurance companies, as newspaper reports are always brief and may in consequence give the public a false impression of the rights and wrongs of the case.

Secondly, arbitration proceedings are less formal than those in open court and the dispute is usually dealt with more quickly. These advantages should not, however, be exaggerated. An arbitration is a 'legal proceeding' (Arbitration Act 1950, s.29 (i)) and differs from other legal proceedings only as to the choice of tribunal. Commonly, counsel are briefed by both sides, rules of evidence and procedure must be followed, and all the normal defences in legal proceedings, for example, that the case is statute-barred, are available.

Thirdly, arbitration proceedings are less expensive than normal litigation. This is true, however, only because litigation is extremely expensive rather than because arbitration is cheap. The costs of arbitration are normally paid by the losing party, and the amount is usually such as to deter people from entering into arbitration proceedings lightly.

Finally, it is said that arbitrators are usually persons well-versed in the technicalities of the matters on which they are asked to adjudicate, and that their verdicts should therefore be fair. This is undoubtedly true, but it must not be inferred from this that the ordinary courts are staffed by judges without specialist knowledge. The Commercial Court, in particular, includes judges with a detailed knowledge of a wide variety of specialised subjects, who are well able to deal with, for example, disputes arising under insurance contracts. Indeed, judges of the Commercial Court often sit as arbitrators, rather than as High Court judges. The advantage of this is that, with the consent of the parties, they can depart from the normal rules of procedure and admissibility of evidence where the interests of justice demand or where it is necessary to expedite business. The hearing is in private and is heard in any place convenient to the parties. The award is also made privately to the parties and is not published like a judgment.

The purpose of the Arbitration Acts 1950–1979 is to ensure that arbitration proceedings are subject to proper statutory control. If a question of law (but not a question of fact) arises out of an award, there is a right of appeal to the High Court. The appeal may be brought by agreement between the parties or with the consent of the court, but the court will not grant leave unless it considers that a ruling on the question of law could substantially affect the rights of the parties. From the decision of the High Court on a question of law a further appeal lies to the Court of Appeal, but only if the High Court or the Court of Appeal gives leave, and this will be given only if the High Court certifies that the question of law is one of general public importance or is one which for some other special reason should be considered by the Court of Appeal.

Until the enactment of the Arbitration Act 1979, it had been considered a matter of public policy that parties to an arbitration agreement should not be permitted to exclude the possibility of judicial review. Section 3 of the 1979 Act, however, does permit such exclusion in certain strictly limited circumstances.

The Act makes a distinction between domestic and international arbitration agreements. Section 3(7) provides that a domestic agreement is: 'An arbitration agreement which does not provide, expressly or by implication, for arbitration in a State other than the UK and to which neither:

(a) an individual who is a national of, or habitually resident in, any State other than the UK, or

(b) a body corporate which is incorporated in, or whose central management and control is exercised in, any State other than the UK

is a party at the time the arbitration agreement is entered into.'

International agreements are those which do not fall within Section 3(7).

In domestic arbitration agreements, exclusion of the supervisory jurisdiction of the courts can come about only if the parties so agree after the commencement of the arbitration. International arbitration agreements are treated differently in that the original arbitration agreement, entered into before a question of actual arbitration arises, may contain an exclusion agreement. Such an agreement is not permitted, however, in connnection with arbitrations relating to maritime matters, insurance, and commodity broking.

Generally, arbitration clauses, such as that in the standard fire policy, refer to the appointment of one arbitrator, though sometimes reference is made to two, one to be appointed by each party to the dispute. Even where the agreement is that one arbitrator only shall be appointed, the parties may not be able to agree as to who the arbitrator shall be, and in these circumstances the Arbitration Acts provide that each party shall appoint an arbitrator. Whenever there are two arbitrators, it also becomes necessary to appoint an umpire, whose role is to deal with the dispute if the two arbitrators cannot agree. Needless to say, every effort is made to agree upon the appointment of a single arbitrator, as the appointment of two arbitrators and an umpire increases the costs involved.

3. The administration of justice – 2

3A.Function and status of judges
  3A1.Lords of Appeal in Ordinary
  3A2.Lords Justices of Appeal
  3A3.High Court Judges
  3A4.Circuit Judges
  3A5.Recorders
3B.The European Court
3C.Magistrates
3D.Other persons exercising judicial
  functions
  3D1.Registrars
  3D2.The Law Officers of the Crown
  3D3.The Director of Public
    Prosecutions
  3D4.Masters of the Supreme Court
  3D5.Coroners
3E.Judicial independence and immunity
3F.The jury system
  3F1.The civil jury

3F2.The criminal jury
3G.The legal profession
  3G1.Solicitors
    3G1A.The Law Society
    3G1B.The Solicitors' Disciplinary
      Tribunal
    3G1C.Qualifications and functions
      of solicitors
  3G2.Barristers
  3G3.Comparison between the two
    branches of the legal profession
    3G3A.Similarities
    3G3B.Differences
3H.Legal aid and advice
  3H1.Legal aid under Part I
  3H2.Legal advice and assistance
    under Part I
  3H3.Legal aid under Part II

3A.Function and status of judges

The judiciary is the collective name given to the judges who preside over the English courts. The main groups of judges are as follows:
— Lords of Appeal in Ordinary;
— Lords Justices of Appeal;
— Judges of the High Court;
— Circuit judges;
— Recorders.

Before going into detail regarding these various groups, it is useful to consider the role of the Lord Chancellor. His position within the British constitution is unique in that:
— He is a member of the Cabinet and the government, and therefore holds office only during the lifetime of a government. As a cabinet minister, he is usually a member of the political party which commands a majority in Parliament, and to that extent is a political figure.
— He is head of the judicial system and in this capacity he is completely non-political. He is the senior judge of the House of Lords in its judicial capacity, and often sits as such. He is also nominal President of the Supreme Court, but in fact never sits in the Court of Appeal, the High Court or the Crown Court.

It may be thought that there is some conflict of interest between the various functions of the Lord Chancellor, and it is certainly true that countries with written constitutions, such as the USA, take great care to ensure that there is a 'separation of powers', that is, that the same people do not exercise executive (or governmental), legislative, and judicial powers. The combination of such powers in the Lord Chancellor cannot be defended on logical grounds, but it can be asserted without hesitation that the Lord Chancellor, to whichever political party he belongs, never allows political considerations to affect his judicial functions, especially his main function of recommending persons for appointment as judges.

3A1.Lords of Appeal in Ordinary

Until 1876, the whole of the House of Lords sat as a judicial body, but now only those members who hold or have held high judicial office carry out this work. For this purpose the Appellate Jurisdiction Act 1876 provided for the appointment of life peers as Lords of Appeal in Ordinary to act in a judicial capacity. They are supplemented by the Lord Chancellor, in his capacity as senior judge in the House of Lords, and other members of the House who have held high judicial office. As mentioned earlier, the Lord Chancellor retains his position as such only as long as the government of which he is a member remains in office, but thereafter he still remains a member of the House of Lords and assists with its judicial work.

Lords of Appeal in Ordinary, or 'Law Lords' as they are commonly called, must have been barristers of at least fifteen years' standing, or have been judges of the Supreme Court for at least two years. They are appointed by the Crown on the advice of the Prime Minister. They include judges from Scotland and Northern Ireland, as the House is the final court of appeal for all civil matters throughout the UK, and for criminal matters in England, Wales, and Northern Ireland.

A court of three judges constitutes a quorum in the House of Lords, but most commonly a court of five sits. In any event there is always an uneven number, as in most courts of appeal, because if the judges are not unanimous (as is often the case in the

House of Lords), the decision depends on the majority. Judgments delivered in the House are known as 'opinions', and are normally delivered to the parties in printed form rather than being read aloud in open court. If a Law Lord wishes to express himself orally he is entitled to do so, in which case he is said to 'make a speech' rather than deliver a judgment, a reminder of the days when decisions were made by the House as a whole after hearing speeches.

In theory, Lords of Appeal in Ordinary can sit in the Court of Appeal, but in practice they never do so.

3A2. Lords Justices of Appeal

In dealing with civil cases, the Court of Appeal normally consists of Lords Justices of Appeal, who are presided over by the Master of the Rolls, who performs a curious role in that, in addition to being the senior judge of the Court of Appeal, he also has supervisory powers over solicitors. Lords Justices of Appeal must be barristers of at least fifteen years' standing, or have been High Court judges for at least one year, and are appointed by the Crown on the recommendation of the Prime Minister.

A normal court consists of three judges, but under certain circumstances there may be a court of only two. Where a point of law of great importance or difficulty is involved, there may be a 'full' court of five judges. In theory there is no difference between a court of three and a court of five – judgment is unanimous or by a majority – but where a precedent is established by a full court it commands greater respect and is less likely to be overruled.

There are 18 Lords Justices of Appeal, and as High Court judges also sit in the Court of Appeal, there may be nine or ten courts of appeal sitting at any one time.

The Lords Justices of Appeal also form the nucleus of the Court of Appeal when it is dealing with criminal cases, but in this capacity they are presided over by the Lord Chief Justice of England, and are supplemented by High Court judges of the Queen's Bench Division as business requires. The Lord Chief Justice must be a barrister of at least fifteen years' standing, and he is appointed by the Crown on the recommendation of the Prime Minister.

A Lord Justice of Appeal may sit in the High Court, exercising the powers of a High Court judge but only on rare occasions does this happen, as the Lords Justices of Appeal are more than fully occupied with the work of the Court of Appeal.

The Supreme Court Act 1981 provides that one of the ordinary judges of the Court of Appeal may be appointed as Vice-President of the Court of Appeal as a whole, or one may be appointed as Vice-President of the Civil Division and another as Vice-President of the Criminal Division to preside in the absence of the Master of the Rolls or the Lord Chief Justice.

Lords Justices of Appeal are not, despite their title, members of the House of Lords. They are in fact knights, so that in private life they are known as, for example, Sir Thomas Robins. Such a person in his official capacity would be known as Lord Justice Robins, and in legal literature this is abbreviated to Robins L.J. (plural L.JJ.)

3A3. High Court Judges

The three Divisions of the High Court are staffed mainly by High Court judges, who must be barristers of at least ten years' standing, and who are appointed by the Crown on the recommendation of the Lord Chancellor. The Lord Chief Justice presides over the Queen's Bench Division; the Vice-Chancellor over the Chancery Division (although theoretically the Lord Chancellor is head of the Division); and the President over the Family Division. The Lord Chief Justice, the Vice-Chancellor, and the President are also all *ex officio* members of the Court of Appeal. When any Division of the High Court is sitting as a Divisional Court, a quorum consists of three judges. When exercising first instance jurisdiction, there is one judge, who usually sits alone, that is, without a jury. The exceptional cases in which a jury is allowed in a civil action in the High Court are considered later in this chapter.

Appeals in the High Court are usually heard in the Divisional Court but in the case of appeals from certain tribunals, such as the Special Commissioners of Income Tax, the case is heard by a single High Court judge.

High Court judges are known as puisne (pronounced 'puny') or junior judges. The term is somewhat misleading, as although High Court judges may be considered junior to Lords of Appeal in Ordinary and Lords Justices of Appeal, they are men of great learning and experience.

High Court judges also deal at first instance with the more serious criminal cases heard in the Crown Court and for this purpose the judges are appointed to one of the following six circuits: North Eastern, Northern, Midland and Oxford, South Eastern, Wales and Chester, and Western. All Class One cases must be heard by a High Court judge; Class Two cases are normally heard by a High Court judge, although the judge may remit the case to a Circuit judge or Recorder; and, occasionally, Class Three cases are heard by a High Court judge. In dealing with criminal cases a High Court judge always sits with a jury.

The increasing work of both the High Court and the Crown Court has necessitated a large increase in the number of High Court judges in recent years. The problem has been aggravated by the fact that there is now a compulsory retiring age of seventy-five, whereas in former years judges very often continued in active life until well into their eighties. On appointment a High Court judge is given a knighthood, so that in private life he becomes known as, for example, Sir John Jones. In his judicial capacity, however, he is known as Mr Justice Jones, which is legal literature is abbreviated to Jones, J. In court he is addressed as 'my lord'.

A High Court judge must retire at the age of seventy-five, but otherwise can be removed from office only by addresses to the Crown moved in both Houses of Parliament or for misconduct, a procedure which in fact has never occurred. The same rules apply to Lords of Appeal in Ordinary and Lords Justice of Appeal. It was mentioned in chapter 2 that the High Court sits in London and in some of the larger provincial cities. Quite often cases outside London are in fact heard by Circuit judges or senior barristers, sitting in the capacity of Deputy High Court judges.

3A4. Circuit Judges

County courts are staffed mainly by Circuit judges, who must be barristers of at least seven years' standing, or Recorders who have been in office for at least three years. They usually sit alone, but in rare circumstances there may also be a jury.

Circuit judges also sit as judges of the Crown Court, and in this capacity are always assisted by a jury.

Despite their title, Circuit judges are usually attached to one court only, and do not go on circuit from one court to another.

The retirement age of a Circuit judge is seventy-two, but he may be asked to continue to serve until the age of seventy-five. He may be removed from office by the Lord Chancellor on the grounds of incapacity or misbehaviour.

The Recorder and Common Serjeant of the City of London, who deal only with criminal cases at the Central Criminal Court, have the rank of Circuit judges.

3A5. Recorders

Cases in the Crown Court may also be heard by Recorders sitting with a jury. A Recorder must be a barrister or solicitor of at least ten years' standing. The main distinction between Circuit judges and Recorders is that the former are full-time judges, and the latter are part-time, being expected to serve for a minimum of thirty days a year. The compulsory retiring age of a Recorder is seventy-five, and appointment may be terminated on grounds of incapacity or misconduct.

Although the main function of Recorders is to deal with criminal cases, they may also, where the need arises, deal with civil cases in the county court.

To summarise the situation in the Crown Court, a case may, depending on its gravity, be heard by either a High Court judge, a Circuit judge, or a Recorder, in each case sitting with a jury. In hearing appeals from magistrates' courts one judge sits, but in this event he is assisted by not fewer than two, nor more than four, magistrates.

The Central Criminal Court is presided over by the Lord Chancellor in theory, and the Lord Chief Justice in practice. It is staffed by High Court judges and the Recorder and Common Serjeant, in each case sitting with a jury. By a quirk of history, the Lord Mayor and Aldermen of the City of London are also entitled to sit.

3B. The European Court

The Court of Justice of the European Communities consists of ten judges, presided over by the President. Each member State appoints one judge, who must have been either a judge or a professor of law in the country from which he is appointed. The judges hold office for a period of six years, but their appointments are renewable. The UK, as one member State, is entitled to appoint only one judge, despite the fact that there are two distinct legal systems in the UK, the English and the Scots.

3C. Magistrates

The office of justice of the peace, or magistrate, dates back to 1361. There are two types of magistrate, lay and stipendiary.

Lay magistrates are appointed by the Lord Chancellor on the recommendation of the Lord Lieutenant of a county, or the Council of a borough. They are usually people with no previous legal experience. On appointment they undergo a course of training, but the main purpose of this is not so much to teach them law as to train them to act in a judicial manner. To advise them on matters of law when sitting, they have the assistance of a clerk, who may be either a barrister or a solicitor, but is usually a solicitor.

The jurisdiction of the magistrates' court has already been dealt with in chapter 2. Lay magistrates are not paid for their work as such, but they are entitled to claim travel and subsistence expenses. They work on a part-time basis, sitting once or twice a week. In the City of London, the Lord Mayor and Aldermen are *ex officio* magistrates.

In many large towns and cities there are, either instead of or in addition to lay magistrates, stipendiary magistrates, that is, paid magistrates who work on a full-time basis. A stipendiary magistrate is a qualified lawyer, appointed by the Crown on the recommendation of the Lord Chancellor, and he has the same powers as a bench of two or more lay magistrates. Stipendiary magistrates in London are known as Metropolitan Stipendiary magistrates.

Both the lay and the stipendiary magistrates must retire at the age of seventy, and both may be removed from office by the Lord Chancellor for incompetence.

Every magistrates' court has a clerk, who is a barrister or solicitor of at least five years' standing, and whose main function is to advise the magistrates on matters of law. He is not concerned with questions of fact, nor with matters relating to findings of innocence or guilt. In some courts magistrates seek the opinion of the Clerk on sentencing policy, but the final decision on sentencing is a matter for the magistrates alone.

When the Crown Court is hearing an appeal from the magistrates' court or a committal for sentence, between two and four magistrates sit with the judge or Recorder, who presides. The decision of the court may be a majority decision, but if the court is equally divided, the judge or Recorder has a casting vote.

3D. Other persons exercising judicial functions

3D1. Registrars

In addition to Circuit judges, there are registrars attached to every County court. The registrar acts as an assistant judge. He is the only type of judge who is also a civil servant, and he must be a solicitor of at least seven years' standing.

The registrar can deal with undefended cases, defended cases where the amount involved is not more than £500 unless either party objects to his doing so, and any case with which both parties agree to let him deal.

He may also deal with cases referred to arbitration. This is a procedure peculiar to the County court, and is not to be confused with arbitration under statute or in accordance with the terms of a contract, as described in chapter 2. In the County court, arbitration is a comparatively informal procedure designed to deal speedily and inexpensively with the smaller cases, thereby saving the time and expense of a full hearing. An application for reference to arbitration may be made by either party, and the terms on which the reference is to take place are decided by the court. The registrar is generally appointed arbitrator, although sometimes the judge or an outside arbitrator is appointed, the strict rules of evidence do not apply, and with the consent of the parties the case may be decided on the basis of statements and documents submitted by the parties rather than oral evidence. The award of the arbitrator is entered as the judgment, and can be enforced by the court. There is no appeal from the award.

Legal representation in arbitration proceedings is discouraged, and any costs of legal representation are not normally allowed. A litigant may, however, bring with him a relative or friend to help present his case. It is by these means that the proceedings are kept as inexpensive and as informal as possible.

Cases involving an allegation of fraud against one of the parties cannot be referred to arbitration except with the consent of that party.

3D2. The Law Officers of the Crown

The Law Officers of the Crown are the Attorney-General and the Solicitor-General.

The Attorney-General. The Attorney-General is a barrister and a member of the government, but not of the Cabinet. By tradition he does not take part in political matters, except to the extent that some judicial matters within his province necessarily have political overtones. The main duties and powers of the Attorney-General are as follows:

— He advises the government on matters of law.
— He conducts civil proceedings, particularly in revenue matters, on behalf of the Crown.
— He leads for the Crown in important criminal prosecutions.
— His consent is required before certain types of proceedings, for example, prosecutions under the Official Secrets Act, can be commenced.
— He can stop a trial on indictment by entering a *nolle prosequi,* that is, a direction to discontinue the proceedings.
— He supervises the work of the Director of Public Prosecutions.
— By virtue of his office he is leader of the Bar and he presides at its general meetings.

The Solicitor-General. The office of Solicitor-General, like that of Attorney-General, is political. The Solicitor-General, despite his title, is always a barrister. His main practical function is to act as assistant to the Attorney-General and he can exercise all the functions of the Attorney-General if the latter is ill or for any other reason cannot carry out his duties. The Solicitor-General also deputises if for any reason the office of Attorney-General is vacant.

3D3. The Director of Public Prosecutions

The Director of Public Prosecutions is appointed by the Home Secretary but he works under the superintendence of the Attorney-General. He is a civil servant and must be a barrister or solicitor of at least ten years' standing. His main functions are to institute and conduct criminal proceedings which are of unusual importance or difficulty, including prosecutions for all offences punishable by death. Although he institutes the proceedings, they are brought in the name of the Crown, for example, *R* (= Rex or Regina) v. *Smith*. It used to be the case that when a criminal appeal was heard by the House of Lords, the Director was both nominally and practically made a party to it, so that it was cited, for example *Smith* v. *D.P.P.* (Director of Public Prosecutions). This practice was discontinued in 1979, so that now the Crown is nominally a party even to criminal appeals in the House of Lords.

3D4. Masters of the Supreme Court

Masters of the Supreme Court are concerned with the following subjects:
— Interlocutory matters, that is, anything which arises in the course of preparation of a case for trial.
— Taxation of costs in civil cases, that is, deciding what costs are to be awarded to a successful litigant. (The word 'taxation' in this context has nothing whatever to do with taxation in the normal sense of the term.)
— The assessment of damages in undefended civil cases.

From the decision of a Master in the matters mentioned, an appeal lies either to a High Court judge or to a Divisional court, depending on the circumstances.

3D5. Coroners

The work of coroners has been described in chapter 2. A coroner must be a barrister, solicitor, or qualified medical practitioner who has practised his profession for at least five years.

3E. Judicial independence and immunity

It is essential that judges in any court and others who exercise judicial functions should administer justice impartially, and without an eye to any personal gain. To ensure as completely as possible that this is so the following conditions operate:

Firstly a judge will never become involved in a case in which he has an interest of any nature. If he has a direct interest he will not hear a case, and by tradition if he has even what might be considered a remote interest he will declare it and ask the parties whether they are content that he should try the case.

Secondly, judges are completely free of control by the government. Although the senior appointments are filled by nominees of the Prime Minister or the Lord Chancellor, judges are appointed until retirement-age and cannot be removed except in the special circumstances noted earlier. Clearly, they are not immune from making mistakes of law, and in some cases may pass sentences which are inappropriate, but ample protection is provided by the system of appeals. Judges are in no respect agents of the government, and they show no bias in favour of the Crown when it is a party to litigation. On the contrary, they see it as one of their duties to protect citizens from the excesses, in this country fortunately rare, of government.

Thirdly, such promotion as is open to judges cannot be achieved by influence or partiality, and does not result in any significant financial gain. By any standards judges are well paid, but it is probably true to say that their salaries are less than they could earn as barristers in private practice. Promotion of a High Court judge to the position of Lord Justice of Appeal, and from Lord Justice of Appeal to Lord of Appeal in Ordinary, does not result in any increase in salary.

A judge of a superior court is immune from any proceedings, either civil or criminal, in respect of any act which is done by him in his judicial capacity, even if it is malicious or in bad faith. A judge could not for example, be sued for false imprisonment by a person whom he had sentenced, even if the person concerned could produce clear evidence that he was innocent. He is not immune, however, if it can be shown that he acted outside his jurisdiction, but, in practice, High Court judges have such wide jurisdiction that it is virtually impossible for them to act outside it.

Judges of inferior courts enjoy similar immunity, with the exception that if it is alleged that the judge acted outside his jurisdiction, the onus is on the judge to prove that what he did was within his jurisdiction.

By the Justices' Protection Act 1848, magistrates may be sued for acts done without jurisdiction and for wrongful acts done maliciously or without cause within their jurisdiction.

A general immunity against civil and criminal liability attaches to other persons taking part in the administration of justice as regards things said or done by them in that capacity, for example, jurymen, witnesses or advocates. A person who gives false evidence, however, is guilty of the crime of perjury.

Although people acting in a judicial capacity are given the immunity mentioned, in their private capacities they have no immunities whatsoever, and they are liable civilly and criminally in the same way as are other citizens. The only person who enjoys immunity from law is the Queen in her personal capacity.

3F. The jury system   The origin of the jury system is a matter of doubt and dispute among legal historians.

3F1. The civil jury   For present purposes it is necessary to go back to the reign of Henry II (1154–89), who introduced the Petty Assizes and the Grand Assizes. (The term Assizes here refers to what today are called juries, and is in no way associated with the system of courts called Assizes which were in existence until 1970.)

The Petty Assizes were twelve freeholders chosen from the district in which a dispute originated, and they were sworn to answer specific questions of fact, rather than to give a decision on a case as a whole. They were not jurors in the modern sense, because there were no witnesses at the trial, and the jurors were expected to answer the questions from their own knowledge, and to find out the truth if they did not know.

The Grand Assizes were a means of settling disputes as to the ownership of land. They consisted of twelve knights of the shire, whose task was to declare whether what was alleged in the writ by which the action was started was true. As with the Petty Assizes, they spoke from their own knowledge.

By the beginning of the fourteenth century it had become the function of juries to decide general issues as distinct from specific questions of fact. Later the practice grew of having witnesses as well as jurors, so that the jury did not act entirely on their own knowledge. However, although in 1562 a statute gave the right to compel the attendance of witnesses at a trial and so recognised the importance of witnesses, it was not until the decision in *Bushell's Case* (1670) that it was finally recognised that jurors should not act on their own knowledge, but should decide cases on the evidence adduced by witnesses.

The current rule is that every person between the ages of eighteen and sixty-five who is on the register for parliamentary and local government elections is eligible for jury service, provided that he has been resident in the United Kingdom for at least five years (although any person with an insufficient command of English, however long he has resided in the country, can ask to be excused jury service). Certain groups of people, however, are not eligible:

— judges and other people concerned with the administration of justice, such as lawyers, policemen, and probation officers;
— clergymen;
— mental patients who are resident in a hospital or similar institution or who regularly attend for treatment by a medical practitioner.

Other people, although eligible, can claim exemption as of right:

— members of either House of Parliament;
— full-time members of the armed services;
— medical practitioners and those in similar professions;
— people who have attended for jury service within the last two years.

Persons who have served a prison sentence of three months or more are disqualified for jury service for a period of ten years, and those who have been sentenced to a term of imprisonment for five years or more are disqualified for life. There is therefore little substance to the criticism which is heard from time to time that "convicted criminals" can serve on juries.

Service on a jury for those who are eligible is compulsory, and a person who ignores a summons to sit on a jury may be penalised. A potential juryman may, however, ask to be excused, and the request will be granted if attendance would impose unusual hardship: if, for example, he is a self-employed business man and the case may last for several weeks, or if a woman has children for whose care it would be difficult to make provision.

The use of juries in civil cases is now comparatively rare. Either party may demand a jury in cases of fraud, defamation, malicious prosecution, and false imprisonment. In all other cases the question of whether there shall be a jury is left to the discretion of the court, which rarely allows one except in defended divorce petitions, of which at present there are very few.

When there is a jury in a High Court case it consists of twelve persons whose verdict must normally be unanimous, but if unanimity cannot be reached after a reasonable period the verdict of ten of a jury of eleven or twelve, or nine of a jury of ten, can be accepted. The original number of jurymen is always twelve, but may be reduced to eleven or ten as the result of, say, sickness in the course of the trial. If the number falls below nine a re-trial may be ordered, but with the consent of both parties the trial may proceed with an incomplete jury.

Very occasionally, a jury is allowed in a case heard by the County court. In this court the jury consists of eight persons. Normally their verdict must be unanimous, but if unanimity cannot be reached, the verdict of seven out of eight is accepted.

Juries also sit in coroners' courts. In such courts the jury is always an uneven number, either seven, nine, or eleven. The verdict need not be unanimous, but the coroner may discharge the jury and summon another if there are more than two dissentients.

In general, it is the function of the jury to decide the facts of a case, matters of law being left to the judge. But a judge may withdraw a case from the jury if he decides that the evidence is so flimsy that no reasonable jury could find for the plaintiff. The relationship between judge and jury was explained in *Metropolitan Rail* v. *Jackson* (1877) (a negligence case, but the same principle would apply in other cases) as follows:

> The judge has a certain duty to discharge, and the jurors have another and different duty. The judge has to say whether any facts have been established by the evidence from which negligence may reasonably be inferred; the jurors have to say whether from these facts, when submitted to them, negligence ought to be inferred. It would place in the hands of jurors a power which might be exercised in the most arbitrary manner, if they were at liberty to hold that negligence might be inferred from any state of facts whatever.

Where a case is heard by a judge alone, he is of course performing the functions of both judge and jury.

3F2. The criminal jury

The Assize of Clarendon, 1166, and the Assize of Northampton, 1176 (in this context 'Assize' means 'decree' or 'ordinance') imposed on a 'jury' drawn from a particular district the duty of ensuring that prisoners were brought before the judges of Assize to be tried for serious crimes. This was the origin of the Grand Jury. Later it became the duty of the Grand Jury to consider all bills of indictment, that is, allegations of crime, preferred against prisoners who had been committed for trial by the justices of the peace in order to discover whether there was a 'true bill', that is, whether the accusations of crime had been genuinely brought, and whether there was a *prima facie* case. Grand Juries were abolished in 1933, and their functions are now performed by magistrates' courts.

The origin of the present criminal jury, the Petty Jury as it was called in the days when there was also a Grand Jury, can be traced back to 1215, when trial by ordeal was abolished and trial by battle, a duel between the parties, was also losing favour. There was need, therefore, for a new form of trial and the practice arose of a man 'putting himself on his country', that is, agreeing to be bound by the verdict of his neighbours.

As with the civil jury, the criminal jury at first acted entirely on their own knowledge. Later they had the assistance of witnesses, and eventually it became accepted that the jury should base their decisions entirely on the evidence adduced before them. An important landmark in the history of the jury was *Bushell's Case (supra)* which established the independence of the jury, with its verdict not being challengeable except on appeal, on the grounds, for example, that it was against the weight of the evidence.

At the present time, all criminal cases dealt with at Crown Courts (except appeals from magistrates' courts) are heard before a jury of twelve. As with civil cases, a procedure requires the jury to try to reach unanimity, but if, after a reasonable time, which must be at least two hours, they cannot agree, the judge may accept a majority verdict of ten in the case of eleven or twelve jurors, or nine in the case of ten jurors. The Crown Court cannot accept a majority verdict of guilty unless the foreman of the jury states the voting figures.

Exceptionally, in cases of murder and offences punishable by death, a trial may not continue if the number of jurors is reduced below twelve unless both prosecution and defence agree. In the event of a jury being unable to agree, and the division of opinion being such as to prevent a majority verdict being entered, they are discharged and a new trial is ordered. If the jury at the second trial also fail to agree, it is the practice of the Crown not to proceed with the case. It is a general rule that jurors are chosen more or less at random from the electoral lists, but any party to proceedings may inspect the panel from which the jurors for his case will be drawn. Normally, either party has very limited rights to challenge jurors. However, for certain types of criminal case, particularly those involving charges of treason, terrorism, or membership of a proscribed organisation, both prosecution and defence may, well before the trial, be given a list of potential jurors whose backgrounds they can investigate, with a view to excluding potential jurors who might be thought not to be impartial. This procedure is looked upon with disfavour by many because it destroys the element of random selection which is one of the main justifications of the jury system, because the investigations are expensive, and because the prosecution has access to information, such as police records, which is not available to the defence.

A person charged with a criminal offence may always challenge up to three jurors without giving any reason for the challenge, and have them replaced. His objection may be completely without justification, for example, that the jurors are young people, or coloured people, or women, but the court will never know his reasons. Since one defendant can challenge only three jurors (unless he can give good reasons for further challenges), the scope for abuse of the system of challenge is limited when there is a single defendant. Where, however, there are a number of defendants involved in the same case and each can have three challenges, they can if they act in collusion sometimes completely distort the composition of the jury so that it is no longer a random selection. It is for this reason that many people feel that the right of challenge without cause, for which there is no logical justification, should be abolished.

As already mentioned, it is the general rule that when a person has served as a juror he or she is automatically exempt from further service for a period of at least two years. The judge also has a discretionary power to release a jury from service for a longer period or even for life. It has long been a practice for judges to exempt juries from further service where they have been involved in a trial which is lengthy or complicated or where the details of the case have been particularly distasteful and unpleasant.

It is generally accepted that in criminal cases the system of trial by jury, as distinct from trial by judge alone, is desirable, but the system does run into problems, of which two may be mentioned. First, when a number of defendants are charged together, and there are perhaps several alternative charges brought against each defendant, trials tend to become prolonged, and the task of the jury in reaching verdicts on various counts against various defendants can be difficult. (There was one case in 1982 where a jury deliberated for nine days to reach verdicts on various charges brought against a total of fourteen defendants.) Secondly, some cases, particularly those involving fraud over a long period, may by their nature be so complicated as to be virtually incomprehensible to ordinary members of the public. Suggestions are made from time to time that long or complicated trials should not be dealt with by ordinary juries, but no alternative suggestions have attracted wide acceptance, and it would perhaps be unwise to alter a generally sound system simply because in certain cases it gives rise to problems.

3G. The legal profession

The legal profession in England and Wales is divided into two branches, solicitors and barristers. The reasons for this division are mainly historical rather than the result of a conscious effort to divide the profession into two distinct parts.

Broadly, it is true to say that under the English system solicitors give their clients legal advice, and obtain advice on specialist matters, that is, they 'seek counsel's opinion', when necessary, from a barrister (counsel), very much in the same way as a general medical practitioner may call in a consultant physician.

If it is necessary to bring or defend an action on behalf of the client, a solicitor may appear on behalf of his client in a magistrates' court, a county court, a Crown Court on appeal from a magistrates' court or where his client has been committed for sentence to the Crown Court, or in the High Court on bankruptcy matters only. In all other cases, only a barrister has a right of audience in the courts.

A lay client who is involved in a legal action requiring the services of both solicitor and counsel very often feels that this system puts him to unnecessary expense. Superficially, it may appear that he is paying twice, but there are strong arguments in favour of the system:

— It is a fact that litigation is not more costly in England than it is in other countries where the dual system does not operate.
— Even where the legal profession is not formally divided, the complexity of law is such that, inevitably, some lawyers tend to specialise, so that it may well be necessary to engage two lawyers in a particular case.
— A very high quality of advice and assistance is available to the litigant, as every solicitor can call on the services of every barrister.

In England, judges are chosen from the most able members of one of the branches of the legal profession, namely, barristers (except that in the Crown Court a solicitor may be a Recorder and as such may later proceed to the position of Circuit judge). There is no separate judicial profession as there is in some countries. It is sometimes argued that it should be possible for eminent solicitors to become High Court judges. It should, however, be remembered that it is possible, by passing the appropriate examinations, for a person to transfer from one branch of the profession to the other and experience of one branch is for certain purposes treated as experience in the other. It is of interest to note that the present Lord Chief Justice, Lord Lane, and his predecessor started their professional careers as solicitors. There can be no doubt that the practice of choosing High Court judges from among practising barristers has resulted in England having a judiciary which, in independence, integrity, and intellectual range and grasp, is unsurpassed by any other country.

3G1. Solicitors

The Law Society was founded in 1825. Its governing body is the Council of the Society, under a President who is elected annually.

3G1A.The Law Society

The Law Society performs a variety of functions:

— With the concurrence of the Lord Chancellor, the Lord Chief Justice, and the Master of the Rolls, it makes regulations regarding the education and training of prospective solicitors.

— It issues the certificates of satisfaction that prospective solicitors require for admission.

— It keeps the roll of solicitors.

— It issues practising certificates to solicitors whose names have been entered on the roll and who wish to practice.

— With the concurrence of the Master of the Rolls, its Council makes rules regarding the professional conduct of solicitors.

— In certain circumstances it may intervene in a solicitor's practice to rescue the business of the client.

— It runs a compensation fund for the victims of certain wrongful acts and defaults by solicitors.

— It supervises the charges made by solicitors for their work.

— It is closely associated with the Legal Aid Scheme, of which details are given later in this chapter.

— It deals with complaints about solicitors made by members of the public through a department under the control of its Professional Purposes Committee. After investigation of the complaint the Society may refer it to the Solicitors' Disciplinary Tribunal, refuse or impose conditions on the solicitor's next practising certificate, or intervene directly in the solicitor's practice. Lay observers, that is, people who are neither solicitors nor barristers, are appointed by the Lord Chancellor to oversee the way in which the Society carries out its investigations.

3G1B.The Solicitors' Disciplinary Tribunal

The Solicitors' Disciplinary Tribunal adjudicates in disciplinary proceedings relating to solicitors. Its members, who are appointed by the Master of the Rolls, include solicitor members, who must be solicitors of at least ten years' standing, and lay members, who are neither solicitors nor barristers. The President of the Tribunal is a solicitor member. The quorum for the Tribunal is three, including at least one lay member, but the solicitor members at any sitting must exceed in number the lay members.

The Tribunal has power to strike the name of a solicitor off the roll, suspend him temporarily from practice, or impose a fine. There is a right of appeal to a Divisional Court of the Queen's Bench Division and thence, with the leave of the court, to the Court of Appeal.

3G1C.Qualifications and functions of solicitors

The majority of people wishing to become solicitors now have law degrees, and can proceed directly to the Final examination of the Law Society after spending nine months at a recognised law school. A person without a degree in law must take the Common Professional Examination, involving one year's attendance at law school, before proceeding to the Final examination. In each case, after passing the Final examination, the would-be solicitor must serve two years' articles (a form of apprenticeship) under a solicitor of at least five years' standing. He may then apply for admission as a solicitor, have his application approved by the Master of the Rolls, and obtain a practising certificate, which must be renewed annually, from the Law Society. A barrister cannot also work as a solicitor. If he wishes to do the work of a solicitor he must first be 'disbarred', that is, formally give up his qualification as a barrister. He must then pass an examination to become a solicitor, but he does not have to be articled.

A practising solicitor may either practise on his own, or in partnership with other solicitors, or as a salaried employee of a firm of solicitors. Solicitors cannot turn their firms into limited companies, and under no circumstances may they advertise for business.

The work of solicitors is varied. Their main functions include conveyancing, that is, dealing with sales and purchases of land; the preparation of wills and the administration of the estates of deceased persons; and litigation, including the preparation of cases for counsel and appearing personally in magistrates' courts and County courts on behalf of their clients. Most solicitors are also 'commissioners for oaths', and in this capacity act as witnesses for people who have to sign documents and swear that they are true. A solicitor is an officer of the High Court, and as such is subject to disciplinary control by the Court as well as by the Law Society.

A solicitor must keep clients' accounts separate from his own, and such accounts must be audited every year and any audit certificate must be supplied to the Law Society.

In their day-to-day work, solicitors are assisted in their offices by clerks of varying grades, the more senior of whom are known as legal executives and are members of the

Institute of Legal Executives, which was founded in 1963. Legal executives do not have to serve articles, and the examinations of the Institute are not as demanding as those of the Law Society, but they provide a professional status and help to equip legal executives to carry quite onerous responsibilities. Legal executives have a limited right of audience in the county court.

3G2. Barristers

Since the end of the fourteenth century, barristers have been organised in Inns, of which there are four: Middle Temple, Inner Temple, Gray's and Lincoln's. Even during the fourteenth century the Temple was a meeting-place for lawyers and a residential college for students of law. The Inns are now administered by 'Benchers', who are generally judges or other senior members of the Bar.

Originally, barristers were known as counsellors, whose practice it was to accompany the judges on circuit, assisting the court itself and plaintiffs and defendants in civil actions and prisoners in criminal actions. Counsellors only acted for a party if they received instructions to do so, and this gave rise to the need for solicitors, who could act as intermediaries between clients and counsellors.

A person who wishes to become a barrister must first obtain a good honours degree (not necessarily in law, but if it is not in law an extra year's study is necessary), must become a member of one of the four Inns, and must 'keep terms' by dining at the Hall of his inn on a number of occasions over a period of one or two years, thus giving him an opportunity to meet judges and senior barristers. He must attend courses of study and then pass the examinations which are organised jointly by the Inns through the Council of Legal Education. He is then 'called to the Bar' as a barrister. If he wishes to practice in the courts he must, shortly before or after being called, commence a period, usually of one year, in the chamber of a barrister with an established practice in order to gain experience. This is known as pupillage: the pupil reads his master's papers, attends his master's conferences, and accompanies his master to court. After six months, although still a pupil, he may take his own cases.

Many barristers do not practise in the courts, but instead they take up positions in industry and commerce. Such persons may serve a 'commercial pupillage' under a practising barrister, and if they do so and later decide that they wish to practise in the courts, they are exempt from three months of the normal period of pupillage. The barrister under whom a pupil serves his pupillage must be a barrister of at least five years' standing.

Practising barristers are divided into Queen's Counsel (Q.C.s) and junior barristers. A barrister who wishes to become a Q.C. must have had long experience and must be recommended by the Lord Chancellor. The process of becoming a Q.C. is known as 'taking silk', because Q.C.s are entitled to wear silk gowns. A Q.C. is also known as a leader, or leading counsel. Normally, High Court judges and Circuit judges are selected from amongst Q.C.s, but there is no rule to this effect, and juniors are occasionally appointed.

The practice of appointing Q.C.s is considered by many to be unsatisfactory. Appointments are at the discretion of the Lord Chancellor, and successive Lord Chancellors have adopted a highly restrictive attitude in making appointments. The result is that in general the demand for Q.C.s exceeds the supply, so that they are able to charge extremely high fees, which is one reason why the cost of litigation is so high.

Barristers have a duty to the court as well as to their clients. In conducting a case a barrister must inform the court of all relevant statutes and precedents, whether or not they support his argument, although, of course, he may criticise the statutes or precedents which are against him. In criminal cases, if prosecuting counsel is aware of facts which support the defendant's case or lessen the gravity of the offence, he must state them: it is his task to see that justice is done, and not necessarily to attempt at all costs to secure a conviction.

Apart from their duties in court in conducting cases, barristers are frequently called upon to give 'opinions' on difficult points of law, possibly on matters unconnected with impending litigation. Juniors are also very often responsible for the drafting of pleadings, that is, the written statements setting out details of a claim or defence, as the case may be, and for giving advice on matters arising during the preliminaries to a trial. Counsel have no direct contact with their lay clients, apart from conferences arranged and attended by the instructing solicitor, through whom all a barrister's work must come. He is not permitted to advertise.

A barrister is expected not to refuse a brief in any case, unless he has a financial interest in the matter or has already been instructed by the opposite party.

Newly-qualified barristers who have not yet built an established practice sometimes accept what are known as dock briefs in criminal cases, where persons are charged with indictable offences and have not instructed anyone to defend them. This is an exception to the rule that counsel can act only on instructions received from a solicitor. Fees for dock briefs are very small.

Unlike the majority of solicitors, each barrister works on his own account, but groups of them commonly share 'chambers' (offices) and collectively employ a barristers' clerk, who is responsible for the administrative work of the chambers. A number of sets of chambers specialise, for example, in criminal matters.

In any particular case, counsel's fee will be fixed by agreement between the client's solicitor and the barrister's clerk, but it is one of the oddities of English law that this agreement is binding in honour only, so that a barrister cannot sue for unpaid fees, although a solicitor who does not pay may be reported to the Law Society. On the other hand, a barrister cannot be sued for negligence in the conduct of a case in court or matters which occur before a trial and which are essentially connected with the conduct or management of the case in court. He is, however, liable for his negligence in connection with other work which he may perform.

Barristers are subject to regulation by the Senate of the Inns of Court and the Bar, whose members include the Attorney-General, the Solicitor-General, and representatives appointed by each Inn. The Senate formulates policy on a variety of matters affecting the profession, including general policy on education, although the day-to-day administration of education is in the hands of the Council of Legal Education.

Complaints against barristers are referred to a committee of the Senate known as the Professional Conduct Committee. The Committee has the following powers:

— it may admonish a barrister;
— it may refer the case to the Treasurer of the barrister's Inn for a reprimand;
— it may refer a case to an *ad hoc* Disciplinary Committee appointed by the President of the Senate. If the Committee finds a case proved, the barrister may be disbarred, temporarily suspended, fined or reprimanded. Against a decision of the Committee there is no appeal to the normal courts, but the Lord Chancellor and all High Court judges sit as 'visitors' to hear appeals and exercise supervisory powers.

3G3. Comparison between the two branches of the legal profession

There are some similarities and some differences between the two branches of the legal profession.

3G3A. Similarities

The main similarities may be summarised as follows:

— Both solicitors and barristers have a legal immunity in respect of actions and statements made during the lawful conduct of their clients' lawsuits. For example, they cannot be sued for slander in respect of anything which they say in the course of a trial.
— Both are bound not to disclose facts affecting their clients which come to their knowledge in the course of professional dealings with their clients.
— Both are liable to censure and penalties for unprofessional conduct, by the Law Society and the Senate of the Inns of Court respectively.

3G3B. Differences

The main differences may be stated as follows:

— A solicitor can make a binding contract with his client for his fee, but a barrister cannot do so, although he can refuse a brief unless paid in advance.
— A solicitor deals directly with his client, but professional etiquette demands that a barrister should deal only through a solicitor.
— A solicitor is an officer of the court, and as such is subject to disciplinary action by the judge presiding in a court. A barrister is not an officer of the court, and therefore is not subject to this control, although he may be disbarred or suspended by the Senate of the Inns of Court if found guilty of professional misconduct.
— The qualifications of solicitors, and control of their conduct, are largely prescribed by statute, but for barristers the qualifications required, and the etiquette to be observed, are dependent mainly on the traditions and customs of the Inns of Court.
— A solicitor has a right of audience only in certain courts, but a barrister may appear in any court.

3H. Legal aid and advice

In theory it is always possible for a litigant to conduct his own case in any court, either civil or criminal, from the magistrates' court right up to the Court of Appeal, but in the majority of cases it is unrealistic for a person to think of doing so, except in small cases in the County court, where legal representation is positively discouraged, and in minor cases in magistrates' courts, where a litigant may well feel, and rightly so, that the penalty which may be imposed if he is found guilty will be so small that the cost of legal representation does not represent value for money; many would feel, for example, that it is better, whatever the merits of the case, to submit to a fine of, say, £5 for an offence under the Litter Act than to engage a solicitor who might secure an acquittal and then submit an account for, say, £50.

For legal proceedings of any consequence, either civil or criminal, legal representation is for all practical purposes essential. Unfortunately, however, many people cannot afford to risk costs, however good a case they think they may have, and it is for such people that the Legal Aid Act 1974 makes provision. The 1974 Act lays down the principles to be followed in the granting of legal aid and advice, and these principles are put into practice by the Legal Aid Committee, a specially constituted committee of the Council of the Law Society.

For the purpose of the scheme the country is divided into a number of areas, each with an area committee comprised of solicitors and barristers. Within each area there are local committees, and it is to such committees that most applications for legal aid are made, but application for legal aid for an appeal must always be made to an area committee.

3H1. Legal aid under Part I

Legal aid under Part I of the Act includes representation by a solicitor and, where necessary, by a barrister, drawn from panels of solicitors and barristers participating in the scheme. Help is given not only in the conduct of the action itself, but also in the preliminary proceedings and in settling or compromising an action.

Legal aid under Part I is available for various types of proceedings, the more important being as follows:

—all civil cases, except defamation and undefended divorce cases, in the House of Lords, the Court of Appeal, the High Court, and the County Court;

—certain civil proceedings in the Crown Court and magistrates' courts;

—criminal cases in the Divisional Court of the Queen's Bench Division and in the House of Lords on appeal from the Divisional Court of the Queen's Bench Division;

—proceedings in the Employment Appeal Tribunal.

Application for legal aid is made on a form which can be obtained from any legal aid area or local office, from a Citizens' Advice Bureau, or from a solicitor on a legal aid panel. The form sets out the purpose for which legal aid is required, the applicant's financial resources, and the name of the solicitor who is to deal with the case. The application is then subjected to two kinds of examination:

Firstly, the committee must satisfy itself that the applicant is entitled to legal aid on financial grounds, and for this reason it investigates his financial resources. The secretary of the local committee sends details of the applicant's financial position to the Supplementary Benefits Commission, who usually interview the applicant to determine his disposable income and capital and, if required to contribute to the costs, the maximum amount which he could pay. Disposable income is the applicant's annual income after deductions have been made in respect of rent, rates, income tax, maintenance of dependents, and other essential expenditure. Disposable capital is the applicant's gross capital less certain deductions, including the value of the applicant's home and his personal and household effects.

Secondly, the local committee enquires into the merits of the applicant's case. It must not pre-judge the case, but it will grant a legal aid certificate only if it is satisfied that the applicant has reasonable grounds for taking, defending, or being a party to the proceedings in question, and that it is reasonable for the applicant to receive legal aid in the particular circumstances of the case.

If the application is accepted on both financial and legal grounds, a written offer of legal aid is made to the applicant, who has twenty-eight days in which to accept the offer. If he accepts, he is provided with a legal aid certificate.

If the committee refuse the application, the applicant can appeal to the area committee. There is no appeal from the decision of an area committee.

The legal aid scheme is financed out of the legal aid fund. This fund receives money from the following sources:

—a grant from public funds;

—the contributions of applicants;

—the costs of successful cases. In fact, the great majority of cases where legal aid is granted are successful. Where an applicant has made a contribution and the costs awarded against the other party are insufficient to reimburse both the legal aid fund and the applicant fully, the applicant receives only the amount in excess of what is required to reimburse the legal aid fund;

—damages and property recovered in successful cases. If the costs recovered for an assisted person and the contribution paid by him do not meet the payments made out of the fund to his solicitor and, where appropriate, counsel, the Law Society normally has a first charge for the balance of any damages or other property recovered in the proceedings.

In addition to meeting the assisted party's costs, the legal aid fund in certain circumstances meets the whole or part of the costs of an unassisted party who succeeds against an assisted party. The reason for this is that an unassisted party, although successful, could otherwise be financially worse off than the assisted party.

3H2. Legal advice and assistance under Part I

A person whose income and capital do not exceed certain limits is entitled to legal advice and assistance financed out of the legal aid fund, up to a limit of £40 on a solicitor's own authority, or a larger sum with the approval of the appropriate area committee. The advice and assistance may take the form of:

— oral or written advice from a solicitor or, if necessary, from a barrister on the application of English law to a problem relating to the applicant;
— assistance in taking any necessary step;
— the actual taking of any necessary step, including the negotiation of any settlement but not the institution or conduct of any legal proceedings.

A person cannot obtain advice and assistance in connection with proceedings for which a legal aid certificate has been issued to him, or where a legal aid order (see below) in respect of criminal proceedings has been made.

When legal advice and assistance are required, an applicant must find a solicitor who participates in the scheme and supply him with such information as will enable the solicitor to determine the applicant's disposable income and disposable capital.

Advice and assistance are available to any person if:

— his disposable income does not exceed a specified amount per week; or
— if he is in receipt of supplementary benefit or family income supplement; and
— his disposable capital does not exceed a specified amount.

A contribution must be made by the applicant if he is not receiving supplementary benefit and his disposable income exceeds a specified amount per week.

Applications for legal advice and assistance must be made on a standard form, which is commonly known as the Green Form. Where money or property is recovered as a result of the advice and assistance given, the cost of the advice and assistance is usually deducted from it, but this rule is not enforced if to do so would cause hardship.

The Legal Aid Act 1979 extends the Green Form scheme to cover representation in magistrates' courts in civil matters, such as the payment of maintenance. This means that the solicitor who has given the advice can also represent his client in court without the need for legal aid as such to be sought.

3H3. Legal aid under Part II

Under Part II of the Legal Aid Act 1974 legal aid is available:

— in criminal cases in magistrates' courts, in the Crown Court, in the Court of Appeal – Criminal Division, and in the House of Lords on appeals from the Court of Appeal – Criminal Division; and
— in certain proceedings relating to children and young persons in juvenile and magistrates' courts and in the Crown Court on appeal from juvenile and magistrates' courts.

The question of whether an applicant must make any contribution towards his costs is normally left until the case has been heard. The court has power to order the applicant and/or any appropriate contributor (which usually means the father or mother of an applicant below the age of sixteen) to make such payment in respect of costs incurred as appears reasonable with regard to their resources and commitments and for this purpose the applicant must furnish a written statement as to his means. Normally this is a contribution, but the court has power to order the applicant to pay the whole of the costs. However, if at the outset it appears that a contribution will have to be made eventually and that the means are available for an immediate payment, an application for legal aid may be refused unless the applicant or other contributor is prepared to make a down payment. There are, however, no rigid financial rules laid down for legal aid in criminal cases as there are for civil cases. It is the merits of the case, rather than a person's financial status, which determine whether or not he will receive legal aid.

A person under the age of 17 may not himself apply for legal aid, but a parent may do so on his behalf. Refusal to grant legal aid in criminal cases may be challenged by applying for review to the Divisional Court of the Queen's Bench Division.

Legal aid under Part II in general consists of representation by solicitor and counsel, and includes advice on the preparation of the case. In magistrates' courts, however, only representation by a solicitor is allowed except in respect of an indictable offence where unusually grave or difficult circumstances make representation by both solicitor and counsel desirable. In certain cases in the Crown Court and the Court of Appeal – Criminal Division, legal aid may consist of representation by counsel only.

Application is made to the appropriate court for a legal aid order. Where the applicant is over sixteen years of age, he must furnish a statement of means. Where he is under sixteen, the court may require him and any appropriate contributor to furnish statements of means. The court will not make a legal aid order unless it appears that the applicant's means are such that he requires assistance in meeting the costs of the proceedings. Subject to this:

— the court must make a legal aid order where a charge of murder or a prosecution appeal to the House of Lords is involved;

— in other cases the court may make a legal aid order where it appears desirable in the interests of justice to do so. Where for any reason a doubt arises as to whether a legal aid order should be made, the doubt must be resolved in the applicant's favour.

4. Legal status and personality

4A.Status	4B2.Corporations
4A1.Minors	4B2A.Corporations sole
4A2.Persons suffering from mental	4B2B.Corporations aggregate
disorder	4B3.Unincorporated associations
4A3.Bankrupts	4B3A.Partnerships
4A4.Husband and wife	4B3B.Lloyd's underwriters
4B.Legal personality	4B3C.Trade unions
4B1.The Queen	4B3D.Employers' associations

As a general rule, every person in England and Wales is subject to English law, and is entitled to the protection of the law. This statement must, however, be heavily qualified. On the one hand, many people, for example, minors, are protected from the full force of the law and, conversely, do not have full legal rights and liabilities. On the other hand, the law controls, not only human beings, but also what are known as 'juristic' persons, or corporations. The most frequently encountered corporations are companies registered under the Companies Acts, but there are also many other types, as will be seen later. Corporations are subject to the law in the same way as are individuals, except where their very nature demands different treatment. Although it can act only through agents, a corporation can be found guilty of some crimes, but obviously not crimes such as murder. There are, however, limits to the penalties which can be imposed; the corporation can be fined but it cannot be imprisoned, and 'you cannot hang the common seal', as it used to be said when death was a comparatively common penalty.

4A.Status Status indicates membership of a particular class of persons, and any particular individual may have several statuses, each of which imposes on him certain obligations and gives him certain rights. Thus, one person may be a British citizen, which imposes on him a duty of loyalty and entitles him to the protection of the Crown; a married man, which imposes on him the obligation to maintain his wife and children, and gives him rights in respect of his children; and a minor, that is, a person under the age of eighteen, who will be treated differently from an adult in, for example, the laws of crime, contract, and torts.

Status must be distinguished from capacity. Status indicates what a person is; capacity indicates what he is legally entitled to do. Thus, a person who has the statuses of British nationality and majority, that is, who is over eighteen years of age, has the capacity to vote in general, local, and European elections. But a person who is an alien does not have this capacity. Certain aspects of status are dealt with below.

4A1.Minors A person under eighteen years of age may be referred to in law as either an infant or a minor; current fashion favours the latter term. The rules relating to minors' liabilities in respect of crime, contract and tort are dealt with in chapters 5, 6 and 8 respectively. Other important rules relating to minors are that:
— a minor cannot vote or sit in Parliament or on the council of a local authority;
— he cannot sit on a jury;
— he cannot make a will unless he is a member of the armed services on active military service or a seaman at sea;
— he cannot take part directly in litigation; he may, however, bring an action through his next friend, or defend an action through his guardian *ad litem*. Normally, it is his father or legal guardian who acts in these capacities.

4A2.Persons suffering from mental disorder Each branch of law has its own rules relating to persons who are of unsound mind, and also its own definition of unsoundness of mind. Each branch must therefore be treated separately.

Contract and torts. The rules relating to unsoundness of mind in the laws of contract and torts are dealt with in chapters 6 and 8 respectively.

The Mental Health Act 1959. The Mental Health Act 1959 makes numerous provisions in respect of people who are suffering from mental disorder which is defined as 'mental illness, arrested or incomplete development of mind, psychopathic disorder, and any other disorder or disability of mind'.

The provisions of the Act may be divided into two categories, depending upon whether or not the patient is before a criminal court. The question of whether a person charged with a crime is suffering from mental disorder is relevant at various stages of the proceedings:

During remand. A person remanded in custody awaiting trial may, if the Secretary of State is satisfied that he is suffering from one of a number of mental disorders as certified by reports from two doctors, be transferred to a mental hospital, and the trial will not proceed.

During trial. Before the opening of the case for the defence, a defendant may be found incapable of understanding the proceedings. If so, he is said to be 'unfit to plead', and he will then be detained in a mental hospital until the Home Secretary, being satisfied that he has fully recovered his sanity, orders his release.

Alternatively, insanity may be pleaded as a defence, in accordance with what have become known as the M'Naghten rules:

> To establish a defence on the ground of insanity, it must be clearly proved that, at the time of the committing of the act, the party accused was labouring under such a defect of reason, from disease of the mind, as not to know the nature and quality of the act he was doing; or, if he did know it, that he did not know he was doing what was wrong.

The burden of proof of insanity rests upon the defence, and if it succeeds, a verdict of 'not guilty by reason of insanity' will be brought. The defendant will then be detained in a mental hospital under his discharge is ordered by the Secretary of State.

There is a special defence of 'diminished responsibility' which is available only on a charge of murder. If a person so charged 'was suffering from such an abnormality of mind (whether arising from a condition of arrested or retarded development of mind or any inherent causes or induced by disease or injury) as substantially impaired his mental responsibility for his acts and omissions in doing or being a party to the killing', he is guilty of manslaughter and not murder.

The burden of proving diminished responsibility rests upon the defendant. A person found guilty of manslaughter by reason of diminished responsibility is not treated as if he were of unsound mind; he will be sentenced to imprisonment rather than to detention in a mental hospital.

After trial. A person found unfit to plead or not guilty by reason of insanity is automatically sent to a mental hospital, as already mentioned. In addition, a person who is undergoing a sentence of imprisonment may be transferred to a mental hospital on the order of the Secretary of State if, in the opinion of two doctors, he is suffering from certain mental disorders which warrant hospital detention. Whatever may have been the length of his original sentence of imprisonment, he will not be released from the mental hospital until the Secretary of State is satisfied that he is no danger to the public, and is fit for release.

Although a person suffering from mental disease is not charged with any crime, it is possible that he will be compulsorily detained in a mental hospital. A person may enter a mental hospital voluntarily, and if he does he is at liberty to leave at any time. Legislation encourages voluntary and informal treatment, both inside and outside hospital, and 90% of mental patients submit to voluntary treatment. There remain, however, some cases where, in the public interest, a patient must be sent to and detained in a mental hospital.

In case of urgent necessity, a relative or a mental welfare officer may apply for the compulsory admission of a patient to a mental hospital. The application must be supported by the recommendation of a doctor, and the patient must be discharged within three days unless a second doctor recommends further observation, in which case the period can be extended to twenty-eight days.

Where there is no urgent necessity a more complex procedure is followed. The nearest relative or a mental welfare officer may apply to the mental hospital for the admission of the patient for observation or treatment.

The grounds of admission for observation must be that the patient is suffering from mental disorder warranting detention for observation. If treatment is sought, the application must show that the patient is suffering from mental illness or severe subnormality, or is under the age of twenty-one and is suffering from psychopathic disorder or subnormality. Detention for either observation or treatment requires the applicant to state that it 'is necessary in the interests of the patient's health or safety, or for the protection of other persons'. The application must be supported by the written recommendation of two doctors.

Where a patient has been admitted for observation, he must normally be discharged after twenty-eight days. Detention for treatment is limited in the first instance to one year, but towards the end of the year the patient is examined and, if necessary, authority for his detention may be renewed.

While a person is being detained for treatment, he or his nearest relative may make an application for discharge to a Mental Health Review Tribunal. Such a tribunal consists of a doctor, a lay person, and a lawyer who presides over the proceedings. There is a tribunal for each Regional Health Board in England and Wales.

Compulsory guardianship. There are cases where mental patients do not need in-patient hospital treatment but do need care and supervision, and the Mental Health Act provides for this through the medium of compulsory guardianship. A guardianship application may be made to a local health authority in respect of a patient of any age who is suffering from mental illness or severe abnormality, or in respect of a patient under twenty-one years of age who is suffering from psychopathic disorder or subnormality. The application names either the local health authority or an individual as guardian, and if the application is successful the guardian has similar powers to those which a father has over a child under the age of fourteen years.

Management of mental patients' affairs. Within the Chancery Division of the High Court there is a Court of Protection 'for the protection and management of the property of persons under disability'. The court has jurisdiction over any patient who in the opinion of the judge is 'incapable by reason of mental disorder of managing and administering his property and affairs'. The court may appoint a receiver who may be given such duties and powers as the judge thinks fit. The receiver is usually a near relative of the mental patient.

Civil actions. As in the case of minors, persons suffering from disability within the meaning of the Mental Health Act cannot directly become involved in civil litigation. Such a person can, however, sue by his 'next friend', and may defend an action through his 'guardian *ad litem*'.

4A3. Bankrupts

A bankrupt is a person who has been adjudicated bankrupt because he has been unable to pay his debts and some or all of his creditors have brought proceedings against him in respect of his debts. A person who is adjudicated bankrupt loses certain rights:

— He cannot sit in either House of Parliament.
— He cannot be a member of a local authority.
— He cannot be a magistrate.
— He cannot be a director of a limited liability company or take part in its management.
— He cannot obtain a loan over a certain figure nor make a contract without declaring that he is a bankrupt.

After ten years a person is automatically discharged from bankruptcy, but the courts keep the situation regarding bankruptcy under review, with the aim of restoring more people to their constitutional rights.

4A4. Husband and wife

Despite the prevalence of divorce in modern society, the status of marriage in English law is still described as the 'voluntary union for life of one man and one woman to the exclusion of all others'. Marriage is a contract, and by strict logic should be dealt with in chapter 6, but it is a contract of such a special kind that it is more suitably dealt with here, as it changes the status of the parties.

The law of the country in which a marriage takes place governs its validity, so that judges are often called upon to deal with matrimonial cases governed by foreign law. For present purposes, however, it will be assumed that all marriages are governed by English law.

A marriage is void, that is, it is treated as having never existed, if:

— the parties are within the prohibited degrees of relationship; for example, a father cannot marry his daughter;
— either of the parties is under the age of sixteen;
— if certain formal requirements have not been complied with;
— if either of the parties at the time of the purported marriage was already lawfully married;
— if a party to a polygamous marriage entered into outside English and Wales was at the time of the marriage domiciled in England or Wales.

A voidable marriage is one which is valid until such time as it is annulled by a competent court on the petition of one of the parties. Under the Matrimonial Causes Act 1973 grounds for annulment are:

— if it has not been consummated owing to the incapacity of either party;
— if it has not been consummated owing to the wilful refusal of the respondent, that is, the party against whom the petition is brought;
— if either party did not validly consent to it, for example, in consequence of duress, mistake, or unsoundness of mind;
— if at the time of the marriage either party was suffering from mental disorder within the meaning of the Mental Health Act 1959 of such a kind and to such an extent as to be unfitted for marriage;
— if at the time of the marriage the petitioner did not know that the respondent was suffering from venereal disease in a communicable form;
— if at the time of the marriage the petitioner did not know that the respondent was pregnant by some person other than him.

Except in the first two categories, proceedings must be instituted within three years of the date of the marriage. The court will refuse a decree, even if the conditions mentioned exist, if the petitioner has knowingly led the respondent into a sense of security, or if from all the circumstances it appears that it would be unjust to grant the decree.

The most important legal consequences of a valid marriage are:

— The parties have a general duty to live with each other, unless separated by agreement, or by a decree of judicial separation obtained from a court, or by an order from a magistrates' court containing a non-cohabitation clause.

— The husband has a normal duty to maintain his wife, and if a husband is destitute a wife has a duty to maintain him if she can.

— Either party may apply to the court for a determination of any questions arising between them as to the title to or possession of property.

— At common law, one of the parties, most usually the husband, has the legal right to occupy the matrimonial home, but the Matrimonial Homes Act 1967 allows the court to give the other party occupational rights.

— Spouses can sue each other either in contract or in tort, but in cases of tort the Law Reform (Husband and Wife) Act 1962 provides that the court may stay the action if it appears that no substantial benefit would accrue to either party.

— Both husbands and wives have rights in respect of testate and intestate succession, that is, where there is a will or no will respectively. When there is no will, detailed rules of statute law provide that if a husband dies a wife is adequately provided for (subject to the limits of the husband's estate). When a husband leaves a will which does not adequately provide for his wife, the widow may petition the court to have the provisions of the will varied in her favour.

— Either party may be charged with stealing the property of the other, but normally only with the leave of the Director of Public Prosecutions.

Present law provides only one ground for dissolution of marriage, commonly known as divorce: that the marriage has irretrievably broken down. The petitioner for divorce will have to demonstrate that one or more of the following sets of circumstances exist:

— that the respondent has committed adultery, and that on that account the petitioner finds it intolerable to live with him (or her);

— that the respondent has behaved in such a way that the petitioner cannot reasonably be expected to live with him (or her);

— that the respondent has deserted the petitioner for a continuous period of at least two years immediately preceding the presentation of the petition;

— that the parties to the marriage have lived apart for a continuous period of at least two years immediately preceding the presentation of the petition and the respondent consents to a decree being granted;

— that the parties to the marriage have lived apart for a continuous period of at least five years.

A petition for divorce cannot normally be presented during the first three years of marriage.

In proceedings for divorce, nullity, and judicial separation the court has wide powers to order financial relief for either party. Such relief, in the normal order of things, is most commonly given in favour of the wife, and there is a growing tendency to hold, wherever possible, that property, particularly the matrimonial home, is owned equally, whatever the strict legal position may appear to be.

A considerable number of marriages are entered into under the laws of a particular religion, or within a religion of a certain denomination, as, for example, the Church of England or the Roman Catholic Church; and marriages may be annulled according to the laws of these bodies. The courts, however, take no notice of such laws. Thus, for example, even although the Roman Catholic Church does not recognise divorce, the English Courts may dissolve a marriage to which one or both parties are Roman Catholics.

4B. Legal personality
4B1. The Queen

The Queen has two capacities: firstly she is an individual capable of owning and disposing of her own property. In her private capacity she is immune from the law, and so cannot be charged with any crime, and she does not have to pay income tax. The reason for these immunities is that she is herself considered to be 'the fountain of justice', and therefore she cannot bring an action against herself. The majority of criminal actions are brought in the name of the Queen (R = Regina (Queen) v. Smith). The immunity of the Queen does not extend to any of the members of her family, who are all subject to the law in the same way as members of the public.

Secondly, the Queen is also the present representative of a corporation sole (this term will be explained later in this chapter) which has perpetual existence irrespective of who actually occupies the throne at any particular moment. In this corporate capacity the Queen is normally referred to as the Crown, an expression which is extended to all those who act under the direct authority of the Queen, such as the armed services, the government, government departments and civil servants, and consular officers. The expression does not include the nationalised industries, nor such organisations as the British Broadcasting Corporation, which are separate legal entities created by Parliament.

Before 1947, the Crown could be sued only by certain archaic methods, the chief of which was the process known as Petition of Right, and in many circumstances there was no remedy at all. The Crown Proceedings Act 1947, however, stated that:

— The Petition of Right and certain other old statutory procedures are abolished.

— A person may now sue the Crown, by ordinary process and under the normal rules of court, in all those cases where he could previously have proceeded only by Petition of Right or one of the other abolished special statutory procedures. Thus, a person can now sue the Crown in contract or for the restitution of property.

— With certain exceptions, which are not important in the present context, the Crown is liable in tort as if it were a natural person of full age and capacity. It is responsible:

(a) in respect of torts committed by its servants or agents where the servant or agent would also be liable;

(b) in respect of any breach of those duties which a person owes to his servants or agents at common law by reason of being their employer;

(c) in respect of any breach of the duties attaching at common law to the ownership, occupation, possession, or control of property;

(d) in respect of breaches of statutory duties expressly binding the Crown as well as other persons.

— An action against the Crown may be begun in either the High Court or the county court as appropriate. The proceedings are instituted against the appropriate government department or, if they are not associated with a particular government department, against the Attorney-General.

Civil servants and members of the armed services are in a special position in that in general they are not entitled to sue the Crown in respect of their service agreements. Most of the provisions of the Employment Protection Act 1975, however, apply to civil servants and allow them to bring actions against the Crown for unfair dismissal. No such remedies are, however, available to members of the armed services.

The Crown differs from other litigants in that there is no method of enforcing judgment against it. This is, however, of academic interest only, as the Crown always abides strictly by the decisions of the Courts, subject to the same rights of appeal as are available to people generally.

The Post Office occupies a peculiar position in law. At one time Post Office employees were Crown servants, but the Post Office Act 1969 established the Post Office as a public authority, which does not enjoy the privileges of the Crown. Nevertheless it is still the case that there is no contractual relationship between the Post Office and any of its customers, and no action lies against the Post Office for anything done or omitted to be done in relation to any postal packet, except that an action can be brought for damages for loss of a registered inland postal packet. The action must be brought within twelve months of the posting of the packet.

Neither the Crown nor the local authority which employs them is responsible for wrongs committed by the police. In these circumstances, the chief officer of police for the area concerned must be sued, and any damages and costs awarded are payable out of police funds.

4B2. Corporations

There are two types of corporation, corporations sole and corporations aggregate. Generally, the term corporation is used to refer to a corporation aggregate, and this practice will be followed here except where the context clearly requires otherwise.

4B2A. Corporations sole

A corporation sole is a legal person representing an official position occupied by a series of successive human beings. As already mentioned, the Queen in her public capacity is a corporation sole, and other examples are the bishops and parish priests of the Church of England, and the Public Trustee. These corporations are in law entities distinct from the human beings who hold the positions at any given time, and who merely act on behalf of the corporation. Thus, the Queen in her personal capacity owns Balmoral Castle, and could sell it in the same way as any other individual can dispose of his property. However, Windsor Castle is owned by the Crown, and the Queen occupies a position akin to a trustee in relation to that particular piece of property, although theoretically, in her public capacity, she could sell it.

The death of the holder of an office which is a corporation sole in no way affects the corporation itself; the corporation cannot die, and its property remains vested in it. Corporations sole can be created only by statute.

4B2B.Corporations aggregate

A corporation aggregate is a legal person consisting of a number of people, but with an existence quite separate from them. Thus, for example, the Chartered Insurance Institute is a corporation which at any particular moment consists of its fifty thousand-odd members. But although the membership is always changing by reason of new admissions, resignations, and deaths, the corporation itself does not change except to the extent that its Charter and Bye-Laws may be altered from time to time and, with obvious exceptions, it has the same legal rights and liabilities as a natural person.

Formation of corporations. One of the rights of the Crown as corporation sole is the creation of corporations aggregate by the grant of a Royal Charter. The majority of such corporations include the word 'chartered' in their titles – the Chartered Insurance Institute, the Chartered Institute of Loss Adjusters, the Institute of Chartered Accountants – but some, such as the British Broadcasting Corporation, do not.

Most corporations, however, come into existence by reason of statute. There are two main methods:

Firstly, a particular corporation may be created by a particular statute, and the corporation thus created may be a corporation aggregate or a corporation sole. Thus, British Rail, British Gas and the National Coal Board are all corporations aggregate, each created by its own Act of Parliament; and the Minister of Education and the three European Communities are by statute created corporations sole.

Secondly, the most common form of corporation is the registered company. These are corporations formed under the various Companies Acts and they are termed registered companies, in contrast to those created by individual Act of Parliament, which are usually styled statutory companies.

Effects of incorporation. The following are the main effects of incorporation:

Firstly, as already mentioned, the corporation has a separate existence distinct from that of its members or shareholders. In *Salomon* v. *Salomon and Co.* (1892) Salomon and some of his acquaintances formed a company which bought a business which previously belonged to Salomon himself. Salomon had £10,000 in debentures (a form of loan which has certain preferential rights if the company becomes unable to meet its liabilities) secured by a charge on the company's assets. The company fell upon hard times and had to be wound up, with assets of £6,000 only and with several creditors, including of course Salomon as debenture holder. In legal proceedings it was argued that Salomon and Co. had never had an existence separate from Salomon, and that the company's debts were his debts. The House of Lords rejected this argument; Salomon and Co. were a legal entity distinct from Salomon himself, and as a debenture holder Salomon as an individual had a prior claim on the company's assets. However, the courts will not allow incorporation to be used as 'a device, a strategem . . . a mere cloak or sham'. In *Gilford Motor Co.* v. *Horne* (1933), a former employee was bound by a restraint of trade, and sought to evade this by establishing a company. He claimed that, although he personally was bound by the restraint, his company, being a separate legal entity, was not. The court rejected this argument, and an injunction was granted against both him and his company.

Secondly, corporations in general have the same rights and duties as private individuals of full age and capacity. Chartered corporations, however, must comply strictly with the terms of their charters, and other corporations are subject to the *ultra vires* rule. This is explained in greater detail in chapter 6.

Thirdly, a corporation may be liable criminally or in tort, in circumstances where the wrongful acts of its human agents can be imputed to the corporation itself. Thus, a company can be found guilty of breach of duty under the Health and Safety at Work etc. Act where machinery is inadequately guarded, but it could not be found guilty of the crime of murder, nor of the tort of false imprisonment, because these are acts which by their nature can be committed only by individuals acting in their private capacity. It is, however, difficult to draw a dividing line; corporations have, for example, been found guilty of the crime of conspiracy.

In *Griffiths* v. *Studebakers Ltd* (1924) the defendants were charged with having used on a public road a motor car carrying more than two persons, which in the circumstances of the particular case was an offence. At the time of the offence the car was being driven by a servant of the defendants, whose express orders he was infringing. The defendants argued that they as a company were not liable, but it was held that they were. Lord Hewart, C.J. said:

'It would be fantastic to suppose that a manufacturer, whether a limited company, a firm, or an individual, would, even if he could, always show cars to prospective purchasers himself; and it would defeat the scheme of this legislation if it were open to an employer, whether a company or a firm, or an individual, to say that although the car was being used under the limited licence in contravention of the conditions upon which it was granted: "My hand was not the hand that drove the car." On these facts there ought to have been a conviction of (the defendants) and also the driver as aider and abetter.'

Fourthly, a corporation has 'perpetual succession', in the sense that it has an existence independent of its members or shareholders, but it can be wound up or liquidated, if, for example, it is unable to pay its debts.

Types of company. It is necessary now to look at the different types of company which can be formed under the Companies Acts. They are of two main types, private companies and public companies.

Private companies. Private companies are companies which by their articles (the rules which govern their internal affairs):
   —restrict the right to transfer their shares;
   —prohibit any invitation to the public to subscribe for their shares or debentures.

Companies which do not subscribe to these rules are public companies. A public company must have at least two members and two directors; a private company must have at least two members and one director. A public company must have an allotted capital of at least £50,000, with at least 25 per cent of the nominal value paid up, but this provision does not apply to private companies. Companies, both private and public, may be further divided into limited and unlimited companies, and limited companies may be even further sub-divided into companies limited by shares or limited by guarantee.

Limitation by shares. Where a company is limited by shares, the liability of a shareholder is limited to the value of his shares. At any given time, shares may be fully or partly paid. Therefore, if a person is the holder of one thousand £1 shares, fully paid, he may, if the company is liquidated, lose the whole of the money which the shares have cost him, but he has no further responsibility for the debts of the company. On the other hand, if he has one thousand £1 shares, 50p paid, his liability is limited to the cost of his shares plus the amount unpaid, which in the example is £500. It should be noted that to speak of a limited liability company is strictly incorrect; it is the liability of the shareholders, not of the company, which is limited.

Limitation by guarantee. Where a company is limited by guarantee, each member undertakes that on the winding-up of the company he will contribute to the assets of the company up to a certain amount, say, £1000, in which case his liability is limited to that amount. It is only rarely that a company limited by guarantee also issues shares to its members, but if it does so they are subject to both forms of limited liability.

Unlimited companies. Where a company has unlimited liability, there is no limit on the liability of members to contribute to the assets of the company to pay the company's debts. For obvious reasons, unlimited companies are rarely found.

Formation of companies. When a company is formed, various documents have to be filed with the Registrar of Companies. The most important are the memorandum of association and the articles of association.

Memorandum of association. The memorandum of association sets out, for all who wish to know, the name, nature, and objects of the company. It must contain the following clauses:
   —The name clause. There can be trouble with names. The name of the company must not be one which is prohibited by statute; it must not be undesirable, which in general means that the name must not be too like that of an existing company; it must not be misleading; and with exceptions for companies formed to promote art and science, for example, the City of London Polytechnic, the last words of the name must be 'public limited company', (abbreviated Plc) or cwmni cyfyngdig cyhoeddus (abbreviated Ccc) in the case of a company with its registered office in Wales, if it is a public company.
   —The registered office clause. This states whether the registered office of the company is to be in England or Scotland.
   —The objects clause. This is perhaps the most important clause of all. It sets out the purpose of the company and the extent of its operations. As already mentioned, a company must not act outside the scope of its objects clause. It is the modern practice of companies to draw their objects clauses in very wide terms, so that if they wish they may engage in activities other than those for which they are primarily formed. The objects clause of an

insurance company, for example, may permit it to engage in the business of banking.

—The limitation of liability clause. Whether the company is limited by shares or by guarantee, there must be a clause stating that the liability is limited.

—The guarantee clause. In the case of a company limited by guarantee, there must be a clause describing the guarantee.

—The capital clause. In the case of a limited company with a share capital, there must be a clause stating the amount of the share capital with which the company proposes to be registered, and describing the division of the capital into shares of fixed amount.

—The association clause and subscription. At least seven persons in the case of a public company, and at least two in the case of a private company, must subscribe their names to the memorandum. If the company has a share capital, each subscriber must take at least one share.

Articles of Association. The Articles of Association regulate the internal affairs of the company, dealing with such matters as the rights and duties of shareholders and directors and the holding of meetings. Every company has its annual general meeting, and meetings of shareholders other than the annual general meeting are termed extraordinary meetings. At the annual general meeting, an account is given of the company's affairs over the past year, the dividend to be paid to ordinary shareholders is agreed, and the directors are elected or re-elected.

Whenever either the memorandum or articles of association of a company are altered, a copy of the instrument embodying the alteration must be sent to the Registrar of Companies, together with a printed copy of the memorandum or articles as altered.

Dissolution of companies. A company is dissolved, that is, its existence ceases, if it is wound up either compulsorily, voluntarily, or under the supervision of the court.

Compulsory winding-up is usually, for practical purposes, the equivalent of the bankruptcy of an individual, although there are other reasons why a company may be wound up compulsorily. It is usually initiated by either the company itself, a creditor, or the Department of Trade, and is carried into effect by order of the court.

A voluntary winding-up is the result of a resolution to that effect by the shareholders, and does not normally involve the court at all. However, creditors and other persons whose interest might be adversely affected by the winding-up may petition the court for the winding-up to be carried out under the supervision of the court, or, alternatively, they may ask the court for a compulsory winding-up.

In whatever way the winding-up is carried out, a liquidator is appointed. The function of the liquidator is to realise all the company's assets, and ensure that all liabilities are met. Where a company is solvent there are no problems; all creditors of the company, including the liquidator for his expenses and fees, are paid, and any surplus is distributed proportionately to shareholders. Where a company is unable to pay all its debts, the position is complicated in that there are detailed rules as to the order in which debts are to be paid. The only point which need be noted here is that unless all other debts of the company are paid in full, the ordinary shareholders of the company will receive nothing.

4B3. Unincorporated associations

Unincorporated associations include any groups of people, however small or large, which do not have the characteristics associated with corporations. They range in size and importance from knitting circles consisting of a few people to trade unions with memberships of a million or more. The only thing which all unincorporated associations have in common is that, unlike corporations, they are not treated as separate legal entities, but as groups of individuals, each individual having certain rights and responsibilities.

Unincorporated associations such as clubs give rise to various legal difficulties. The main difficulties are as follows:

—*Contract.* A member who makes a contract on behalf of a club is usually personally liable. The other members of the club are liable only if they authorise the making of the contract, for example, if the rules of the club so provide, or if later they ratify the contract.

—*Tort.* Where a person is injured as a result of the dangerous condition of the club premises, it would appear that all members, and not just, say, the secretary or the committee, are liable. But if a person is injured as a result of the negligence of a servant of the club, it is thought that whoever employed him (for example, the secretary, the committee or the trustees) is vicariously liable.

—*Property.* While a club is functioning, the individual members have no rights in its property. However, if the club is dissolved, its assets are sold, and after any liabilities have been discharged, the surplus is divided amongst all those persons who are members at the time the assets are distributed, subject to any contrary provision in the rules of the club.

— *Rights of members*. The rights of members depend on the rules of the club, and every member is deemed to be in contractual relationship with every other member. If a member is denied a right, he will in theory be able to bring an action for breach of contract against all the other members of the club. In fact, this would be quite impracticable, and he therefore asks for a representative order against certain members of the club, for example, the officers. If he is successful and damages are awarded, they will be payable by the officers, who in turn are entitled to an indemnity against the funds of the club.

Some of the more important types of unincorporated association are now considered.

4B3A. Partnerships

The bulk of the law regarding partnerships is contained in the Partnership Act 1890, which defines a partnership as the 'relationship which subsists between persons carrying on a business in common with a view of profit'. The law does not prescribe that any particular form is necessary to bring a partnership into existence, but a partnership is usually created by a formal Deed of Partnership. (It is appropriate at this point to note that it is correct to refer to a partnership as a 'firm', but this term should not be used in reference to a corporation.)

The agents of a partnership are in law all treated as one another's agents, and the firm as such may be sued, irrespective of which partners were involved in the subject-matter of the litigation; and this applies even where one or more partners have acted without the authority of the partnership as a whole. Conversely, if any partner in the course of the business has a right of action, this right may be exercised for the benefit of the partnership as a whole.

The fact that the Rules of the Supreme Court make it possible for a firm to sue or to be sued as such does not, however, mean that the firm has a legal personality of its own.

A peculiar feature of partnership is that the law requires that, after the partnership has been formed, each individual partner has the duty of utmost good faith in his dealings with the other members of the partnership. Apart from negotiations leading to the formation of insurance contracts, this is the only instance where the law imposes so onerous a duty. In particular, the duty requires that where a partner makes any profit in connection with the business, it must be shared amongst all the partners in accordance with the terms of the partnership agreement.

Generally, the liability of each partner for the debts of the partnership is unlimited. Under the Limited Partnership Act 1907, however, it is possible to create a limited partnership. Under such an arrangement, the liability of some, but not all, of the partners may be limited to the amount of capital which they subscribe. Thus, such partnerships include 'limited partners' with limited liability and 'general partners' with unlimited liability. Limited partnerships are rare.

The number of people involved in a partnership must generally not exceed twenty.

The death of a partner automatically dissolves the partnership, and the surviving partners must account to his personal representatives for the amount of his interest in the firm. This could put the partnership in financial difficulties, and so it is common for funds to be provided from the proceeds of a life policy on the deceased partner's life. If no arrangement such as this is made, the business of the firm may be dislocated, or perhaps even ended, and there is also the danger that the remaining partners will be tempted to admit another partner simply because he can provide the necessary finance, rather than because he can take an active part in the running of the business.

Because of the existence of unlimited liability, and also because the number of partners is restricted by law, there is a tendency for partnerships to turn themselves into limited companies. However, persons in certain professions must work either on their own account or in partnership, and those in certain other professions, although they may form limited companies, may prefer to work as partnerships. The law therefore allows for partnerships of more than twenty in a number of professions, including solicitors, chartered accountants, architects and chartered loss adjusters.

It is useful to draw comparisons between a partnership and a company:

— A company is a legal entity distinct from its shareholders, whereas a partnership has no corporate existence.

— What a company can do is limited by the scope of its objects clause, whereas partners can by mutual agreement at any time change the scope of their activities. It is important, however, that there be mutual agreement; where, at any given time, an individual partner purports on behalf of the firm to make a contract in connection with an activity which is altogether outside the scope of the activities of the firm, he alone will be liable under it.

— In a company, the liability of a shareholder is limited to the nominal value of his shareholding or the extent of his guarantee, whereas, except in the case of a limited partner, the liability of a partner is unlimited.

— The management of a company is in the hands of its board of directors rather than its shareholders, whereas normally all the members of a partnership play an active part in the running of the business.

— The possible number of members of a company is not subject to any legal restriction, whereas generally the maximum number of members of a partnership is twenty.

— In the case of companies, particularly public companies, details relating to their affairs, and particularly their accounts, must be made public, but a partnership is allowed to operate with very little publicity.

— By definition (see earlier) a partnership is formed with a view to engaging in activities which it hopes will make a profit. Although most companies aim to make profits, it is not essential that this should be their aim.

— A partner may not introduce a new partner into the partnership without the consent of the existing partners, but the shares, and therefore the ownership, of a public limited company may be freely bought and sold.

4B3B. Lloyd's underwriters

It is appropriate here to note that Lloyd's underwriters do not, and cannot, work in partnership. It is well-known that they form themselves into syndicates as a matter of convenience, but a Lloyd's syndicate, although it has some of the marks of a partnership, is not recognised by law as such.

There are two main features which distinguish a Lloyd's syndicate from a partnership. The first is that the day-to-day affairs of the syndicate are usually in the hands of an underwriting agent, the members of the syndicate, or 'names', being concerned almost solely with the provision of financial backing. The second is that, although the liability of each member of a syndicate is unlimited so far as his own share is concerned, no member has any liability for the debts of any other member of the syndicate.

It follows that a Lloyd's syndicate as such can neither sue not be sued, and in theory a person with a right of action against a syndicate must sue each member of the syndicate individually. However, in practice, and this applies not only to Lloyd's syndicates but to all unincorporated associations, the Rules of the Supreme Court provide that a person may, on obtaining a 'representation order', sue a representative or representatives of the syndicate, and the decision of the court will be binding on all of them.

4B3C. Trade unions

Although trade unions are unincorporated associations, the law has always accorded them special treatment. This has varied from treating them as unlawful conspiracies in their early days to the present position in which they are not only legally recognised as lawful associations, but also accorded specially favourable treatment in certain respects.

The legal position of trade unions is now governed by the Trade Union and Labour Relations Acts 1974–76. Although they are not corporate bodies the Acts provide that:

— they are capable of making contracts;

— their property is vested in trustees, to be held on their behalf;

— they can sue or be sued in their own names, and be prosecuted in their own names for crimes committed by them or on their behalf;

— they are not to be treated as unlawful simply because they act in restraint of trade;

— a court order may be enforced against any property held in trust for a union 'in like manner as if the union were a body corporate';

— despite the fact that in general they can be sued, they have a wide immunity in certain matters; they cannot be sued in tort in respect of any act alleged to have been done, threatened or intended to have been done on their behalf. This immunity extends not only to the unions themselves but also to their trustees, members and officials acting on their behalf. This special protection does not, however, apply – unless the act in question is done 'in contemplation or furtherance of a trade dispute' – to actions involving negligence, nuisance, or breach of statutory duty resulting in personal injury to any person, or to any breach of duty owed in connection with the ownership, occupation, possession, control, or use of any property;

—in respect of collective agreements between unions and employers, there is an irrebuttable presumption that the parties did not intend to enter a legally enforceable contract unless the agreement is in writing and states that it is to be legally enforceable. (It will be seen in chapter 6 that in the absence of such a statutory provision the courts would assume that such an agreement would be intended to be legally binding.)

4B3D.Employers' associations

Under the Trade Union and Labour Relations Act 1974 an employers' association is defined as an organisation of employers whose principal purposes include the regulation of relations with workers or unions, or a federation of such organisations (such as the Confederation of British Industries). Such an association may be either a body corporate or an unincorporated association. Where such an association is unincorporated, it is subject to the same provisions of the Trade Union and Labour Relations Acts 1974–76 as apply to trade unions.

5. Classification of English law

5A.Distinction between civil and
   criminal law
   5A1.History
   5A2.The Courts
   5A3.Civil and criminal proceedings
5B.General principles of criminal liability
5C.Qualifications to criminal liability
5D.Civil and criminal remedies
   5D1.Contemptuous, aggravated and
      exemplary damages
   5D1A.Contemptuous damages
   5D1B.Aggravated damages
   5D1C.Exemplary damages
   5D2.Punishment of criminal offences
   5D2A.Death

5D2B.Imprisonment
5D2C.Youth Custody
5D2D.Other punishments for
   young persons
5D2E.Fines
5D2F.Probation
5D2G.Recognizance
5D2H.Community service order
5D2I.Deprivation of property
5D2J.Disqualification for driving
5D2K.Conditional and absolute
   discharge
5D2L.Deferral of sentence
5D2M.Rehabilitation of offenders

It was seen in chapter 1 that law is divided into public law and private law, each having various sub-divisions. For the purpose of this chapter, it is necessary to consider only that part of public law called criminal law, and those parts of private law called contract and torts, here collectively referred to as civil law.

The law of contract is dealt with in detail in chapters 6 and 7; rights and liabilities under a contract arise as a result of agreement between the parties, and as in the other branches of civil law already mentioned, the common law remedy for a breach of contract is an award of compensatory damages.

The law of torts is dealt with in chapters 9 and 10. Torts are breaches of rights owed to people as a whole, as distinct from breaches of contract, which can affect only parties to the agreement. As with contract, the common law remedy in tort is an award of damages. The law of torts differs from other branches of civil law, however, in that, as will be seen below, some torts are very closely associated with criminal law, and it is often difficult to draw the line between them.

5A. Distinction between civil and criminal law

In general terms, the purpose of civil proceedings is to enable persons to enforce their rights or to recover their property for their own benefit. Whether a person wishes· to pursue his rights is a matter for him alone; he can compromise an action or, if he so wishes, fail to bring proceedings or even discontinue proceedings in the course of the trial of a case. The purpose of criminal proceedings, on the other hand, is to enforce law and order in the interests of the community, generally by punishing the offender. Proceedings are usually undertaken by the Crown (private prosecutions are possible but very rare) and once started can be discontinued only by the Attorney-General entering what is known as a *nolle prosequi*.

At first sight, therefore, it would seem that a civil offence is a wrong against an individual, whereas a criminal offence is a wrong against the community, but such a line is difficult to draw. Treason, the most serious of all crimes, is clearly an offence against the community, but most of the other serious crimes, such as murder, manslaughter and rape, are equally clearly offences whose victims are individuals. Nevertheless, they are deemed contrary to the public interest, and so are treated as criminal offences – proceedings will be brought irrespective of the wishes of the victim or his or her relatives. On the other hand malicious prosecution, which strikes at the root of constitutional freedom, is the subject-matter of civil proceedings only.

In truth, it must be said that certain matters are crimes because over the years the courts, and more importantly Parliament, have decreed that they shall be treated as such, and the seriousness or otherwise of a particular matter is of no great relevance. Thus, in the early days of English law even murder was treated as a civil matter, redressible by the payment of compensation on a scale which varied with the rank of the victim. In the twentieth century, on the other hand, Parliament has by legislation decreed that it is a criminal offence, punishable by fine, to throw an empty cigarette packet out of the window of a car.

The fundamental distinctions between crimes and civil wrongs are to be found, not in the nature of a particular act, but in the nature of the proceedings taken and in the consequences which follow.

5A1. History

In the early days of English law all proceedings were treated as what would now be called civil proceedings – as mentioned above, even murder was treated as a matter for compensation rather than punishment (the fact that having to pay compensation might itself be a punishment being incidental). When the royal courts became established, however, they began to treat the more serious offences as crimes punishable by the State. Less serious matters involving interference with persons or property were known as trespasses, for which the wrongdoer had to pay compensation, but in course of time some trespasses came to be known as 'trespasses against the King's Peace' for which fines, forfeited to the State, had to be paid as well as compensation. Thus, some acts, such as assault and battery, became recognised as the subject of both civil and criminal proceedings, and even today many crimes are also torts.

Civil law has tended to develop more by case law than by statute, whereas the converse applies to criminal law. The reason for this is that an individual who has suffered a wrong has a close personal interest in bringing proceedings to obtain redress, and thus there is no lack of decisions to aid the growth of the law. In criminal matters, on the other hand, very often no individual has a sufficiently personal interest to bring proceedings, and it is therefore left to Parliament to legislate on criminal matters, and to see that there is proper machinery for the enforcement of the law. This point however, should not be over-emphasised for much criminal law is based on case law, and virtually the whole of the law relating to murder is based on common law rather than statute.

5A2. The Courts

In chapter 2 it was seen that the systems of courts dealing with civil and criminal matters are largely separate. Nearly all minor civil cases are heard in the County Court, a purely civil court, and the more serious cases are heard in the High Court, which is mainly a civil court. Appeals from the County Court and the High Court lie to the Court of Appeal – Civil Division, and thence to the House of Lords, the only court which has equal jurisdiction in both civil and criminal matters (although the procedure when hearing a civil case is different from that when hearing a criminal case). Magistrates' courts deal with the great majority of minor criminal matters, and have very little civil jurisdiction. Major criminal cases are heard in the Crown Court, a purely criminal court, with appeal to the Court of Appeal – Criminal Division, and thence to the House of Lords.

It must be noted, however, that although the systems of courts are more or less distinct, very often the same judges sit in both civil and criminal courts. A High Court judge, for example, may find himself hearing an appeal from a VAT Tribunal decision one week, and a murder case the next.

5A3. Civil and criminal proceedings

It has been mentioned that many crimes are also civil wrongs, usually torts, examples of which are assault and battery, and theft. In such circumstances both civil and criminal proceedings can usually be taken, although there are exceptions. For example, the Offences Against the Person Act 1861 provides that where a person has been prosecuted criminally for assault and battery in a court of summary jurisdiction (a magistrates' court), then, whether he has been acquitted or convicted, he cannot be sued in civil proceedings for the same incident.

Either the civil or the criminal proceedings may be taken first or, in theory, both sets of proceedings may be begun concurrently. In practice, so great are the delays in preparing civil cases for trial and awaiting a date for hearing that almost invariably the criminal proceedings are heard first. Also in practice, it is comparatively rare for a convicted person to be sued, as it is most unlikely that any damages awarded against him will be paid – few criminals are men of wealth, and even if the criminal is wealthy, it may be impossible to discover the whereabouts of his wealth.

Where both civil and criminal proceedings are taken, the findings in criminal proceedings can be used as evidence in the civil court, but not vice versa. The reason for this is that a much higher standard of proof is required in criminal than in civil proceedings; in criminal proceedings guilt must be established beyond any reasonable doubt, whereas in civil proceedings a plaintiff need prove his case only on a balance of probabilities. Therefore, if evidence has satisfied a criminal court it will satisfy a civil court also, but the converse does not apply. Thus if A is prosecuted for and found guilty of careless driving, he may also be sued in tort for negligence by B, who was injured as a result of his careless driving, and his conviction will be evidence against him in the action for negligence. If, on the other hand, the action in negligence preceded the criminal proceedings, a finding of negligence would not be admissible evidence in subsequent criminal proceedings. It should be noted also that an acquittal in criminal proceedings is not evidence of innocence for the purpose of subsequent civil proceedings.

In some circumstances, civil and criminal proceedings become merged, because certain statutes provide for civil remedies to be given in what are substantially criminal proceedings. The most important statute in this respect is the Powers of Criminal Courts Act 1973.

Under the Act a court by which a person is convicted of an offence may make a compensation order against him requiring him to pay compensation for any personal injury, loss or damage which may have resulted from his offence. In determining whether to make a compensation order the court must have regard to the means of the offender, and no order may be made if the result might be to induce him to commit another crime in order to pay the compensation awarded against him. Orders made by magistrates' courts are generally subject to a limit of £1000, but there is no limit to the amount of an order which may be made by the Crown Court. Compensation may not be made by the criminal courts to the dependants of a person killed as a result of a crime, nor for loss or damage due to an accident arising out of the presence of a motor vehicle on a road.

If a compensation order has been made, the person who has suffered the injury, damage, or loss may nevertheless bring a civil action over the same subject. If he does so the civil court will assess the full damages in the normal manner, but the aggrieved person may receive only the amount by which the damages as so assessed exceed the amount of the compensation order; in other words, the amount which he receives in total must not exceed the amount assessed by the civil court.

In cases of theft, the stolen goods, or some of them, are often recovered, and the Theft Act 1968 provides that where a person is convicted of theft, the court may make a restitution order under which the goods are returned to their owner.

The Crown Court may also make an order of criminal bankruptcy against a person who has been convicted. Such an order may be made where a person has been found guilty of offences which have caused loss or damage of more than £15,000. Where such an order is made, the Director of Public Prosecutions in his capacity of Official Petitioner decides whether it would be in the public interest for him to present a petition for bankruptcy. If he does, the bankruptcy proceedings will follow the normal course.

It is relevant here to mention the work of the Criminal Injuries Compensation Board, which was established in 1964. Where, as happens all too frequently, a criminal uses violence in the course of committing crime, his victim may suffer personal injury, sometimes severe. In such cases, it may be impossible to obtain redress against the criminal himself, either because he has not the means to satisfy any award which might be made against him, or in many cases because he cannot be traced.

The Board is entitled to award *ex gratia* payments from public funds to such victims provided that the victim, or his representatives if he has been killed, make application promptly. The injury must be sufficiently severe as to involve at least three weeks' loss of earnings.

The Board is not concerned with injuries caused by motor vehicles unless they are used as weapons of offence. The reason for this is that, however dangerously or recklessly a car is used, the insurers of the vehicle will pay any claim in respect of injury to a third party, or the claim will be met by the Motor Insurers' Bureau if no insurance is in force.

There are a number of cases where, although crimes and torts do not strictly coincide, criminal and civil proceedings may arise out of the same incident, although the bases of the actions are different. For example, dangerous driving is a crime under the Road Traffic Act 1972, but not a tort; however, the conduct which constitutes dangerous driving may also amount to the common law tort of negligence. Thus, a driver may be prosecuted under the Act for dangerous driving, and on the same facts he may be sued in tort for negligence by, say, a person who has been injured as a result of his dangerous driving. In such a case the proceedings are distinct, the criminal prosecution being for a statutory offence and the civil action being based on a common law tort, and the civil proceedings may well succeed although the prosecution for dangerous driving fails. (In practice, if the prosecution for dangerous driving were brought first and the driver were convicted, it is highly unlikely that the driver would attempt to defend himself against an action of negligence, as he would almost certainly fail. The matter would probably be settled out of court, although there could be litigation over the amount to be paid, known as quantum, as distinct from liability.)

If a duty is imposed on one person by statute and thus a right is conferred upon someone else, the question arises whether the right is enforceable by civil action. The answer depends on a consideration of the Act as a whole. If the Act expressly or by clear implication provides that the right can be enforced by civil action, no difficulty arises. Often, however, an Act is silent on this point, and it is for the courts to determine the intention of Parliament from the wording of the Act.

In the past the courts have expressed conflicting views. According to one view a person who has suffered loss or injury as a result of breach of statutory duty *prima facie* has a right to recover damages unless the wording of the Act clearly indicates that no such right was intended to be given. The other view is that where a statute creates an obligation, and enforces its performance in a specified manner, as by a fine, performance cannot in general be enforced in any other manner.

At the present day the courts tend not to take either of these extreme views, and generally adopt the following guidelines:

(*a*) If a statute is passed for the benefit of an ascertainable class of persons, such as factory workers, it is assumed that members of that class have a civil right of action. On the other hand, if statutes are passed for the benefit of the public as a whole, such as the Road Traffic Acts, they do not give rise to civil rights of action.

(b) A person who is not one of the class for whose benefit the legislation has been passed cannot derive any advantage from it. If, for example, a fireman is injured while fighting a fire at a factory, he cannot bring an action for breach of a statutory duty which the factory owner owed to his employees.

(c) The fact that a statute provides for a penalty, such as a fine, does not mean that civil proceedings are necessarily precluded.

(d) Where before the statute a person had the right to bring a civil action at common law, there is no presumption that the common law right is extinguished by the statute. In many statutes this is made clear by a wording such as 'nothing in this Act shall be taken to prejudice any liability or remedy to which a person guilty of an offence thereunder may be subject in civil proceedings'. However, such a wording does not actually create a civil liability.

(e) A civil remedy may be refused on the grounds that existing common law remedies are adequate, but this is by no means always the case. Nor does the converse necessarily apply: the fact that no common law remedy exists does not mean that one is created by any particular statute.

It must be admitted that these guidelines are vague, sometimes contradictory, and in general unsatisfactory: the truth is that the courts often purport to attempt to find the intention of Parliament on points to which in fact Parliament gave no consideration at all. The result is that to understand the law on this matter a very large number of cases have to be considered and the principles laid down in them mastered, and this is outside the scope of this book.

Where a person can bring an action for breach of statutory duty rather than at common law, he has an advantage in that he does not have to prove fault. He merely has to show that there has been a breach, and that injury or damage has resulted from the breach.

5B. General principles of criminal liability

Before considering the purposes of civil and criminal sanctions, it is desirable first to consider briefly the general principles of criminal liability.

The most important common law maxim of criminal law is *actus non facit reum nisi mens sit rea* (the doing of an act does not make a person guilty unless he has a guilty mind). This embodies the common law principle that a person should not be found guilty of a crime unless it can be proved that, in addition to doing a prohibited act (*actus reus*), he also intended to do it, that is, he had *mens rea*. Since one of the most important reasons for imposing criminal sanctions is to deter, it would generally be pointless to punish a person for doing something which he had not intended to do, or possibly for something which he did not even know he had done.

Actus reus presents little difficulty, as it is contained in the definition of every crime and it is for the prosecution to prove that the accused did the prohibited act. For example, in the case of murder, if A is charged with murdering B, the prosecution must show, *inter alia*, that A did in fact kill B. Sometimes an omission, rather than an act, may constitute the *actus reus* of a crime. For example, in *Fagan v. Metropolitan Police Commissioner* (1968), a constable asked the defendant driver to draw into the kerb, and the defendant did so but stopped with one wheel of his car resting on the constable's foot. He was slow in restarting the engine and moving off when asked to do so, and it was held that his omission to move the car immediately amounted to an assault. (This ruling was based on the assumption that the defendant did not deliberately drive on to the constable's foot, which would have been an example of an act creating an assault.)

The act or omission of the defendant must be the cause of the crime, although it is a general rule that the defendant must take his victim as he finds him. In *R v. Jordan* (1956), the defendant stabbed his victim so that the victim's intestine was penetrated in two places. He was taken to hospital where he died a few days later. Medical evidence showed that the stab wounds had mainly healed at the time of death, and the main cause of death was the abnormal quantity of liquid which had been injected into the victim's lungs while he was in hospital, resulting in pulmonary oedema. The defendant's conviction on a charge of murder was quashed: the cause of death was not the stabbing, but pneumonia resulting from the condition of oedema.

With advances in medicine, there have been cases where victims of crime have been kept 'alive' by life support machines but later, when brain death has been established beyond doubt, have had the life support machines withdrawn. In such cases the courts have held that there has been no break in the chain of causation, and that death has resulted from the original injuries rather than from withdrawal of the life support systems.

Mens rea presents much more difficulty as it is concerned with a person's state of mind, and only an individual himself can with absolute certainty know his own state of mind.

In general, two ingredients are necessary to constitute *mens rea*:

—The act must have been done voluntarily.

—There must have been some foresight of consequences. There may have been intention to do the act, or recklessness, with the defendant foreseeing the consequences of his act, and not caring whether those consequences were brought about or not.

Some crimes are defined so as to require from the prosecution proof that a particular form of *mens rea* was in existence. For example, in murder, the *mens rea* to be proved is 'malice aforethought', that is, an intention to kill or to cause grievous bodily harm. Section 8 of the Criminal Law Act 1967 provides that the court must decide whether the defendant did intend or foresee the result which occurred. In other words, it is a question of fact, not a presumption of law, that the defendant did foresee the results.

Although, as already mentioned, *mens rea* must be proved, it is a rule of law nevertheless that every man is presumed to intend the natural consequences of his acts, for it is impossible to prove a state of mind conclusively. Thus, if it is shown that a man has killed his daughter in cold blood, he is *prima facie* guilty of murder, and it is no defence to say that he intended merely to chastise her and not to kill her. However, this presumption does not displace the onus on the prosecution to prove its case beyond all reasonable doubt. In *Woolmington* v. *D.P.P.* (1935) the defendant killed his wife by shooting her. Although there was some evidence that this was an accident, the trial judge held that it was for the defendant to prove that it was an accident. The House of Lords ruled that this was wrong: as there was some evidence to show that there had been an accident, the prosecution must prove that this evidence could not be relied upon, and that the defendant had murdered his wife. The rule, therefore, is only a rule of construction which applies in the absence of evidence to the contrary, but if challenged by a defendant, the prosecution must prove that it applies.

The common law rule that every crime requires *mens rea* does not always apply to crimes created by statute. There is a presumption that *mens rea* is required, but this may be rebutted by the words or obvious intention of the statute, which may impose strict liability, that is, the defendant may be found guilty even though he has no *mens rea*. For example, in *Meah* v. *Roberts* (1977), two children were, by mistake, served with glasses full of caustic soda instead of lemonade. Although the defendant was not the person who had put the caustic soda in the lemonade bottle, and did not know what the bottle contained, he was nevertheless found guilty of selling food unfit for human consumption, which is an offence under the Food and Drugs Act 1955.

In *Cundy* v. *Le Cocq* (1884) the defendant was convicted of unlawfully selling liquor to a drunken person, although he did not know that the person was drunk. Stephen, J. said: '. . . we have been quoted the maxim that in every criminal offence there must be a guilty mind; but I do not think that maxim has so wide an application as it is sometimes considered to have. In old time, and as applicable to the common law or to earlier statutes, the maxim may have been of general application; but a difference has arisen owing to the greater precision of modern statutes. It is impossible now . . . to apply the maxim generally to all statutes, and the substance of all the reported cases is that it is necessary to look at the object of each Act that is under consideration to see whether and how far knowledge is of the essence of the offence created. Here . . . the object of this part of the Act is to prevent the sale of intoxicating liquor to drunken persons, and it is perfectly natural to carry that out by throwing on the publican the responsibility of determining whether the person supplied comes within that category. I think therefore the conviction was right and must be affirmed.'

Another important maxim of criminal law is *nulla poena sine lege*. This means that a person must not be made to suffer criminal penalties except for a clear breach of existing criminal law, and that the law must be precise and well-defined. This involves the following propositions:

—Statutes involving criminal responsibility do not operate retrospectively, so that a person cannot be found guilty of a crime for doing an act which was not unlawful, however reprehensible, at the time when he did it.

—Case law cannot be widened to increase by analogy crimes which do not directly fall within it. In this there is a fundamental difference between criminal and civil law: in some branches of civil law development has been by extension of broad principles to cover new circumstances.

—Criminal laws ought not to be formulated in wide and vague terms.

In *Shaw* v. *D.P.P.* (1966), the defendant's appeal against conviction for the offence of 'conspiring to corrupt public morals' was dismissed by the House of Lords. However, the minority judgment of Lord Reid is now widely considered to be preferable to that of the majority. Lord Reid said that in his view there was no offence known to the law as 'conspiring to corrupt public morals', and in convicting the defendant of it the courts were creating a new crime on the basis of public policy. He felt that if the courts had stopped creating new heads of public policy in civil law, then they certainly should refrain from doing so in criminal law.

5C. Qualifications to criminal liability

The following qualifications to and exemptions from criminal liability should be noted:

Minors. There is an irrebuttable presumption that a child under ten years of age cannot be guilty of a crime. There is a presumption that a child between ten and fourteen years of age is incapable of committing a crime, but this presumption may be rebutted. Over the age of fourteen, a person is in general fully responsible for his crimes, but there are special provisions for the treatment of young offenders.

Insane persons. The position of insane persons in connection with crimes, and the special defence of diminished responsibility in connection with the crime of murder, have already been dealt with in chapter 4.

Drunkenness. In itself, drunkenness is not a defence in criminal proceedings, and indeed in some cases it is an essential part of an offence, for example, driving a motor vehicle while under the influence of drink. However, where a particular intent is an element of a crime, the defendant may be able to show that he was so drunk as not to be able to form that intent. On the other hand if, for example, a person forms an intention to kill another and then drinks heavily to give himself 'Dutch courage' to carry out the act, he is not allowed to plead drunkenness as a defence. In *Attorney General for Northern Ireland* v. *Gallagher* (1963) a man, with a deliberate intention to kill his wife, drank a bottle of whisky before doing so. His plea of drunkenness was rejected. In this case Lord Denning took the opportunity to summarise the law on drunkenness as a defence:

'If a man is charged with an offence in which a special intention is essential (as in murder though not in manslaughter), then evidence of drunkenness, which rendered him incapable of forming the intention is an answer. . . . If a man by drinking brings on a distinct disease of the mind such as *delirium tremens*, so that he is temporarily insane within the M'Naghten rules, that is to say, he does not at the time know what he is doing or that it is wrong, then he has a defence on the ground of insanity . . . (but) if a man, while sane and sober, forms an intention to kill and makes preparation for it . . . and then gets himself drunk so as to give himself Dutch courage to do the killing . . . he cannot rely on this self-induced drunkenness as a defence to a charge of murder, nor even as reducing it to manslaughter.'

Mistake. It is well known that a mistake as to the law is usually no defence. Where there is a mistake of fact, a person is judged according to whether or not he would have been liable if the facts had been as he thought them to be. For example, if A shoots B, whom he thinks to be C, he is nevertheless guilty of murder, but if he shoots at what he thinks to be a rabbit, but is in fact a man, he may not be guilty of any crime. In *R* v. *Tolson* (1889), a woman went through a form of marriage with another person during the lifetime of her husband and was charged with bigamy. Her husband had been reported drowned at sea and had been missing for five years, and she pleaded successfully that she honestly believed that her husband was dead.

Compulsion. There is a statutory defence available to a wife that a crime, other than treason or murder, was committed under the coercion of her husband. Otherwise, the position is not clear, but it is generally accepted that it is a defence to show that an act was committed under actual compulsion, but that fear induced by threats is not a defence. Duress − that is, illegal constraint − by threats is a defence to some crimes.

Necessity. Necessity has never been recognised as a defence in English law. A startling example is *R.* v. *Dudley and Stephens* (1844) where two ship-wrecked seamen on a raft were so weak with hunger that they killed and ate a cabin-boy who was with them. They were found guilty of murder, but it should perhaps be added that the sentence of death which was passed on them was commuted to six months' imprisonment.

Corporations. The liability of corporations in criminal law has been discussed in chapter 4.

5D. Civil and criminal remedies

It has already been mentioned that the main purpose of civil law is to compensate by an award of damages, whereas criminal law aims to punish. The question of damages generally in contract and tort is dealt with more fully in later chapters, but before dealing here in detail with the concept of punishment, it is necessary to note three exceptional cases where civil law aims to provide something other than compensation; indeed, something more akin to punishment.

5D1. Contemptuous, aggravated and exemplary damages
5D1A. Contemptuous damages

The three exceptional forms of damages are contemptuous, aggravated, and exemplary.

In some cases in tort, the plaintiff may win his case, but the court may decide that in equity his case is entirely without merit, and award contemptuous damages, the amount of which is commonly referred to as 'the smallest coin of the realm', currently $\frac{1}{2}$p. As the plaintiff is not awarded the costs of the action in such cases, the court will in effect have imposed a penalty upon him, despite the fact that his action has been successful.

Contemptuous damages are rarely awarded, but are sometimes considered appropriate where a person of generally bad reputation brings an action for defamation which technically he is entitled to win. In such a case, in awarding contemptuous damages, the court is in effect indicating that his reputation was already so bad that the libel or slander did little or nothing to make it worse.

5D1B. Aggravated damages

Sometimes damages are fixed to compensate not so much for pecuniary loss as for indignity which a person has suffered, particularly where the defendant has been motivated by malice. As Lord Devlin has said: 'There may be malevolence or spite or the manner of committing the wrong may be such as to injure the plaintiff's proper feelings of dignity and pride. These are matters which the jury can take into account in assessing the appropriate compensation.'

In *Ansell* v. *Thomas* (1973) the plaintiff, the managing director of a company, was in dispute with his co-directors, who asked him to leave the premises, and when he refused, called the police, who threatened to use force if the plaintiff did not leave. The plaintiff brought an action against his co-directors for assault and conspiracy, and it was held that he was entitled to aggravated damages for indignity, mental suffering, disgrace and humiliation.

5D1C. Exemplary damages

The greatest departure from the principle that damages are intended to compensate the plaintiff rather than punish the defendant is the award of exemplary, sometimes called punitive, damages. At one time exemplary damages were awarded fairly frequently, but the civil courts now firmly take the view that punishment ought to be the concern only of the criminal courts, and that only in rare cases should exemplary damages be awarded.

The current law relating to exemplary damages is to be found in the judgments in *Rookes* v. *Barnard* (1964) as adopted and amplified in *Cassel and Co. Ltd* v. *Broome* (1972). The rules may be summarised as follows.

—Exemplary damages can only be awarded in connection with certain torts, probably only trespass, defamation, and intimidation. They cannot be awarded in respect of breach of contract in any circumstances.

—There are only three categories of case where such damages can be awarded. The first is where there has been 'oppressive, arbitrary or unconstitutional action by the servants of the government'. The second is where 'the defendant's conduct has been calculated by him to make a profit for himself which may well exceed the compensation payable to the plaintiff'. *Cassell and Co. Ltd* v. *Broome* was an example of this; the defendants had published a book which was defamatory of the plaintiff, and the profits which they might have expected from the sale of the book might well have been in excess of compensatory damages awarded to the plaintiff. The third category is where a statute expressly authorises the award of exemplary damages.

In *Rookes* v. *Barnard* Lord Devlin said that, when a decision in principle has been taken that exemplary damages should be awarded, three points should be borne in mind. First, 'the plaintiff cannot recover exemplary damages unless he is the victim of the punishable behaviour'. Second, 'the power to award exemplary damages constitutes a weapon that, while it can be used in defence of liberty . . . can also be used against liberty'. Third, 'the means of the parties, irrelevant in the assessment of compensation, are material in the assessment of exemplary damages'. In connection with this last point, it may be noted that insurance policies often cover the liability of the insured to pay compensatory damages, but do not cover liability to pay exemplary damages; to cover this latter liability would be almost equivalent to agreeing to pay a fine imposed by a criminal court, which is not permissible as it would be contrary to the public interest.

5D2. Punishment of criminal offences

The punishment of an offender is the purpose of criminal justice, but it is relevant to enquire what aim or aims are intended by imposing punishment, and then to see what punishments are awarded to achieve these aims.

Before going into detail, it is to be noted that for many years Parliament has set its face against two forms of punishment – capital punishment (with minor exceptions which will be mentioned later) and judicial corporal punishment, not so much because they would be ineffective (a matter of considerable dispute), but because there can be no place for them in modern civilised society.

In legal theory, a particular punishment is designed to achieve one or more of four aims:

— Vengeance.
— Deterrence.
— Protection of the community.
— Reformation.

Many people would like to think that vengeance is so base a motive that it should not be the purpose of any form of punishment, and indeed some writers on the subject omit mention of it altogether. Whatever may be the ideal, a considerable sector of the public still sees merit in the principle of 'an eye for an eye', and this public feeling is reflected in sentencing policy.

There can be no doubt that the main purpose currently served by punishment is deterrence. Deterrence has two aspects. First, it is hoped that a criminal who is punished will thereby be deterred from committing the same offence again. Secondly, and more important, the mere threat of punishment is sufficient to deter most people from attempting to commit crime.

It is obvious that some people must be punished, particularly by imprisonment, for the protection of the community. It could hardly be argued, for example, that a fine, of whatever amount, would ever be a suitable punishment for murder.

By any standards, reformation of the criminal is the most useful purpose of punishment; it is in the interests both of the criminal himself and society at large that he should mend his ways and therefore no longer be a danger to, nor a burden on, the community as a whole. Unfortunately, there is scant evidence that the main forms of punishment which are intended to reform achieve any notable success in this respect.

The main forms of punishment imposed by the English courts are now considered.

5D2A. Death

Since the abolition of the death penalty for murder, this punishment can now be imposed only in cases of:

— treason;
— piracy with violence;
— setting fire to Her Majesty's ships or arsenals.

It is inconceivable that the sentence would in fact be executed in respect of the latter two offences. Treason can be committed only in time of war (technically, the intentional killing of the Queen in time of peace is treason but it would in fact be treated as murder) and it is therefore highly unlikely that the sentence of death will ever be carried out in the future.

The death penalty cannot be imposed on a person under the age of eighteen.

5D2B. Imprisonment

With the exception of fines, imprisonment is now the most common form of penalty imposed by the criminal courts. For some crimes, the chief being murder, life imprisonment is a fixed penalty. The judge has no discretion in the matter, but many life prisoners are released on licence under the Royal Prerogative, and with this in mind, the trial judge can indicate the minimum term which he thinks a murderer should in fact serve.

Where there is no fixed term, there is a maximum term laid down by statute for particular offences (Parliament has never followed the practice prevalent in other countries of fixing minimum terms of imprisonment) and a judge has considerable discretion as to the term, subject to the sentence being reduced on appeal if it is out of line with similar cases. For example, the maximum penalty for manslaughter is life imprisonment, but the sentence actually imposed may, according to the circumstances, be only a few months or, exceptionally, as little as one day.

The Criminal Justice Act 1967 introduced into English law the concept of the suspended sentence. Where imprisonment would be an appropriate punishment, the court may impose such a sentence but order that it is not to take effect unless the offender commits another offence punishable by imprisonment within a prescribed time, which must not be less than one year nor more than two years. Thus, a person may be sentenced to six months' imprisonment suspended for two years. If, during the two years, he keeps free from crime punishable by imprisonment, the sentence will never be put into effect. But if he does commit a crime punishable by imprisonment during that period, he will be sentenced for the second crime and the suspended sentence will also come into effect. A suspended sentence must not be imposed unless the punishment of imprisonment, although not actually brought into force, would be appropriate. It must not be imposed, for example, where a fine would be the more appropriate punishment.

Another concept introduced by the Criminal Justice Act 1967 is that of parole. On the advice of a Parole Board, the Home Secretary may release on licence a prisoner who has served at least one-third of his sentence, subject to a minimum of one year.

5D2C. Youth Custody

There is a special punishment for young offenders who have committed offences which, if committed by adults, would be punished by imprisonment. It is known as Youth Custody, and is only imposed on males between fourteen and 21 and females between fifteen and 21 who:

— are unable or unwilling to respond to non-custodial penalties; and/or
— are persons from whom the public need to be protected; and/or
— are persons whose offences are so serious that a non-custodial sentence cannot be justified.

The minimum sentence of Youth Custody is normally four months and one day, and if the offender is under seventeen the maximum sentence is twelve months. A longer sentence may be imposed (by the Crown Court only) if the offender is over seventeeen and it is considered that the offence, or combination of offences, is such that a longer sentence is merited.

5D2D. Other punishments for young persons

Where a custodial sentence, but not Youth Custody, is merited, a young person aged fourteen or over may be sent to a Detention Centre for a minimum period of 21 days and a maximum period of four months.

Where a custodial sentence is not merited, or in any case where the offender is under fourteen, a supervision order may be made. The young person continues to live at home but under the supervision of the local authority social services department. In the case of persons aged fourteen or over, the Probation Service carries out the supervision.

5D2E. Fines

By far the most common penalty for crime is the imposition of a fine. Some offences are punishable only by imprisonment, but the majority are punishable either by imprisonment and/or a fine, or by a fine only.

A fine is a suitable penalty for an offender who is not a 'criminal', but is a dangerous penalty to impose on a person of very limited means, who might be tempted to commit further crime to raise the money to pay the fine. Fines are also of limited value as penalties where they are of small amounts; this applies particularly to fines imposed for minor traffic offences, which are looked upon by some people as part of the running costs of a car rather than as penalties for the infringement of the criminal law.

5D2F. Probation

Instead of being sent to prison or fined, a person, particularly if he is a first offender, may be made subject to a probation order for a period of not less than one, nor more than three, years. Probation is particularly suitable for those who are socially inadequate rather than criminally inclined. The probationer is placed under the supervision of a probation officer, who is an officer of the court, and who will help the probationer in any way he can, particularly in such matters as obtaining employment. If a probationer commits a breach of the probation order he may be both fined for the breach and punished for the original offence.

5D2G. Recognizance

Recognizance is better known by its colloquial title of 'binding over'. It is an order of the court to do or refrain from doing something, usually simply to 'keep the peace'. Failure to comply with the instructions of the court results in the forfeiture of a sum of money.

5D2H. Community service order

Under the Powers of Criminal Courts Act 1973, an offender aged seventeen or over who has committed an offence punishable by imprisonment may, if he consents, be made subject to a community service order. Under such an order he must do between 40 and 240 hours of useful work for the community, the work to be completed within one year. This punishment has been found particularly appropriate for 'football hooligans', the timing of their community work being fixed to coincide with the times of football matches which they might otherwise attend.

5D2I. Deprivation of property

Also under the Powers of Criminal Courts Act 1973, a person may be deprived of his property where it has been used in connection with the commission of a crime. Thus, where a person has used his own vehicle to transport stolen goods, he may forfeit the vehicle.

5D2J. Disqualification for driving

For some motoring offences the offender, as well as some other penalty, may be disqualified for driving for a fixed period, or even for life. This penalty, or the threat of it, often has a much greater deterrent value than fines, particularly if the offender must have the use of a vehicle for his work. He may be disqualified not only for a single serious offence, but also for a series of minor offences under what is known as a 'points' system. Various offences carry a number of points, depending on their seriousness, and when a given number of points has been reached, disqualification is automatic.

5D2K. Conditional and absolute discharge

Sometimes the court may feel that there are special circumstances which justify failure to impose a penalty despite the fact that a person has been found guilty, or it may be felt that the prosecution ought not to have been brought. In such circumstances the offender may be granted either a conditional discharge, the condition being that he does not commit any similar offence again during a prescribed period not exceeding three years, or an absolute discharge, which has no conditions attached. If a person commits a further offence during the period of a conditional discharge, he may be sentenced for the original offence as well as for the further offence.

5D2L. Deferral of sentence

With the consent of the defendant, the court may defer sentence for a period of six months to find out how the defendant behaves, for example, whether he makes any reparation in respect of his offence. If he is of good behaviour during the period of deferral the court may then impose a lenient sentence such as a conditional discharge.

5D2M. Rehabilitation of offenders

The Rehabilitation of Offenders Act 1974 aims to restore the reputation of convicted persons who have not committed another crime for a specified period after their convictions. A convicted person who has received a sentence of not more than 30 months' imprisonment and who has not committed another offence during the rehabilitation period is under no obligation to reveal the offence for any purpose, for example, when seeking employment or when applying for insurance: the conviction is said to be spent. The benefit is lost if he commits another serious offence.

The rehabilitation period varies depending on the length of sentence which has been served, and is a maximum of ten years. It should be noted, however, that a sentence of more than 30 months is never spent, so that a person who has committed a very serious crime is never freed from the necessity to disclose it under appropriate circumstances.

6. Contract – 1

6A.Privity of contract
6B.Types of contract
   6B1.Contracts of record
   6B2.Simple contracts
   6B3.Contracts under seal
6C.Offer and acceptance
6D.Consideration
   6D1.It must be real
   6D2.The promiser must not already
      be bound
   6D3.Consideration must not be past
   6D4.Consideration must move from
      the promisee
   6D5.Consideration must be legal
6E.Estoppel
6F.Capacity to contract
   6F1.Minors
   6F2.Insanity and drunkenness
   6F3.Corporations
6G.Legality
6H.Void, voidable and unenforceable
   contracts
   6H1.Void contracts
6I.Consensus ad idem

6I1.Mistake
   6I1A.Mistake as to the nature of
      the transaction
   6I1B.Mistake as to the identity of
      the other party
   6I1C.Mistake as to the identity of
      the subject matter
   6I1D.Mistake as to the quality of
      the subject matter
   6I1E.Common mistake as to the
      basis of the contract
   6I1F.Mistake as to fundamental
      fact
6I2.Rectification
6I3.Misrepresentation
6I4.Representations and terms
6I5.Duress
6I6.Undue influence
6J.Assignment
   6J1.Transfer of rights
   6J2.Transfer of obligations
   6J3.Assignment by operation of law
   6J4.Assignment and negotiability

A contract is a legally binding agreement, that is, an agreement which the parties recognise shall give rise to legal obligations, enforceable at law. Anson defines a contract as 'an agreement enforceable at law made between two or more persons by which rights are acquired by one or more to acts or forebearances on the part of the other or others'.

For convenience, it will be assumed throughout this chapter, unless specifically stated, that the contract is between two parties only.

It is not necessary that an agreement should contain an express provision that it is intended to be enforceable by law. All agreements are legally enforceable unless:

— the terms of the agreement expressly disavow any intention to create a legally binding agreement;

— the agreement is one of a class to which legal obligations do not normally attach;

— the agreement is one which in the eyes of the law is of no legal effect.

An example of an express term negativing an intention to create a legally binding agreement is to be found in the case of *Rose & Frank Co.* v. *Crompton Bros* (1925). An agreement between the parties contained a term that 'this arrangement is not entered into . . . as a formal or legal agreement, and shall not be subject to legal jurisdiction in the Law Courts'. It was held that such an agreement did not give rise to any legal rights and obligations. In *Jones* v. *Vernon's Pools Ltd* (1938) it was held that a clause in an agreement ousting the jurisdiction of the courts was not contrary to public policy. In this case, a football pools coupon contained a printed condition that the entry should not 'give rise to any legal relationships, rights, duties or consequences whatsoever or be legally enforceable'. It was decided that this condition prevented the plaintiff from bringing an action for payment in respect of a winning coupon which, the defendants alleged, had been lost in the post.

Agreements relating to purely social or domestic matters are examples of those to which legal obligations do not normally attach. In *Balfour* v. *Balfour* (1919) a husband, on leaving the country, agreed to make periodic payments to his wife for her maintenance. When he failed to make the payments as agreed, his wife sued him for the arrears, but it was held that she had no cause of action, as this was solely a domestic arrangement, and was not intended to have legal consequences. This case must be contrasted with *Merritt* v. *Merritt* (1970) where a married couple separated and the husband agreed that the ownership of their house should pass to the wife when she had completed all the mortgage repayments. It was held that there was an intention to be legally bound because the parties had separated and consideration (see later) had been provided. It is also possible that a wife may be her husband's employee, or *vice versa*, in which case a contract of employment may exist between them.

An example of an agreement which is of no effect in the eyes of the law is an agreement to marry. A so-called contract of engagement is not enforceable at law by the Law Reform (Miscellaneous Provisions) Act 1970, which creates a statutory presumption that there is no intention in such circumstances to form a legally binding agreement.

Unless an agreement falls within one or other of the exceptions mentioned above, it will rarely be held ineffective on the grounds that no intention is shown to create legal rights and obligations. For example, in *Simpkins* v. *Pays* (1955) an informal agreement under which three people arranged to enter a newspaper competition on terms that they would each contribute towards the expenses and share any prize money received was held to constitute a valid contract. Therefore, although the prize-winning entry was in the sole name of one only of three, the others were legally entitled to a one-third share of the prize each.

Since contract is a matter of agreement between persons (including corporations), there is generally complete freedom for people to enter into contracts or not as they wish and, if they do so, to decide between them the terms and conditions which are to apply to the contract. This, however, assumes that the parties contract on equal terms, but in many cases they do not. One party, for example a monopoly supplier of a particular type of goods, may be in a much stronger bargaining position than the other, say, an ordinary member of the public. It is for this reason that consumer protection legislation has been passed in recent years, particularly the Unfair Contract Terms Act 1977, the purpose of which is to redress the balance where the parties to certain types of contract are not of equal bargaining strength.

The Act takes away some of the freedom of the parties to a contract to settle the terms of the agreement. It does this by preventing them altogether from relying on certain types of exclusion clause, and by making other types of exclusion clauses subject to a requirement of reasonableness.

The Act is confined almost entirely to what is called 'business liability', rather than purely private transactions and is concerned mainly with consumer contracts and contracts where one party deals with another on the written standard terms of the other. Certain types of contract are exempt from the provisions of the Act, the most important in the present context being contracts of insurance.

For reasons which will later become apparent, section 1 of the Act provides a statutory definition of negligence:

'1. (1) For the purpose of this part of the Act, "negligence" means the breach –
    (a) of any obligation, arising from the express or implied terms of a contract, to take reasonable care or exercise reasonable skill in the performance of the contract;
    (b) of any common law duty to take reasonable care or exercise reasonable skill (but not any stricter duty);
    (c) of the common duty of care imposed by the Occupiers' Liability Act 1957 or the Occupiers' Liability Act (Northern Ireland) 1957.'

It is immaterial whether the breach of duty or obligation was inadvertent or intentional.

The section also makes it clear that subsequent sections apply only to business liability, that is, liability for breach of obligations or duties arising –
(a) from things done or to be done by a person in the course of a business; or
(b) from the occupation of premises used for business purposes of the occupier.
Thus, if a person in his private, as distinct from his business, capacity, sells his car to another person, he is not caught by the Act.

Section 2 of the Act reads as follows:

'2. (1) A person cannot by reference to any contract term or to a notice given to persons generally or to particular persons exclude or restrict his liability for death or personal injury resulting from negligence.
(2) In the case of other loss or damage, a person cannot so exclude or restrict his liability for negligence except in so far as the term of notice satisfies the requirement of reasonableness.
(3) Where a contract term or notice purports to restrict liability for negligence a person's agreement to or awareness of it is not of itself to be taken as indicating his voluntary acceptance of the risk.'

Section 11 deals further with the test of reasonableness mentioned in Section 2 (2). The requirement of reasonableness is that a term should have been a fair and reasonable one to be included in the contract having regard to the circumstances which were or ought reasonably to have been known to the parties when the contract was made. If the term was reasonable at the time of the contract, it will not be deemed unreasonable as a result of circumstances which arise later. Where a contract term or notice restricts liability to a specified sum, whether such sum is reasonable will depend on the resources available to meet the liability and the availability of insurance. If a person claims that a term or notice satisfies the reasonableness test, the onus is on him to show that it does.

Section 3 reads as follows:

'3. (1) This section applies as between contracting parties where one of them deals as consumer or on the other's written standard terms of business.
(2) As against that party, the other cannot by reference to any contract term –

(a) when himself in breach of contract, exclude or restrict any liability of his in respect of the breach; or

(b) claim to be entitled –

(i) to render a contractual performance substantially different from that which was reasonably expected of him, or

(ii) in respect of the whole or any part of his contractual obligations, to render no performance at all,

except in so far as (in any of the cases mentioned above in this subsection) the contract term satisfies the requirement of reasonableness.'

The phrase 'deals as consumer' is concerned mainly with contracts for the sale of goods.

It is to be noted that Section 3 applies in two cases which may or may not be distinct:

(a) where one party deals as consumer;

(b) where he deals on the other's standard terms of business.

Thus, a consumer may deal with the other party not on the other's standard terms, or on the other's standard terms, but the Section also applies when the contract is between two businesses where one party deals on the standard terms of the other, but not where both parties are businesses and standard terms are not used. In the latter case, it is accepted that the parties are free to contract on whatever terms they may agree.

Section 12 of the Act provides that:

'(1) A party to a contract deals as consumer in relation to another party if:–

(a) he neither makes the contract in the course of a business nor holds himself out as doing so; and

(b) the other party does make the contract in the course of a business; and

(c) in the case of a contract governed by the law of sale of goods or hire-purchase, or by Section 7 of this Act, the goods passing under or in pursuance of the contract are of a type ordinarily supplied for private use or consumption.

(2) But on a sale by auction or by competitive tender the buyer is not in any circumstances to be regarded as dealing as consumer.

(3) Subject to this, it is for those claiming that a party does not deal as consumer to show that he does not.'

So far as the test of reasonableness in relation to contracts for the sale of goods is concerned, Schedule 2 to the Act lays down detailed guidelines which the courts should take into account:

(a) the relative strength of the bargaining position of the parties;

(b) whether an inducement to enter the contract was offered;

(c) the knowledge of the customer of the existence and extent of the term;

(d) if the contract excludes or restricts liability if the other party fails to comply with a condition, the feasibility of so complying;

(e) whether the goods were part of a special order.

Section 5 of the Act deals with the supply of goods for use or consumption involving a guarantee. It governs the position of manufacturers, wholesalers and distributors who give guarantees, but where there is no retailer/buyer relationship.

Where loss or damage:

(a) arises from the goods proving defective while in consumer use; and

(b) results from the negligence of a person concerned in the manufacture or distribution of goods;

liability for the loss or damage cannot be excluded or restricted by reference to any contract term or notice contained in or operating by reference to a guarantee of the goods.

Under the Section:

(a) goods are 'in consumer use' when a person is using them in his possession for use otherwise than exclusively for the purpose of a business; and

(b) anything in writing is a guarantee if it contains or purports to contain some promise or assurance (however worded or presented) that defects will be made good by complete or partial replacement, or by repair, monetary compensation or otherwise.

The way in which the Act affects contracts can be seen from a consideration of two cases. In *Woodmans* v. *Dixons Photographic* (1981), a person took some photographs (in fact the only photographs) of a wedding as a present for the bride and bridegroom. The film was sent to processors but was lost, and the plaintiff claimed compensation. The defendants attempted to rely on a clause which read: 'All photographic materials are accepted on the basis that their value does not exceed the loss of the material itself. Responsibility is limited to the cost of replacement of film.' It was held that the clause did not pass the test of reasonableness, and that the plaintiff was therefore entitled to damages of £75. And in *Waldron-Kelly* v. *British Railways Board* (1981) a suitcase was accepted 'at owner's risk' by the defendants, and was lost on a journey. The defendants offered compensation of £27, based on the weight of the suitcase and its contents, but the real value of the goods was £320. It was held that the plaintiff was entitled to recover the full value, as the clause restricting the liability of the defendants to £27 was unreasonable.

Freedom to enter into a contract is also modified by statutory provisions which oblige a person to enter into a contract whether he wishes to or not. For example, subject to comparatively minor exceptions, motor insurance and employers' liability insurance are compulsory; the motorist or employer must insure, although of course he has a choice of insurers.

6A. Privity of contract

As an agreement is made between two parties, it is a general rule that only the parties can have rights and obligations under it, and that it cannot benefit, or act to the detriment of, third parties. To this general rule there are a number of qualifications and exceptions:

— If A sues B for breach of contract, the court may award damages to C, or order B to perform the contract for the benefit of C. For example, in *Jackson* v. *Horizon Holidays* (1975), a man booked a holiday for himself and his family, but the facilities which were provided were not in accordance with those described in the holiday brochure on which he had relied. It was held that he was entitled to recover damages, not only for his own loss and disappointment, but also for that suffered by his family.

— A principal, even if undisclosed, may sue upon a contract entered into on his behalf by his agent.

— The assignee of a debt or chose in action, if the assignment is a legal assignment (see later in this chapter), can sue the original debtor.

— The holder for value of a bill of exchange can sue prior parties and the acceptor.

— In a few cases, a supplier of goods may enforce against a person not a party to the sale a condition as to resale price. This is not a general rule, but it does apply, for example, to the sale of books: a publisher can sell books to a wholesaler, who in turn sells them to a retailer, and the retailer is bound by a condition imposed by the publisher that the books may not be sold in their new condition at less than a specified price.

— If a man insures his life for the benefit of his wife, or *vice versa,* the wife or the husband, as the case may be, is entitled to the proceeds of the policy. This, however, is an aspect of the law of trusts rather than of the law of contract.

— Benefits or liabilities attached to or imposed on land may in certain circumstances follow the land into the hands of other owners.

— An exporter often asks a buyer to open with his bank a credit for the benefit of the exporter. When this is done the exporter can sue the banker if he refuses payment.

— Conveyances of land are often made subject to restrictive covenants. A subsequent buyer may enforce a restrictive covenant even although he was not a party to the original agreement.

— If A makes a contract with B for the benefit of C, and B brings an action against C, C will not be able to claim the benefit of the contract as such, but A can apply for an injunction to prevent the action between B and C coming to trial. For example, in *Snelling* v. *John G. Snelling Ltd* (1972) two brothers were the directors of a company which they financed by loans. Later a finance company provided further finance and it was agreed that the brothers would not reduce their loans until the finance company's loan had been repaid. The brothers also agreed between themselves that if either of them should resign from the company, the money due to him from the company should be forfeited. One of the brothers did in fact resign and claimed the amount owing to him from the company, but it was held that although the company was not a party to the contract, the brothers could enforce the contract as between themselves, so that the company in effect benefited by the forfeiture of the loan made by the resigning brother.

6B. Types of contract

A contract may be:

— a contract of record;
— a simple contract;
— a contract under seal, otherwise known as a specialty contract or deed.

An alternative classification is into executed and executory contracts. A contract is executed when one or both of the parties have done all that the contract requires. For example, if I ask a tobacconist for a packet of cigarettes and he gives them to me and I pay the price, the contract is executed: everything is done which needs to be done. If, on the other hand, the obligation of one or both parties remains to be carried out, the contract is said to be executory. Thus, there is an executory contract if I order a case of wine to be delivered next week, cash on delivery. The contract then only becomes executed when the wine is delivered and I pay for it.

6B1. Contracts of record

Contracts of record are not in any true sense agreements, and their inclusion in the classification is purely an historical accident. All that need be said about them here is that they include judgment debts and recognizances, and that a recognizance is an obligation imposed by a court, for example, an order to pay the costs of an action.

6B2. Simple contracts

A simple contract is an express or implied agreement creating legal rights and obligations. Generally, a simple contract need have no special form, that is, it may be made in writing, or orally, or its existence may be implied from conduct, as where a person boards a bus and, by so doing, indicates both his wish to be carried to his destination and his willingness to pay the appropriate fare.

There are, however, certain contracts which must be in writing and others which, although they need not be in writing, must be supported by written evidence.

The following are the more important contracts which must be made in writing:
— contracts of marine insurance;
— bills of exchange and promissory notes;
— contracts for repayment of money borrowed from a money-lender or of interest on the loan;
— acknowledgments of statute-barred debts;
— consumer credit transactions where the amount involved is less than £5000;
— transfers of shares in a company registered under the Companies Acts.

Such contracts, unless in writing, are void, that is, without any legal effect.

The following contracts must be evidenced by writing:
— contracts of guarantee;
— agreements for the sale or other disposition of land.

It is necessary to distinguish a contract of guarantee, which must be evidenced by writing, from an indemnity, which need not (although it nearly always is). A guarantee is a promise to answer for the debt, default, or miscarriage of another person. There are three parties concerned in a guarantee, namely, the creditor, the debtor, and the guarantor. In simple terms, the guarantor says in effect to the creditor, 'If the debtor does not pay you, I shall'. Under a contract of indemnity there are only two parties, and the indemnifier in effect says to the creditor 'Let him have the goods and I shall see that you are paid'. In other words, a guarantor is only secondarily liable, that is, he is liable only if the debtor does not pay, but an indemnifier is primarily liable. So, in a commercial fidelity insurance, if an employee defaults he is the primary debtor, but insurers undertake to pay the employer if the amount cannot be recovered from the defaulter.

An agreement for the sale or other disposition of land (including buildings) must, as indicated above, normally be evidenced by writing. There is, however, an exception to this rule: the equitable doctrine of part performance permits a party who had partly performed the contract to obtain from the court an order of specific performance to enforce the contract, even although there is no evidence in writing. In *Rawlinson* v. *Ames* (1925) the defendant orally agreed to take a lease of the plaintiff's flat, and the plaintiff carried out alterations to the flat at the request and under the supervision of the defendant. The defendant then refused to take the lease, and the plaintiff claimed specific performance of the contract. It was held that the plaintiff was entitled to succeed, as the carrying out of the alterations in the circumstances of the case amounted to unequivocal acts of part performance.

Where evidence in writing is required, the following rules apply:
— the writing must be in existence at the time when the writ beginning the action is issued, but not necessarily at the time when the contract is made;
— the writing must identify the parties with sufficient clarity;
— the consideration (consideration is dealt with later in this chapter) must be shown, except in the case of guarantees;
— the writing must indicate the subject-matter of the contract and all the material terms of the contract must be stated;
— the memorandum must be signed by the party against whom it is desired to bring the action, or by his authorised agent. Only the party who has signed the memorandum is bound by its terms.

The memorandum need not be a single document. It may be a series of connected documents, and oral evidence is admissible to connect them if one refers to another or the documents are *prima facie* connected.

Failure to comply with the requirement regarding evidence in writing does not make a contract void; the law recognises the existence of the contract, but no action may be brought to enforce its terms. The distinction is important. If, for example, A orally agrees to buy a house from B and pays a deposit, and A later decides not to go through with the transaction, A cannot by law claim repayment of the deposit as there was no evidence in writing of the contract and it is thus unenforceable. If the contract were void, that is, if the law treated it as never having been in existence, A could take legal action to recover the deposit.

Despite the common law requirement of a written memorandum, equity will grant specific performance for the sale or other disposition of land where one party has partly performed his agreement. This is based on the maxim that 'equity will not allow a statute to be used (in this case the Law of Property Act 1925) as an engine for fraud.'

6B3. Contracts under seal

A contract under seal, otherwise known as a specialty contract or deed, must be in writing and must be signed, sealed, and delivered. The sealing and delivery are now as a rule mere formalities; a small disc of red paper is affixed to the document and the party executing it places his finger on the seal saying 'I deliver this as my act and deed'. The really important features of a contract under seal are that it must be in writing and must be signed by both parties.

Corporate bodies, however, each have a distinctive seal upon which must be engraved the name of the corporation; this seal is impressed upon any document requiring execution.

The use of contracts under seal is not widespread, but there are certain types of contract which must be under seal. The most important are as follows:

— Gratuitous promises. These are promises made by a person to give or do something for which he receives nothing in return. Normally, both parties to a contract have rights and obligations.
— Conveyances of land or leases of land for periods of more than three years.
— Transfers of British ships or of shares in such ships.

Sometimes a deed is delivered subject to a condition, for example, that it will not become effective until the purchase money has been paid; or it is delivered now, but it will not become operative until some future date. In each case it is known, until it comes fully into force, as an escrow.

An escrow is useful where a person is buying or selling property, but will be abroad when the transaction is completed. He will complete the formalities before he leaves the country and will usually deposit the deed with his solicitor, although if he wishes he may hand it over to the other party to the transaction.

The differences between a simple contract and a contract under seal may be listed as follows:

— With one exception, a contract under seal need not be supported by consideration, but consideration is always required in a simple contract. The exception is a contract in restraint of trade; for example, an agreement between the seller and the purchaser of a business that the seller will not open another business in competition with the purchaser for a certain period within a defined geographical area. Such an agreement, even if under seal, must be supported by consideration.
— Under the Limitation Act 1980, an action under a speciality contract must be brought within twelve years from the time when the right of action arises. Under a simple contract the general period of limitation is six years, except in respect of an action for damages for personal injuries, in which case the period of limitation is generally three years.
— The doctrine of estoppel applies to specialty contracts. This means that a statement made in a specialty contract is conclusive evidence of its truth, and cannot be contradicted unless fraud, duress, or mistake can be proved. In a simple contract a statement is only presumptive evidence of its truth, and the presumption that it is true can be rebutted by evidence to the contrary.
— The doctrine of merger applies to specialty contracts. This means that if a simple contract is afterwards embodied in a deed, the simple contract ceases to exist.
— Stamp duty of at least 50p is payable on a deed.

6C. Offer and acceptance

Before a valid contract comes into existence there must be an unrevoked offer by one party, the offerer, and an unqualified acceptance by the other, the offeree. A distinction must be drawn between an offer and an invitation to treat. If A says to B, 'I am prepared to sell you my car for £1000', this is an offer which B is entitled to accept. But if B sees in a second-hand car showroom a vehicle on which there is a label indicating a price of £1000, he cannot demand that this car be sold to him at that price. Normally the seller will be only too pleased to sell, but it may be that a mistake was made in putting the label on the car and that the price should have been, say, £2000 rather than £1000. The law has always treated the price-labelling of goods as in invitation to treat rather than as an offer. By displaying goods the shopkeeper merely indicates that he is prepared to consider offers; the customer may offer less than the price marked, and the shopkeeper on the other hand may refuse to accept the price marked. There may be a certain amount of haggling, and the eventual offer may come from either the shopkeeper or the customer.

In *Pharmaceutical Society of Great Britain* v. *Boots Cash Chemists* (1953) the defendants had a self-service store in which customers placed the goods which they required in wire baskets and then took them to the cash desk and paid for them. It was held that the contract of sale was made not when the customer selected goods from the shelves, but when the defendants' employee at the cash desk accepted the customer's offer to buy.

In *Fisher* v. *Bell* (1961), a criminal case, the defendant had displayed a flick-knife with a price marked on it in his shop window. It was an offence to 'offer for sale' an offensive weapon. The defendant was found not guilty on the grounds that, following the rules governing the law of contract, there had been no offer for sale, only an invitation to treat. (This case was an example of the courts following the precise wording of a statute and completely ignoring its intention, which was to prevent the sale of such weapons as flick-knives. To give effect to its intention, Parliament had to pass amending legislation.)

Similarly, in *British Car Auctions* v. *Wright* (1972) it was held that auctioneers did not 'offer for sale' goods which they put up for auction as the offer came from the bidder and acceptance from the auctioneer on the fall of the hammer. Consequently, the auctioneers escaped a conviction for 'offering for sale' an unroadworthy car.

The two most important rules relating to offer and acceptance are: firstly, an offer is not made until it is communicated to the other party. In *Taylor* v. *Laird* (1856) the master of a ship gave up his command during a voyage, but helped to work the ship on its passage home. He claimed remuneration for this work from the owners of the ship, but it was held that he was entitled to nothing, as the offer of his services had not been communicated to the defendants, who therefore had no opportunity to accept or reject his offer.

Secondly, conditions may be attached to the offer, but to be effective they must be communicated to the offeree. This raises the important question of what may be considered to constitute sufficient communication. This point has been discussed in several cases where tickets were sold subject to conditions which were not printed on the tickets themselves.

Although the following cases relate to travel tickets, the same principles apply in other cases where a document does not contain the whole of the terms of a contract, such as a motor insurance cover note.

In *Henderson* v. *Stevenson* (1875) a steamer ticket had on its face only the words 'Dublin to Whitehaven', while on the back of the ticket was printed a condition that the company would not be liable for loss, injury, or delay to the passenger or his luggage. It was held that this condition was ineffective as the passenger's attention had not been drawn to it and he had not assented to it.

In another case, however, *Penton* v. *Southern Railway Co.* (1931), the plaintiff obtained an excursion ticket on the face of which were the words 'for conditions see back'. Although the plaintiff did not read the conditions it was held that he was bound by them, as the company had done all that could reasonably be expected to bring them to his notice.

The matter is summarised by Anson as follows:

> *Prime facie* a person cannot be said to have agreed on terms in a contract of which he was not even aware. On the other hand, if he has exhibited the ordinary external signs of assenting to certain terms, the law will regard him as having assented to them ... we have to ask whether the reasonable inference to put upon his conduct is or is not that he has accepted all the terms which the document contains. We cannot lay down as a rule of law that such an inference is always to be drawn from the fact of accepting a document containing terms. The document, for example, may be defective in the manner in which it calls attention to the terms which it purports to incorporate in the contract.

The problem of conditions is of particular importance in connection with insurance contracts. It is probably true to say that only a small minority of policyholders read their policies and the conditions. If a policyholder could escape his liabilities under the contract simply on the grounds that he had not read the conditions, he would have a valid defence in the large majority of disputes between insurers and insured. The insured, therefore, is bound by the conditions of an insurance policy, whether he has read and understood them or not, provided that the insurers have done all they could reasonably be expected to do to bring the condition to the notice of the insured.

When claims arise under third party insurance policies, it is common for insurers to try to reach a negotiated settlement with the third party in order to avoid litigation. In this connection, an offer of an amount in settlement is often made 'without prejudice'. In *Tomlin* v. *Standard Telephone & Cables Ltd* (1969) it was decided that where such an offer was accepted, there was a binding contract. The words 'without prejudice' meant 'without prejudice to the position of the writer if the terms which he proposed were not accepted.'

Acceptance must be unconditional. If, for example, a proposer for a particular class of insurance has been quoted the standard rates and completes a proposal form on the basis that standard rates will apply, the insurers may accept the offer. If, however, the risk turns out to be more hazardous than normal and they demand an enhanced premium, the proposer is not bound to accept the new terms. In effect, the insurers have rejected the original offer and made a counter-offer which the proposer is free to accept or reject.

In *Hyde* v. *Wrench* (1840) the defendant offered to sell his farm to the plaintiff for £1000. The plaintiff in turn offered £950, which was refused. The plaintiff later increased his offer to £1000, but this was also refused by the defendant. It was held that the plaintiff was not entitled to specific performance of the contract, or to damages, because the original offer was terminated by his counter-offer of £950 and could not therefore be accepted later.

On the other hand, in *Branca* v. *Cobarro* (1947) the defendant agreed to sell to the plaintiff his mushroom farm. The written agreement between them ended with the words: 'This is a provisional agreement until a full legalised agreement, drawn up by a solicitor and embodying all the conditions herewith stated is signed.' It was held that this was a binding agreement which would remain in force until superseded by a more formal agreement between the parties.

Acceptance must be communicated. It is a general rule that acceptance must be communicated to the offeror. The offeror may prescribe a particular mode of acceptance, but he may not attempt to dispense with acceptance altogether. In *Felthouse* v. *Bindley* (1862) the plaintiff wrote to his nephew offering to buy a horse, and adding 'If I hear no more about him I consider the horse mine at £30/15/0d'. The horse was one of a number which the nephew had asked an auctioneer to sell for him, and on receiving his uncle's letter he asked the auctioneer to withdraw the horse from the sale. By mistake the auctioneer sold the horse. In an action for conversion brought by the uncle against the auctioneer, it was held that there was no contract between the uncle and the nephew, as acceptance had not been communicated, and the action for conversion therefore failed.

Acceptance may, however, be communicated by conduct in appropriate circumstances. In *Carlill* v. *Carbolic Smoke Ball Co.* (1893), the defendants advertised a medical preparation known as the 'Carbolic Smoke Ball' at a cost of 10/- (refills 5/-), and offered £100 to any person who, having used the preparation in accordance with directions, should have the misfortune to catch influenza. Mrs Carlill bought a smoke ball, used it in accordance with directions for fifty-eight days, caught influenza, and claimed the £100. The defendants resisted the claim on several grounds, one of them being that Mrs Carlill had not communicated to them her acceptance of their offer. The Court of Appeal, however, held that where a promise is made in return for the doing of an act, the doing of the act is itself sufficient to indicate acceptance. Mrs Carlill was therefore entitled to £100.

It should be noted that this case is exceptional in that advertisements are not usually offers in the legal sense of the term. The special feature here was that £1000 had been deposited by the defendants with a bank to meet any claims which might arise, and the court held that this showed that it was a firm offer and that a legal relationship was intended.

An offer cannot be accepted if the acceptor did not know of the existence of the offer. For example, if a person advertises that he will pay a reward to the finder of property to which he has lost, and some person who is unaware of the offer of the reward finds the property and returns it to its owner, he is not entitled to the reward. (Incidentally, if a police officer finds lost property and returns it to its owner, he is not entitled in any circumstances to a reward, even if he knows that a reward has been offered, as in finding and returning the property he is doing no more than his normal duty.)

An exception to the rule that acceptance must be communicated is where acceptance is by post. In this case acceptance is complete at the moment when the letter is posted, even if it never reaches its destination, provided that the letter is properly addressed and properly posted. This does not apply however, if the agreement indicates that the offer is not accepted until notice of acceptance is actually received.

In *Holwell Securities* v. *Hughes* (1974) the appellants had the right 'exercisable by notice in writing to' the respondent to purchase a property from him. They wrote to him purporting to exercise this right, but their letter never arrived. It was held that there was no contract, as there had been no notice in writing to the respondent.

The use of telex in making contracts is increasing, and the question arises whether the normal rule or the postal rule applies to acceptance by telex. In *Brinkibon Ltd* v. *Stahag und Stahlwarenhandelsgesellschaft mbH* (1982) the plaintiffs were an English company who wished to purchase steel bars from the defendants, who were an Austrian company based in Vienna. The negotiations took place through a series of telexes to and from London and Vienna, and the telex which constituted the acceptance of the offer was sent by the plaintiffs from London to Vienna. The House of Lords held that this was an instantaneous communication between the parties and that the contract was concluded when and where the acceptance of the offer was received by the offeror, that was, in Vienna. In the event, the defendants did not make delivery of the goods, but it was held that the plaintiffs could not bring an action against them in the English Courts, as the contract was not made within their jurisdiction.

This decision followed the rule in *Entores Ltd* v. *Miles Far East Corpn.* (1955). Its main interest lies in the fact that the court made it clear that there is no hard and fast rule that where negotiations are by telex the contract is completed when and where the telex is received. The rule does apply where the telex can be considered to be an instantaneous communication, for example, a telex sent by the offeree from his office to the offeror at his office during normal working hours. Where, however, the communication is not instantaneous as, for example, where the message is sent out of office hours or at night, or through a telex machine belonging to a third party, the time and place of the formation of the contract can only be resolved by reference to the intention of the parties, by sound business practice, and in some cases by judging where the risk should lie, and not by applying a universal rule.

Explaining the need to consider further the decision in the *Entores* case, Lord Wilberforce said:

> 'Since 1955 the use of telex communication has been greatly expanded, and there are many variants on it. The senders and recipients may not be the principals to the contemplated contract. They may be servants or agents with limited authority. The message may not reach, or be intended to reach, the designated recipient immediately: messages may be sent out of office hours, or at night, with the intention, or on the assumption, that they will be read at a later time. There may be some error or default at the recipient's end which prevents receipt at the time contemplated and believed in by the sender. The message may have been sent and/or received through machines operated by third persons. And many other variations may occur. No universal rule can cover all such cases . . .'

An offer may be general or specific. It may be made to people generally, and accepted by any person in the class to whom it is addressed. This is so where the offer is made by newspaper advertisement as in *Carlill* v. *Carbolic Smoke Ball Co.* (*supra*). But where the offer is made to a specific individual, as where A offers to sell his car to B, it can be accepted only by B.

An offer is open until it is accepted (which has already been explained) or until it is revoked or lapses. An offer may be revoked, that is, withdrawn, by the offeror at any time before it is accepted. In transactions by post, the offer is complete only when it reaches the offeree, but as mentioned above, acceptance is usually effective from the moment when the letter is posted. Revocation, like offer, is only effective from the moment it reaches the offeree. Therefore, if A offers by post to sell goods to B, and B, after a few days' delay, accepts the offer by post, a revocation by A in the meantime will be of no effect unless it has reached B before B posted the letter of acceptance.

In *Henthorne* v. *Fraser* (1892), A offered to sell property to B for £750. On the day following that on which B received the offer, B at 3.30 p.m. posted a letter of acceptance. In the meantime, at noon on the same day, A had written a letter withdrawing the offer, but this did not reach B until 5.50 p.m. It was held that the contract was complete when the acceptance was posted, and that A was bound.

In *Dunmore* v. *Alexander* (1830) a letter accepting an offer of employment was followed by a letter withdrawing the acceptance. Both letters reached the offerer by the same post. It was held that the acceptance was validly cancelled.

There is an exception to the rule that an offer may be revoked at any time before acceptance, namely, when valuable consideration has been given to keep an offer open for a certain time. This is what is usually called an option, as where A offers to sell property to B and B, wishing to have time to consider the matter, pays A small sum in return for A's promise to keep the offer open for, say, fourteen days. In *Mountford* v. *Scott* (1974), the defendant, in consideration of a payment of £1, signed an agreement giving the plaintiff the right to purchase his house for £10,000 at any time within six months. When, three months later, the plaintiff sought to exercise the option, the defendant tried to resile from the agreement as the value of the house had increased considerably, but it was held that he was bound by it. Sometimes the offeror, when making the offer, stipulates that it must be accepted within a specified time; if it is not accepted within that time, the offer lapses. However, an offer may be revoked within the time stated unless valuable consideration has been given. In *Routledge* v. *Grant* (1828) the defendant offered to take a lease of the defendant's premises 'a definitive answer to be given within six weeks from 18 March 1825'. It was held that the defendant was entitled to withdraw the offer within the six weeks, as the plaintiff had given no consideration to keep the offer open.

Where no period is stipulated the offer lapses unless it is accepted within a reasonable time. What is reasonable depends on the circumstances of each case. In *Ramsgate Victoria Hotel Co.* v. *Montefiore* (1866) an offer to buy shares, made on 28 June, was accepted on 23 November. It was held that the acceptance was invalid, as an unreasonable time had elapsed between offer and acceptance.

An offer lapses on the death of the offeror if it involves some element personal to the offeror, such as an offer to write a book, and also where the offeree actually knows of the offeror's death, but otherwise the death of the offeror has no effect on the offer. The death of the offeree terminates the offer, which cannot therefore be accepted after his death for the benefit of his estate.

As the contract is complete after acceptance has been made, the death of either the offerer or the offeree after acceptance has no effect on the contract, which can be enforced by or against the personal representatives of the deceased. An obvious exception is that a contract for personal services lapses on the death of the person concerned.

6D. Consideration

A contract must have either form, that is, be made under seal, or have consideration. The one exception to this general rule has already been noted; a contract in restraint of trade must always be supported by consideration, whether or not it is made under seal.

Consideration was defined in *Currie* v. *Misa* (1875) as: 'Some right, interest, profit or benefit accruing to one party, or some forbearance, detriment, loss or responsibility given, suffered or undertaken by the other.'

Another, and perhaps better, definition is that of Sir Frederick Pollock: 'An act or forbearance of one party, or the promise thereof, is the price for which the promise of the other is bought, and the promise thus given for value is enforceable.'

This means that where a person wishes to enforce a promise made to him by another he must show that he gave something to, or did something for, that other, in return for the promise. For example, a contract of insurance is a promise by insurers to indemnify or compensate the insured on the occurrence of a specified event, in return for which the insured gives consideration, that is, pays a premium. In the absence of consideration there is a mere gratuitous promise, which is enforceable only if in the form of a specialty contract.

Examples of consideration are:
— payment of, or promise to pay, money;
— performance of, or promise to perform, personal services;
— transfer of, or promise to transfer, land or goods.

There are five rules to be noted in connection with consideration.

6D1. It must be real

Consideration must be real, but need not be adequate. It is not for the court to decide whether the parties have made a good or bad bargain, and the court therefore will not enquire whether the consideration was adequate. For example, evidence that the price paid for goods was below the current market price will not be taken into account. But the court must be satisfied that the consideration was real, that is, that it had some value, although not necessarily an adequate value.

In *White* v. *Bluett* (1863) a son sued his father's executors, claiming that his father had offered to pay him money if he, the son, would cease from complaining that he had been unfairly treated by the father. The court held that a consideration of this sort was too insubstantial to have real value, and that therefore no valid consideration existed.

On the other hand, in *Thomas* v. *Thomas* (1842) the executor of the plaintiff's husband agreed to allow the plaintiff to have the use of her late husband's house on a payment of £1 a year, but later refused to convey the property to her on the grounds that there was no consideration. It was held that the plaintiff's promise to pay £1 a year was real, although not adequate, consideration, and that she was therefore entitled to have the house conveyed to her. This decision in practice means that what are virtually gratuitous promises can be enforced even if they are not embodied in a deed. It has been said that 'a peppercorn does not cease to be good consideration if it is established that the promisee does not like pepper and will throw away the corn.'

6D2. The promisor must not already be bound

The consideration must not be something which the promisor is already bound to do. Three possibilities may arise under this heading:

Firstly, the promisor may already be under a legal obligation towards the promisee, in which case the consideration is inadequate. In *Foakes* v. *Beer* (1884) Julia Beer obtained judgment against John Foakes for £2090. Later, the parties made an agreement under which Foakes agreed to pay £500 down and half-yearly sums of £150 until the full £2090 had been paid off. When the full debt had been paid in accordance with this agreement, Beer sued Foakes for interest on the debt. It was held that she was entitled to succeed as there was no consideration for the agreement to pay by instalments; it related to something which Foakes was already bound to do.

Secondly, the promisor may already be under an obligation to a person other than the promisee, in which case the consideration is good. In *Shadwell* v. *Shadwell* (1860) an uncle promised to give to a nephew an annuity if the nephew would marry the lady to whom he was already engaged. It was held that the agreement between uncle and nephew was binding, even though at the time it was made the nephew was under an existing legal obligation to marry the lady. (At the time of this case an agreement to marry, that is, an engagement, was legally binding, but this is no longer so.)

Thirdly, the promisor may be under a legal obligation towards the public in general, as in the circumstances mentioned earlier where a policeman finds lost property and has a legal duty to return it to its owner.

6D3. Consideration must not be past

Consideration must not be past. In this connection, it is necessary first to explain that consideration may be either executed or executory. Consideration is executed when a party to the contract can show that he has already paid for goods which he has ordered. It is executory when a party to the contract has promised to perform his part of the contract and is ready and willing to perform it if the other party is also willing to perform his part. For example, if a life assurance office issues a letter of acceptance agreeing to give life cover if the proposer will pay the first premium within a certain time, the consideration of the life office is executory. If the proposer then pays the premium within the stipulated time the consideration is executed by both parties.

A promise now to do something in return for services previously rendered is not binding. There is here no consideration at all, as the promisor receives nothing beyond what he already has. In *re McArdle* (1951) the occupants of a house had repairs and decorations carried out at a cost of £488. Later the beneficial owners of the house agreed in writing to pay the £488. It was held that the consideration was past, and therefore an action to recover the £488 must fail.

There are certain true or apparent exceptions to this rule:
— Where A asks B to carry out work for him and B reasonably assumes that the price will later be fixed, a subsequent agreement fixing the price will be binding. Here there is implied a promise at the time of the request to pay a reasonable amount for the work to be done.
— In actions upon bills of exchange, the Bills of Exchange Act 1882 provides that any consideration is sufficient which would be sufficient in a simple contract, and this is also the case with an antecedent debt or liability.

6D4. Consideration must move from the promisee

The consideration must move from the promisee. This means that a person cannot enforce an obligation unless he himself has given consideration. This can be put another way by saying that only the parties to a contract can have rights or obligations under it and that a third party cannot claim under a contract. in *Scruttons Ltd* v. *Midland Silicones Ltd* (1962) stevedores damaged a drum of chemicals which they were loading. The goods were carried subject to a bill of lading which limited the amount of compensation for damage by the carriers to £500. The House of Lords held that as the stevedores were not parties to the contract of carriage they could not rely on this limitation clause.

6D5. Consideration must be legal

The consideration must be legal. Illegality is dealt with later in this chapter.

6E. Estoppel

Closely associated with consideration is the doctrine of estoppel. The purpose of consideration was originally to act as a test for the court to find out if there had been a bargain between the parties which it could enforce. In time, however, the requirements regarding consideration went further than this and were applied also to the discharge of contractual liabilities, so that if A and B entered into a contract and A carried out his part, but was prepared to waive performance by B, if there was no consideration for the waiver A could call upon B at any time to perform his obligations in spite of A's promise which, being gratuitous, had no effect in law unless it was embodied in a deed of release.

However, in *Central London Property Trust Ltd* v. *High Trees House Ltd* (1947) Denning J. (as he then was) held that where a party has waived his contractual rights against another party and the other party has changed his position by relying on the waiver, the courts would regard it as unjust to permit an action against him to succeed on the basis of the original obligation. In other words, the party who waived his rights will be estopped, that is, prevented, from denying that he intended the waiver to have a legal effect.

The doctrine of estoppel does not give rise to a cause of action but only provides a defence in certain cases where an action is being brought against a party when he thought the other party had waived his rights under an existing contract. This is what is meant by the saying that estoppel is only a shield, not a sword.

Without going into detail, it may be mentioned here that for many years the doctrine of consideration has been thought by many lawyers to be unsatisfactory in many respects, and as long ago as 1937 a Law Revision Committee recommended that it should be dispensed with entirely in connection with written contracts. The law of contract is at present under detailed scrutiny by the Law Commission with a view to codification and it may be that in the not too distant future the law regarding consideration will be radically altered.

6F. Capacity to contract

The general rule is that any person may enter into any type of contract. There are however, certain classes of people to whom special rules apply.

These are:
— minors, that is, people under eighteen years of age;
— people who are of unsound mind or who are drunk;
— corporations.

6F1. Minors

The Family Law Reform Act 1969 fixes the age of majority at eighteen. A person under the age of eighteen is legally a minor and contracts entered into by him are either:
— binding;
— void, that is, in law there is no contract at all; or
— voidable, that is, the minor may affirm or repudiate the contract as he wishes.

The law takes the view that persons under age should have the protection of the law of contract because of their immaturity. Even a minor who misrepresents his age cannot be sued under a contract, but he has no immunity in criminal law in such circumstances.

Three types of contract are binding on a minor: Firstly, contracts for the supply of necessaries which have been delivered. Necessaries are goods suitable to the condition in life of the minor and to his requirements at the time of sale and delivery. The minor must pay a reasonable price, not necessarily the contract price, for them, and he is not liable until the goods are in fact supplied. In *Nash* v. *Inman* (1808) Inman, a Cambridge undergraduate, ran up a bill of £145 (perhaps £2000 at current prices) with a Savile Row tailor. The tailor was unsuccessful in his claim for the amount, the Court of Appeal holding that, while clothes in reasonable quantities are necessaries, Inman was already adequately supplied. The purchases from Nash were sheer extravagance, and thus could not be considered necessaries.

It is not always easy to decide what is a necessary. In *Clyde Cycle Co.* v. *Hargreaves* (1898) the court decided that a racing bicycle was a necessary for a seventeen-year-old apprentice.

Where a person supplies goods to a minor, the onus is on him to prove that they are necessaries.

Secondly, contracts of education and service. These include articles of apprenticeship and contracts of employment, although the terms under which minors can be employed are subject to various restrictions. In *Doyle* v. *White City Stadium Ltd* (1935) Doyle, who had been granted a licence to box by the British Boxing Board of Control, was held bound by the conditions under which the licence was granted, for although some of the conditions were not for his benefit, the contract was for his benefit when looked at as a whole.

Thirdly, contracts of marriage. A person who has not attained majority may enter into a contract of marriage, but the consent of his parent or guardian, or, failing that, the consent of the court, is required.

A trading contract where the minor's capital is at risk is never enforceable, however beneficial it may be to him. Thus, in *Mercantile Union Guarantee Corporation* v. *Ball* (1937) it was held that the buying on hire purchase terms of a lorry by a minor for use in connection with his business as a haulage contractor was not binding on him, although the owner could recover the lorry, as a hire purchase contract is not a contract of sale.

Under the Infants Relief Act 1874 the following types of contract made by minors are said to be void, but the term void in this context is a misnomer. In fact a better description would be 'irrevocably voidable at the wish of the minor'. If they were void the minor could not sue on them, but in fact he can adhere to them if he so wishes or otherwise avoid them. They include:
— contracts for the repayment of money lent or to be lent;
— goods supplied or to be supplied, other than necessaries;
— accounts stated, where the minor admits that he owes money to another person.

Thus, agreements to pay by instalments are not enforceable on a minor.

In these circumstances, although he cannot be sued, the minor cannot recover money which he has paid unless there has been a total failure of consideration.

All contracts made by minors which do not fall within the categories already mentioned are voidable. A distinction must, however, be made between contracts of a continuing nature and other types of contract. Contracts of a continuing nature are voidable but, unless repudiated by the minor during minority or within a reasonable time of coming of age, they become binding upon him. Such contracts include covenants attached to a lease, liability for a call on shares, and partnership agreements.

In *Davies* v. *Beynon-Harris* (1931) a minor took a lease of a flat. Three years later, after he had attained his majority, he was sued for arrears of rent. It was held that he was liable to pay the arrears of rent because the contract was voidable, not void, and he had not repudiated it during minority or within a reasonable time after attaining majority.

All other contracts are voidable at any time, and cannot be ratified by the minor on his attaining his majority so as to become binding on him. This is the effect of s. 2 of the Infants Relief Act 1874: 'Any purported ratification of a contract made during infancy in unenforceable, even though new consideration is given for such . . . ratification'.

6F2. Insanity and drunkenness

A person certified as mentally disturbed may be subject to the control of the Court of Protection. If so, contracts are made on his behalf by a receiver appointed to look after his affairs. Apart from this, a contract made by an insane or drunken person is binding upon him if it is for necessaries. All other contracts made by people in these classes are voidable, but only if at the time of the making of the contract the other party to it was aware of the insanity or drunkenness. For this purpose, a person is not to be considered insane or drunk unless at the time of making the contract he was incapable of realising the effect of what he was doing.

Where such a contract is voidable, it becomes binding on the erstwhile insane or drunken person unless he repudiates it within a reasonable time of the cessation of the disability.

6F3. Corporations

Corporations, as has been noted earlier, come into existence by Royal Charter, by special Act of Parliament, and, most commonly, by registration under the Companies Acts. There is a distinction in their contractual capacities between corporations formed by Royal Charter and others:

A corporation formed by Royal Charter may enter into contracts to the same extent as may a private individual, although the Charter may impose limitations on what the corporation may do. If the corporation in making a contract exceeds its powers, the contract is valid, although the corporation may be liable to forfeit its charter.

However, if a chartered body does something which is outside its powers, a member may ask the court to issue an injunction restraining it. For example, in *Jenkin* v. *Pharmaceutical Society* (1921) a chartered society proposed to form a committee to regulate conditions of work between employers and employees who were members of the society, and also proposed to spend money on an insurance scheme for its members. Both these schemes were outside the terms of its charter, and the plaintiff, a member of the society, was held entitled to an injunction restraining the society from implementing them.

All other corporations are subject to the *ultra vires* (beyond the powers of) rule, which means that they cannot make contracts relating to matters other than the business for which they were formed. For example, a trading company incorporated under the Companies Acts has a Memorandum of Association stating the objects for which the Company was formed, the scope of its operations, and the extent of its powers. Any contract entered into outside these powers is void as being *ultra vires*.

In *Ashbury Railway Carriage and Iron Co. Ltd* v. *Riche* (1875) the company agreed to assign to another company a concession which they had bought for the construction of a railway in Belgium. The Memorandum of Association made no mention of the construction of railways, and it was therefore held that the agreement to assign was *ultra vires* and void.

The *ultra vires* rule could be harsh on a person who in good faith makes a contract with the corporation not knowing the contract is *ultra vires*. The European Communities Act 1972 therefore provides that where a contract is made between A and B and A is acting *ultra vires*, provided B is acting in good faith and A's action was the result of a decision of its board of directors, B can enforce the contract against A, but not vice versa.

6G. Legality

A contract which is illegal is generally destitute of legal effect. But if a contract is legal in part and illegal in part, the part which is legal can be enforced if it can be severed from the part which is illegal. The three most important categories of contracts which are illegal are as follows:

Firstly, agreements to commit a crime or a civil wrong. In *Allen* v. *Rescous* (1676) A gave R £1, on R's promising to assault X, it being agreed that if R failed to carry out his promise he would pay A £2. R did not carry out his promise, and A sued him for the £2. It was held that the transaction was illegal and void.

In *Napier* v. *National Business Agency Ltd* (1951) the defendants agreed to pay the plaintiff a salary of £13 a week plus £6 expenses. This was a device, known to both parties, to avoid payment of income tax on the £6, as the plaintiff's expenses in fact never amounted to more than £1 a week. When the plaintiff was summarily dismissed he claimed £13 in lieu of notice. His claim failed, as the agreement between him and his employer was contrary to public policy and illegal.

Secondly, agreements which are contrary to public morality. Morality here appears from decided cases to be confined to sexual morality. In *Pearce* v. *Brooks* (1866) the plaintiffs hired a brougham to a woman whom they knew to be a prostitute, and who would use the carriage in connection with her trade. On her refusing to pay the cost of hire, they sued her for the amount due but it was held that the contract could not be enforced, as it was entered into for an immoral purpose.

Thirdly. contracts interfering with the administration of justice. These include contracts to compromise criminal proceedings.

In *Clubb* v. *Hutson* (1965) the plaintiff charged the defendant with the crime of obtaining goods by false pretences but agreed not to institute criminal proceedings on the defendant's giving him a promissory note (an I.O.U.). In an action on the note it was held that payment could not be enforced, as it was not in the public interest that such a charge should be suppressed.

6H. Void, voidable and unenforceable contracts

It is convenient at this point to draw distinctions between void, voidable and unenforceable contracts. A void contract is treated in law for all purposes as if it did not exist, and so is something of a contradiction in terms. If a contract is voidable it is binding, but one party to it has the option to set it aside. An unenforceable contract is valid, but cannot be enforced in a court of law if one of the parties refuses to carry out his obligations under it. An unenforceable contract can, however, be used as a defence to a claim.

A statute may make an agreement unlawful. For example, under the Resale Prices Act 1976, collective agreements between suppliers of goods to blacklist people who sell at prices below those fixed by the suppliers are unlawful.

6H1. Void contracts

Certain contracts, although not illegal, are void. Examples of void contracts are:

— Contracts made void by statute. These include contracts of gaming or wagering, which are made void by the Gaming Act 1845, and contracts made with a moneylender who does not hold a licence under the Moneylenders Act 1927.

— Agreements affecting the freedom and sanctity of marriage. An agreement in total restraint of marriage is void, but not a partial restraint, for example, a promise not to marry a Welshman. Marriage brokage contracts, under which a person agrees to introduce another to a person of the opposite sex, with a view to marriage, are void, as also are contracts providing for the future separation of husband and wife. In *Herman* v. *Charlesworth* (1905) the defendant agreed to introduce men to the plaintiff with a view to marriage, and she made a payment to him of £25. He introduced several men to her, but no marriage took place. The plaintiff successfully sued for the return of the payment.

— Certain contracts in restraint of trade. There are various types of contract in restraint of trade, the two most important, for present purposes, being agreements which restrict the right of a person to follow his trade, profession, or calling, and those which relate to the sale of a business, where the seller agrees to restrictions on his right to compete in business with the buyer. Such contracts are void unless the following conditions are fulfilled: the restrictions must be fair and reasonable as between the parties; they must be reasonable from the point of view of the public interest; and the agreement must be supported by consideration even if it is under seal. The courts are less willing to enforce contracts of this type involving employees than they are to enforce contracts relating to the sale of a business.

In *Eastes* v. *Russ* (1914) the defendant was employed by the plaintiff as a microscopist on terms that he would not engage on similar work within ten miles of the plaintiff's laboratory. It was held that this restriction, which was unlimited in time, was wider than was necessary to protect the plaintiff's interests and was therefore void.

In *Nordenfelt* v. *Maxim Nordenfelt Guns and Ammunition Co. Ltd* (1894) Nordenfelt sold his business to a company and agreed not to enter into competition with the company for a period of twenty-five years from its incorporation. It was held that, although the restraint was worldwide, it was valid as being necessary to protect the company's interests, and was not contrary to the public interest.

In *Herbert Morris Ltd* v. *Saxelby* (1916) the respondent, as a condition of his service with the appellants, agreed that if he left the appellants' service he would not engage in work similar to that undertaken by them for a period of seven years anywhere in Britain or Ireland. It was held by the House of Lords that such a covenant was too wide and could not be enforced.

An employee will, however, be restrained if he is in breach of his implied term of fidelity towards his employer. In *Sanders* v. *Parry* (1967) the defendant was employed by the plaintiff as an assistant solicitor. During the course of his employment he was given the task of looking after the legal affairs of an important client. After several months the defendant and the client agreed that the defendant would set up in practice on his own account, and that the client would then transfer all his work to the defendant. It was held that the plaintiff was entitled to damages, as the defendant had acted contrary to the interests of his employer and was in breach of the implied term of fidelity.

In partnership agreements there are often clauses restricting an outgoing partner from practising within a defined area. Such clauses are enforced if they are reasonably necessary for the protection of the practice even if they restrain competition as such. To this extent, the position as between partners is different from that as between employer and employee.

A number of cases have come before the courts involving solus agreements, under which a trader agrees to buy all his supplies of a particular commodity from one supplier. Whether such agreements are enforceable depends on whether the court considers them to be reasonable. In *Esso Petroleum Co. Ltd* v. *Harpers Garage Ltd* (1967) it was held that an agreement to buy petrol from one company only for 21 years was too long, but that an agreement for five years was reasonable.

Restraints imposed by trade associations or professional bodies on their members are void unless they are reasonable. In *Pharmaceutical Society of Great Britain* v. *Dickson* (1968) the society passed a resolution the effects of which were that the opening of new pharmacies would be restricted and the services which they could provide would be curtailed, the aim being to stop pharmacies entering into new fields of trading. It was held that the resolution was void as being an unreasonable restraint of trade.

By the provisions of Article 85 of the Treaty of Rome, agreements between undertakings and practices which have as their object the prevention, restriction, or distortion of competition within the EEC countries are generally void. This may render certain types of contracts in restraint of trade void under community law.

6I. Consensus ad idem

The requirement of *consensus ad idem* means that there must be complete agreement between the parties to the contract. This involves consideration of the rules relating to mistake, rectification, innocent and fraudulent misrepresentation, non-disclosure and concealment, and duress and undue influence.

6I1. Mistake

Mistakes will not in all circumstances make a contract void. A mistake of law will never make a contract void, as the legal maxim is that ignorance of the law is no excuse. A mistake of fact will make a contract void only if it falls within one of the following categories, in which case it is known as an operative mistake.

6I1A. Mistake as to the nature of the transaction

If a person signs a document, having been misled as to the fundamental character of the document, he will not be liable under it. But if he has been misled only as to details, he will be liable.

In *Foster* v. *Mackinnon* (1869) the defendant was sued on a bill of exchange for £3000. The jury found that when Mackinnon endorsed the bill of exchange he did so under the mistaken belief that it was in fact a guarantee. It was held that he was not liable on the bill of exchange.

The plea of mistake in such circumstances, however, is available only if the person making the mistake can show that he was not negligent in so doing.

In *Howatson* v. *Webb* (1908) the defendant executed a document which he knew transferred property of his to one Whitaker, although he did not know that in fact it was a mortgage deed. It was held that the plaintiff, who had innocently accepted an assignment of the mortgage, was entitled to sue under the deed.

The law on this point was reviewed in *Saunders* v. *Anglia Building Society* (1970). In that case an elderly widow signed a document which she was told was a deed of gift of her house to her nephew. She did not read the document which was in fact an assignment of her interest in the house to the person who had told her that it was a deed of gift. It was held that the plea of mistake was not available to her, as the transaction intended and carried out was the same, namely, an assignment. In giving judgment the House of Lords laid down the following rules:

— A plea of *non est factum* (mistake as to the nature of the transaction) will rarely succeed when a person signs a legal document without reading it.

— A mistake as to the identity of the person in whose favour the document is executed will not support a plea of *non est factum* unless the mistake is regarded by the courts as fundamental.

— The distinction between the character of a document and the contents of a document (which was drawn in *Howatson* v. *Webb* (*supra*)) is confusing and illogical. The better test is whether the document is fundamentally different from what it was thought to be. Under this test it would be possible to hold, for example, that a person who signs what he thinks to be a guarantee for £1000, but is in fact a guarantee for £100,000, will not be bound by it. But carelessness on the part of the person signing the document in such circumstances will prevent him from raising the plea.

611B. Mistake as to the identity of the other party

Mistake as to the identity of the other party makes a contract void only if the identity of the other party was material, in the sense that the first party thought that he was contracting with A, and would not have entered into the contract if he had known he was contracting with B. This rule will be better understood by considering these three cases:

In *Cundy* v. *Lindsay* (1878) one Blenkarn, fraudulently misrepresenting himself to be the respectable firm of Blenkiron & Co., obtained goods from Lindsay and Co., did not pay for them, and sold them to the appellants. Lindsay and Co. sued the appellants for conversion. It was held that there was no contract between Lindsay and Co. and Blenkarn, from which it followed that he could not lawfully transfer the goods to the appellants. The appellants therefore were in unlawful possession of the goods, and must pay damages for conversion.

In *Ingram* v. *Little* (1960) a swindler who called himself P.G.M. Hutchinson obtained from the plaintiffs a car which they had for sale. They agreed to let him have the car only because they were satisfied that he was P.G.M. Hutchinson whom they had reason to believe was trustworthy. It was held that the plaintiffs had placed reliance on the identity of the customer and that in the circumstances there was no contract.

In *Lewis* v. *Averay* (1971), on the other hand, the plaintiff sold his car to a person who signed a cheque in payment in the name of R.A. Green, after having given the impression that he was a well-known actor, Richard Green. The cheque was dishonoured and it was discovered that R.A. Green was an imposter.

The defendant had purchased the car in good faith and it was held that the contract between the plaintiff and Green was valid, and that the defendant had therefore obtained a good title. The distinction between this case and *Ingram* seems to be that in *Ingram* the plaintiff relied on the fact that the 'buyer' was Hutchinson, whereas in *Lewis* the court considered that the plaintiff, although assuming that the buyer was Richard Green, did not consider this fact to be of vital importance.

A contract is more likely to be held void for mistake if it has been concluded in writing or by telephone than if the parties have met face-to-face.

611C. Mistake as to the identity of the subject matter

In *Scriven Bros. and Co.* v. *Hindley and Co.* (1913) an auctioneer sold bales of hemp and tow on behalf of the plaintiffs. The defendants made a bid for one lot which they thought was hemp, but was in fact tow. The plaintiffs sued the defendants for the amount of the bid, but it was held that the action must fail, as the plaintiffs knew they were selling tow, whereas the defendants thought that they were buying hemp. The defendants' mistake was reasonable, as there was an ambiguity in the auction particulars.

611D. Mistake as to the quality of the subject matter

Mistake as to the quality of the subject-matter makes a contract void only if the mistake is common to both parties, and the absence of the quality concerned makes the subject-matter fundamentally different from what it would have been if that quality were present.

In *Strickland* v. *Turner* (1852) the plaintiff purchased an annuity in respect of a person who, unknown to either party, was already dead. It was held that there was no contract and the plaintiff was therefore entitled to recover the purchase money.

611E. Common mistake as to the basis of the contract

A contract is void if there is a mistake as to the existence of a state of facts forming the basis of the contract, where the mistake is common to both parties. In *Cooper* v. *Phibbs* (1867) Cooper, having obtained a three-year lease of a salmon fishery, later discovered that he himself was in fact the owner of the fishery. It was held that he was entitled to have the lease set aside.

611F. Mistake as to fundamental fact

If one of the parties to a contract is mistaken as to some fundamental fact concerning the contract and the other party knows or ought to know this, the contract is void. In *Legal and General Assurance Society* v. *General Metal Agencies* (1969) a tenancy had been terminated but the plaintiffs, as landlords, by mistake sent out a computerised account asking for payment of the next quarter's rent, and when the rent was paid by cheque, banked the cheque, which was cleared. The defendant claimed that the demand for and acceptance of the rent created a new tenancy, but the court held that this was not so, as the plaintiffs had acted by mistake and the defendant knew or ought to have known of the mistake.

612. Rectification

It sometimes happens that the parties make an agreement which is then reduced to writing, and later discover that the written document does not set out fully or accurately the terms of the agreement between the parties. In such circumstances the court may rectify the document to express the true agreement between the parties, provided that there is sufficient evidence of the true intention. Alternatively, the parties may themselves consent to rectify the document.

In *Thos. Bates and Son* v. *Wyndhams (Lingerie)* (1981) the intention, known to both parties, was that a lease should contain an arbitration clause, but this was omitted from the lease, a fact which was known to the tenant, but not the landlord, when the tenant signed the lease. It was held that the lease could be rectified at the request of the landlord to include the arbitration clause.

613. Misrepresentation

A representation is a statement made with the purpose of inducing another person to enter into a contract. If such a statement is false, it is called a misrepresentation, which may be made either innocently or fraudulently. An innocent misrepresentation is a false statement made by a person who honestly believed it to be true. If such a statement was material, that is, if it was a statement which induced the other party to enter into the contract, and the other party suffers damage by entering into the contract in reliance upon it, the contract is voidable at his option. He may either sue for the contract to be rescinded, or plead the defence of innocent misrepresentation in any action which may be brought on the contract. By the Misrepresentation Act 1967 a plaintiff is entitled to sue for damages when rescission is either inappropriate or impossible, for example, when a contract has been performed.

A fraudulent misrepresentation is a false statement made by a person who knows it to be untrue, or does not believe it to be true, or is a statement made recklessly by a person not caring whether it is true or false. The difference in effect between innocent and fraudulent misrepresentation is that with the latter the party who has been fraudulently induced to enter the contract is entitled not only to rescission of the contract, but also to damages.

In *Edgington* v. *Fitzmaurice* (1885) the plaintiff lent money to the defendant after he had said that he required the money to expand his business. In fact, he needed the money to pay off existing debts. The plaintiff sued the defendant for damages for fraud, and it was held that he was entitled to succeed. Rescission is an equitable remedy, and will not be awarded where:

— the injured party was aware of the misrepresentation and carried on with the contract;
— the parties cannot be returned to their original positions;
— another party has acquired an interest in the goods;
— the injured party has waited too long before claiming his remedy.

Although a party to a contract must not make misrepresentations as to material facts, there is in general no duty upon him to disclose material information. In other words, if he says nothing at all he is not liable, but if he does make a statement he is liable if it is false. The general rule is often expressed as *caveat emptor* – let the buyer beware; it is for each party to satisfy himself that he has obtained all the information which he requires before entering into the contract.

There are, however, exceptions to the *caveat emptor* rule. The first is that all insurance contracts are contracts of the utmost good faith (*uberrimae fidei*) which means that both parties to such contracts have a duty to disclose all material facts. This means that a proposer for insurance must disclose to the underwriter all facts which would affect the decision of a prudent underwriter whether to accept the insurance or on what conditions or at what rate of premium. Whether the failure to disclose is innocent (known simply as non-disclosure) or fraudulent (known as conceal-ment), the effect is to give the party who has suffered from the failure to disclose the right to repudiate the contract.

The second is that contracts of suretyship or partnership are not themselves con-tracts *uberrimae fidei,* but when such contracts have been formed the creditor in his dealings with the surety, and the partners in their dealings with each other, must display the utmost good faith.

A misrepresentation may give rise to both criminal and civil proceedings. For example, the Trade Descriptions Act 1968 provides that 'any person who, in the course of a trade or business, applies a false trade description to any goods or supplies or offers to supply any goods to which a false trade description is applied shall be guilty of an offence'. In addition to suffering a fine or imprisonment, a person guilty of an offence may be ordered to pay up to £1000 in compensation to a person who has been misled by the false description.

614. Representations and terms

It is sometimes necessary to decide whether a statement is a representation or a term. If there has been a misrepresentation the position is as already described, but if there has been a breach of a term, the aggrieved party can claim damages for breach of contract. The following rules apply in determining whether a statement is a representation or a term:

— If a contract indicates that a statement is to be considered a term, the courts will treat it as a term.
— Statements in written contracts are usually treated as terms, but an oral statement may be either, depending on the intention of the parties.
— An oral statement is likely to be treated as a term if it is intended to prevent a buyer of goods from discovering whether the goods are defective, as where a car dealer says that a car is in very good condition and does not require inspection.
— If an aggrieved party would not have entered into the contract had the statement not been made, it will be treated as a term.
— Statements made during preliminary negotiations tend to be treated as representations.
— Oral statements not later included in a written contract tend to be treated as representations.

615. Duress

Duress makes a contract voidable at the option of the party who has been subjected to it. Duress may take the form of actual violence or threats of violence to the party himself or towards members of his family, but the detention of goods with the purpose of coercing another to enter into a contract is not duress.

616. Undue influence

Undue influence means that one party to the contract enters into it in such circumstances that he cannot be said to be exercising his own free judgment. This arises where one party is in a dominant position.

In *Welch* v. *Cheesman* (1974) a woman lived with a man of violent disposition in a house which she owned, and as a result of threats and violence by him she agreed to sell him her house for £300. When he died his widow claimed the house, then worth £3000, but it was held that the contract of sale had been induced by duress.

Where the threat is to property rather than to a person the law is not clear, but the better opinion is that a threat to property, such as a threat to destroy a person's house unless he agrees to enter into a contract, will render the contract voidable.

Certain relationships give rise to a presumption of undue influence, and it is then for the defendant to prove that in fact undue influence was not exercised. Such relationships include:

— doctor and patient;
— parent and child;
— solicitor and client;
— religious adviser and a member of his congregation;
— trustee and beneficiary.

In all other circumstances it is for the plaintiff to prove that he was in fact subjected to undue influence.

There is no presumption that a husband exercises undue influence over his wife, but it is open to her in any particular case to show that he has in fact done so. In *Cresswell* v. *Potter* (1978), for example, a wife, in the course of divorce proceedings, made over to her husband her share in the matrimonial home for a small amount. The transaction was set aside and she was awarded half of the proceeds of the sale of the house on the grounds that she was comparatively poor and ill-educated, and that she had not had the benefit of any independent advice.

Another interesting case is *Clifford Davies Management* v. *W.E.A. Records* (1975) where the manager of a 'pop' group, an astute businessman, made each member of the group sign a contract assigning the copyright in all their compositions for a period of ten years over to him. It was held that the assignment was invalid as undue influence had been exercised.

Undue influence makes a contract voidable at the option of the party suffering from it, provided that he repudiates the contract within a reasonable time.

In *Allcard* v. *Skinner* (1887) the plaintiff had been a member of a sisterhood bound by a vow of poverty, and had given all her property to the lady superior of the order. She left the sisterhood, and, six years later, sued to recover her property from the lady superior. It was held that she had been subject to undue influence, but her delay in bringing the action disentitled her to relief.

6J. Assignment

For present purposes, assignment means the transfer of rights and obligations under a contract from one person to another. If a person has a right to receive something under a contract, or on the other hand a duty to perform some obligation, he may, in certain circumstances, transfer this right or duty to another person. The rules relating to assignment are rather complicated, and in studying them the reader should keep in mind the basic rule that in general only the parties to a contract can acquire rights or be made subject to obligations under it.

6J1. Transfer of rights

A right under a contract is considered in law to be a piece of property of the type known as a 'chose in action' as distinct from a 'chose in possession', which is a piece of tangible property. Choses in action may be either legal or equitable. A legal chose in action is one which is enforceable at common law, for example, the right to be paid for goods sold and delivered. An equitable chose in action is one which, before the passing of the Judicature Act 1873, could be enforced only in the Court of Chancery, but which can now be enforced in all courts.

At common law, neither a legal nor an equitable chose in action could be assigned, although either could be assigned in equity. There could thus be no legal assignment of a legal chose in action nor a legal assignment of an equitable chose in action; but there could be an equitable assignment of a legal chose in action, or an equitable assignment of an equitable chose in action. If there was an equitable assignment of a legal chose in action, the assignee, that is, the person to whom the right had been assigned, could not bring an action to enforce his right in his own name; he had first to bring an action in the Court of Chancery to compel the assignor, that is, the original owner of the right, to lend his name to an action, and an action was then brought in the common law courts in the name of the assignor, but for the benefit of the assignee. The situation was less complicated with an equitable assignment of an equitanble chose in action; the assignee could simply bring an action in his own name.

The Judicature Act 1873 provided that there could be a legal assignment of a chose in action. There are, therefore, now four possibilities:

— a legal assignment of a legal chose in action;
— a legal assignment of an equitable chose in action;
— an equitable assignment of a legal chose in action;
— an equitable assignment of an equitable chose in action.

The rules relating to legal assignment of either a legal or an equitable chose in action are now to be found in the Law of Property Act 1925 s. 136:

> any absolute assignment by writing under the name of the assignor . . . of any . . . legal thing (chose) in action, of which express notice has been given to the debtor, trustee or other person from whom the assignor would have been entitled to claim such . . . thing in action, is effectual in law . . . to pass transfer from the date of such notice:
> *(a)* the legal right to such . . . thing in action;
> *(b)* the legal and other remedies for the same; and
> *(c)* the power to give a good discharge for the same without the concurrence of the assignor.

Thus there is no difference in law between the legal assignment of a legal chose in action and the legal assignment of an equitable chose in action. Consideration is not necessary for a legal assignment, and there can therefore be a valid assignment by way of gift.

The assignor of a chose in action cannot transfer a better title than he himself possessed. If the person liable under a contract would have had a valid defence in an action brought by the assignor, he has a similar right against the assignee. In *Young* v. *Kitchin* (1878) a builder, who was entitled to money under a building contract, assigned his rights under the contract to the plaintiff. It was held, in ascertaining the amount to be paid to the plaintiff, that the debtor was entitled to make a reduction on account of certain breaches of contract by the builder.

It should be noted that, to be valid, a legal assignment must be in writing, signed by the assignor, and that written notice must be given to the person liable under the contract.

If the requirements of the Law of Property Act 1925, s. 136 are not complied with, there can be no legal assignment, but there may be an equitable assignment, either of a legal chose in action or of an equitable chose in action. Where there is an equitable assignment of a legal chose in action, proceedings must always be brought in the name of the assignor, although for the benefit of the assignee. Otherwise, the rules for equitable assignment are the same, either for legal or equitable choses in action, and are as follows:

Firstly, consideration is not necessary to support an assignment provided that the transfer is complete, but there must be consideration where the transfer is not complete. An example of an incomplete transfer is the assignment of an expectancy under a will.

Secondly, as with a legal assignment, the assignor cannot transfer a legal title better than he himself possessed.

Thirdly, no special form, such as writing or signature, is required for an equitable assignment, but there must be sufficient proof that the assignor intended to transfer his rights to the assignee. As between the assignor and the assignee, it is not necessary that notice be given to the party liable under the contract. The person liable under the contract, however, provided that he has not been given notice of the assignment, is entitled to continue to deal with the assignor as if the assignor were still entitled to the rights under the contract, and if he does so the assignee has no rights against him, although the assignee would have a right to sue the assignor. It is highly desirable, therefore, that notice of the assignment be given to the person liable under the contract, not only for the reason already mentioned, but also because if notice is given the assignee secures priority over the other assignees.

Fourthly, an equitable assignment of a chose in action, unlike a legal assignment, need not be absolute, but where it is conditional, or relates to part only of the obligations under a contract, the assignor must be made a party to any action, and the action must be brought in his name.

Certain choses in action can only be assigned in a particular way, but it is unnecessary to go into detail here.

It is not possible to assign a personal right. If a party enters into a contract with a particular person, and might not have been willing to enter into the contract if another person had been concerned, the person with whom he enters into the contract cannot unilaterally assign his rights in the contract to another. A good example of this is where an insurer enters into a contract with an individual requiring a motor insurance policy. The age of the proposer, his driving and accident record, the type of car he drives, and other factors are essential to the insurer's decision whether to accept the proposal, and the decision might be very different were the proposer someone else. The policyholder cannot therefore assign the policy to another person without the consent of the insurer.

An assignment is ineffective if the effect of it would be to increase the obligations on the other party to the contract. In *Kemp* v. *Baerselman* (1906) the defendant promised to supply Kemp, a cake manufacturer, with all the eggs which he might need for a year. It was held that Kemp's right could not be assigned, as the contract was a personal one and the assignment of the right could have the effect of increasing the burden on the defendant.

A person cannot assign a right where the assignment is considered to be contrary to public policy. Two examples may be given:

— A pension payable to public officers may not be assigned, as it is considered to be a payment provided to enable the holder to maintain himself in a manner suitable to the dignity of his former office.

— Where a breach of contract has already occurred the person entitled to sue may not then assign his right, although even then he is still entitled to assign the proceeds, if any, of the action.

6J2. Transfer of obligations

A person is not entitled to transfer his obligations under a contract without the consent of the other party and of the assignee. If they do consent, the result is not strictly an assignment of the contract, but is what is known as novation, the coming into existence of a new contract between the person entitled to the benefit of the contract and the person to whom the obligations have been assigned.

Cases do, however, arise where people enter into contracts in circumstances in which they know that the person with whom they actually contract will delegate or sub-contract some part of his obligations. If A, a would-be purchaser, asks B, a builder. to build a house for him, he knows that in the ordinary course of business B is likely to sub-contract some of the work to, say, plumbers, electricians and decorators. This is not a transfer of liabilities on the part of B, but rather delegation. B is still liable to A in full under the terms of the contract, and if there is any breach of contract in respect of any of the work done by the sub-contractors, B is liable to A who, in turn, has no rights against the sub-contractors.

In *British Wagon Co.* v. *Lee* (1880) the plaintiffs hired wagons to the defendants, and contracted to keep them in repair. The repair work was in fact done by sub-contractors, and the defendants claimed that this was a breach of contract. It was held that there was no breach of contract and that the plaintiffs were entitled to delegate the work, because the only thing that mattered to the hirers was that the wagons should be kept in repair; it was quite immaterial to them whether the work was done by the plaintiffs themselves or was sub-contracted. On the other hand, if one party employs another, relying on the personal skill or special qualifications of the other, then the other is not entitled to delegate the work to sub-contractors.

In *Edwards* v. *Newlands and Co.* (1950) the plaintiff had entered into a contract with the defendants for the storage of his furniture. It was held that the work could not be delegated because it was of a personal nature: 'Much skill and care is necessary in appointing the men who are to handle the goods, in selecting the place where they are to be stored, in seeing that it is reasonably fireproof and burglar-proof, and in choosing the caretaker.'

6J3. Assignment by operation of law

Sometimes assignment of rights and obligations under a contract arises, not as a result of the action of the parties to the contract, but automatically, by operation of law, without the consent, express or implied, of either party to the contract. The two cases of assignment by operation of law which must be considered are those which arise when one or other of the parties to the contract dies or becomes bankrupt.

In the case of the death of a party to a contract, the normal rule is that the benefit of any rights, and the burden of any liabilities, under the contract pass to his personal representatives (executors or administrators) for the benefit, or to the detriment, of his estate, as the case may be. The liability of the personal representatives thus assigned is, however, limited to the amount of the estate; they are not themselves personally liable.

There are two exceptions to this general rule, one in respect of rights and the other in respect of liabilities. Firstly, where a person on his death had a right to bring an action which might have resulted in an award of exemplary damages, that is, damages in excess of the actual loss which he has suffered, the right of action still survives but only ordinary damages may be awarded.

And secondly, where a person on his death owed obligations of a purely personal nature, the obligation is extinguished by his death. For example, if an opera singer had entered into a contract to take a leading part in an opera, and died before carrying out the work, it would hardly be reasonable (although it might lead to some interesting results) to expect his personal representatives to undertake the obligation.

When a party to a contract is adjudicated bankrupt, the benefit of any rights, except purely personal rights, and the burden of any liabilities, pass to his trustee in bankruptcy. A trustee in bankruptcy is, however, entitled to disclaim any onerous contracts, and if he does so, the bankrupt's rights and liabilities under the contract are immediately discharged. Where the other party to the contract suffers loss as a result of disclaimer of liability by the trustee in bankruptcy, or had a right against the bankrupt in respect of a breach of contract, he cannot sue the trustee in bankruptcy. Instead, he must prove in the bankruptcy; in other words, he must establish his right against the bankrupt and then he, along with other creditors, will share in any dividend declared out of the bankrupt's estate.

There are two cases in which a bankrupt's right under a contract do not pass to the trustee in bankruptcy, but remain with the bankrupt personally:
— when a breach of contract causes injury to the bankrupt's person or feelings;
— where the bankrupt has suffered loss as a result of a breach of contract of personal service after the bankruptcy.

6J4. Assignment and negotiability

The nature of assignment has already been discussed, but before considering the distinction between assignment and negotiability, it is necessary to be clear exactly what negotiability means.

An instrument is said to be negotiable when any person who has acquired it in good faith and for value can enforce the contract contained in it against the person originally liable, although the person from whom he acquired it may have had a defective title or no title at all.

Negotiable instruments include cheques, bills of exchange, promissory notes, bearer debentures, and bearer bonds. They are not subject to two of the rules relating to consideration mentioned earlier in this chapter, namely, that consideration must move from the promisee and that consideration must not be past. A negotiable instrument is not valid, however, if it can be shown that at no time was consideration given for it.

The nature of negotiability is shown clearly in the following case:

In *Miller* v. *Race* (1758) the plaintiff in good faith purchased a bank note, which is a negotiable instrument. The note had in fact been stolen in a mail robbery. When he presented it to a bank, payment was refused. It was held that the bank was liable in respect of the bank note.

It should be noted that the holder of a negotiable instrument, to obtain a good title, must have acquired it in good faith. In the case just mentioned, if the plaintiff had known that the note had been stolen he would have obtained no title to it. It should also be noted that if the document had been an instrument which is not negotiable, such as a postal order, rather than a bank note, the plaintiff, even if he had obtained it in good faith, would have had no title to it.

If a negotiable instrument is made payable to bearer it can be negotiated by simple delivery, as where one person hands to another a bank note. If it is made payable 'to order', as in the case with a cheque, it must be endorsed before delivery; if it is not, there is no negotiation but only a simple assignment.

The holder of a negotiable instrument does not in any circumstances need to give notice to the person liable under it.

As a negotiable instrument is a written document, transfer of it must necessarily be absolute. The Bills of Exchange Act 1882 provides that an endorsement purporting to negotiate only part of a debt is invalid.

The distinction between assignment and negotiability can be summarised as follows:

— An assignor can assign to an assignee only the title which he has; the holder in due course of a negotiable instrument may obtain a title superior to that of the transferor.

— As a result, a party liable under a contract may use against an assignee any defence which would have been available to him against the assignor; but the holder in due course of a negotiable instrument takes it 'free from equities' and the party liable under it would not be able to use against the holder any defence which would have been available against the transferor.

— Notice of a legal assignment is necessary, and notice of an equitable assignment, although not necessary, is highly desirable; but no notice is necessary of the transfer of a negotiable instrument.

— Virtually all choses in action are assignable, but only a limited category of documents are negotiable.

7. Contract – 2

7A. Discharge of contract	7B1B. Minimisation of loss
7A1. Performance	7B1C. Remoteness of damage
7A2. Breach	7B1D. Pre-contract expenditure
7A2A. Conditions	7B1E. Prospective loss
7A2B. Warranties	7B1F. Liquidated damages and
7A3. Frustration	penalties
7A4. Release	7B1G. Interest
7A5. Accord and satisfaction	7B2. Quantum meruit
7A6. Merger	7B3. Specific performance
7B. Remedies	7B4. Injunctions
7B1. Damages	7C. Limitation
7B1A. Income tax	7D. Interpretation of contracts

7A. Discharge of contract

There are various ways in which a contract may be discharged, that is, the contractual rights and obligations of the parties come to an end. They are:
—performance;
—breach;
—repudiation and frustration;
—release;
—accord and satisfaction;
—merger.

7A1. Performance

Performance is the usual way in which a contract is discharged; each party to the contract carries out his obligations in accordance with its terms. There are, however, certain rules in connection with performance which must be noted:
—If there is a time fixed for performance of the contract, it must be performed at or within that time. If no time is fixed, it must be performed within a reasonable time. What is reasonable is for the court to decide in case of dispute.
—Where a particular mode of performance is stipulated by the contract it must be observed, but if there are several different ways in which a contract may be performed, a person may choose whichever mode is most convenient to him.
—Where one party to the contract owes money to the other party, he must make a valid legal tender of the money. He must offer the correct amount in cash and in proper legal form, that is:
(a) Bank of England notes up to any amount;
(b) not more than £5 in cupro-nickel coins of denominations up to 20p;
(c) not more than £10 in cupro-nickel coins of a denomination over 20p, that is 50p pieces;
(d) not more than 20p in bronze coins.
—If a valid tender is refused, the debtor is not discharged from his obligation, but in subsequent legal proceedings a successful plea of tender will mean that the other party will have to pay the whole of the costs of the action. However, if a party is under an obligation to deliver goods rather than to pay money, a proper tender of the goods which is refused will operate as a complete discharge.
—When payment is made by cheque, the debt is discharged when the cheque is honoured. If the cheque is dishonoured, the creditor has the option of suing either under the contract or on the dishonoured cheque.
—Where a party has substantially, but not exactly, performed his part of a contract, as, for example, where a builder under contract builds a house in which there are slight deficiencies or flaws, he is entitled to payment of the full contract price less a sum representing damages for the defects in the work.

7A2. Breach

A breach may be either a breach of condition or a breach of warranty, with each having differing consequences. It is important, therefore, to distinguish between conditions and warranties, and the effects of each.

7A2A. Conditions

A condition is a term of contract which is of such vital importance that failure by a party to observe it will entitle the other to treat the contract as discharged, thus relieving him of his obligations under it. Conditions may be conditions precedent or conditions subsequent, and in some contracts there may be implied conditions.

A condition precedent is one upon which the coming into operation of the contract depends:

In *Behn* v. *Burgess* (1863) there was an agreement that the defendant would load coal into the plaintiff's ship 'now in the port of Amsterdam'. In fact the ship was not in Amsterdam at the time of the contract, and when it arrived the defendant refused to load it. It was held that he was entitled so to do, as the words 'now in the port of Amsterdam' amounted to a condition precedent.

Where there is a condition subsequent, the contract is in force until a particular event which is the subject of the condition occurs, and on its occurrence the contract may be discharged.

In many contracts there are conditions which the law treats as implied, although they are not specifically expressed in the contract. For example, under the Sale of Goods Act 1979 various conditions are implied in a contract of sale, including the conditions that the seller has a right to sell the goods and, in a contract for sale by sample, that the bulk shall correspond in quality with the sample.

Where there is a breach of condition by one party to a contract, the other party may:

— treat the contract as discharged and/or claim damages; or

— affirm the contract and, treating the breach as a breach of warranty, claim damages for the breach.

7A2B. Warranties

A warranty is a term of a contract which is not of such fundamental importance as a condition, relating as it does only to a collateral matter, that is, a matter not at the root of the contract.

In *Street* v. *Blay* (1831), the defendant bought a horse from the plaintiff, its soundness being a term of the sale. Before paying for it, the defendant sold it to a third party, who in turn sold it to someone else, who sold it back to the defendant. The defendant then discovered that the horse was unsound when he originally bought it. He therefore sought to rescind the contract. It was held that he had lost his right to rescind by selling the horse, but nevertheless there had been a breach of warranty which entitled him to damages.

Warranties may be express or implied. The Sale of Goods Act 1979 for example, provides that in every contract of sale there is an implied warranty that the buyer will have undisturbed possession of the goods.

Where one party to a contract is in breach of warranty, the other party is entitled to claim damages for the breach, but he is not entitled to treat the contract as discharged.

The position with regard to conditions and warranties, as outlined above, applies to contracts generally, but in an insurance contract a warranty is equivalent to a condition in other contracts and vice versa. For example if, as a term of a fire insurance contract, the insured 'warrants' that he will supply and maintain specified fire extinguishing appliances and fails to do so, the insurers are entitled to repudiate all liability under the policy.

The distinction between breach of condition and breach of warranty is illustrated by two somewhat similar cases:

In *Poussard* v. *Spiers and Pond* (1876) the plaintiff was due to sing in an opera, but was unable to appear for the first few nights as she was ill. The defendants hired another singer whom they retained even after the plaintiff recovered from her illness and was ready and willing to perform. When the plaintiff sued for breach of contract it was held that she had been in breach of condition, and the defendants were therefore within their rights in terminating her contract.

In *Bettini* v. *Gye* (1876) a singer was engaged for a number of concert performances commencing on 30 March 1875, with a stipulation that she would attend six days' rehearsals before that date. She was taken ill, and did not recover until 28 March, so that she missed the rehearsals although she was in full health by 30 March. It was held that the defendant was not entitled to reject the plaintiff's services: she had been in breach of warranty, not condition, as the rehearsals were subsidiary to the main purpose of the contract. The plaintiff did, however, have a right to damages resulting from her late arrival.

Apart from breaches of condition and warranty, there are other forms of breach of contract which will bring the contract to an end:

— A party may simply fail to perform his part of the contract, as where a shopkeeper fails to deliver goods which have been ordered.

— A person may simply state that he does not intend to perform his part of the contract.

— A party may take some action which makes performance impossible. For example, in *Omnium D'Enterprises* v. *Sutherland* (1919) the defendant agreed to hire a ship to the plaintiff, but later sold the ship unconditionally so that it could not be hired. It was held that there was a repudiation of the contract by the defendant.

The remedy for breach of contract in any of the above circumstances is an action for damages, and the action may be brought as soon as it is clear that the breach has occurred.

7A3. Frustration

The subject of frustration, or impossibility, is important and more than a little complicated. First, a distinction must be drawn between an agreement to do something which is impossible either in law or in fact, which is in effect no contract at all, and subsequent impossibility or frustration, where circumstances arise after the contract has been formed which make it impossible to carry out the contract.

The general rule is that subsequent impossibility or frustration is no defence to an action for breach of contract; if a party wishes to avoid liability arising out of frustration he should make special provision in the contract relating to this contingency. In the following exceptional cases, however, frustration will terminate a contract, and a party unable to perform his obligations under it will not be liable for breach of contract.

> *Where the contract is based on an assumption that a particular event will occur, and the event does not take place.* In *Krell* v. *Henry* (1903) the defendant agreed to hire rooms from the plaintiff to view the coronation procession of Edward VII. The procession was cancelled and the defendant on that account refused to pay the balance of rent due. It was held that the plaintiff was not entitled to the rent, as the holding of the procession as arranged must be assumed to have been the basis of the contract.

On the other hand, in *Herne Bay Steamboat Co.* v. *Hutton* (1903) the defendants agreed to hire a boat to take passengers to see the naval review at Spithead on the occasion of Edward VII's coronation. The review was cancelled, but the boats forming the review were assembled, and the tour of them could therefore have gone ahead but was in fact cancelled. It was held that the contract was not frustrated, and the defendant was therefore held liable for the loss caused to the plaintiff.

> *Where the performance of the contract depends upon the continued existence of a particular thing, and that thing is accidentally destroyed.* In *Taylor* v. *Caldwell* (1863) the plaintiffs agreed with the defendants for the hire of a hall in which was to be given a series of concerts. The hall was destroyed by fire before the concerts were given. It was held that in these circumstances neither party was bound to perform his obligations under the contract.

On the other hand, there is the case of *Matthey* v. *Curling* (1922) where the plaintiff leased premises to the defendant on the condition that if they were damaged or destroyed by fire the defendant would make good the loss. Later the premises were requisitioned by the military authorities during World War I and during the period of requisition they were destroyed by fire. The defendants contended that the lease had been terminated by the requisition and that they were therefore no longer under any duty to repair, but it was held that they were bound by the contract as the requisition had not made it impossible to carry out the terms of the contract.

> *Where there is a fundamental change of circumstances affecting a commercial venture.* (The line between what is and what is not sufficient to discharge a contract under this heading appears to be finely drawn.) In *Metropolitan Water Board* v. *Dick, Kerr and Co. Ltd* (1918) the appellants, in July 1914, undertook to construct some reservoirs, but, on the outbreak of World War I the work was stopped by order of the Minister of Munitions. It was held that this order had put an end to the contract and the appellants were therefore released from their obligations under it. But in *Tsakiraglou and Co. Ltd* v. *Noblee Thorl* (1961) the appellants agreed to sell to the respondents 300 tons of Sudanese groundnuts, shipment to take place during November/December 1956. As the Suez Canal was blocked the voyage had to be made via the Cape of Good Hope, with consequent extra expense and delay. It was held, nevertheless, that the parties were bound by their original contract, Viscount Simonds saying 'an increase of expense is not a ground for frustration'.

> *Where the frustration is caused by a change of the law, but not where it is caused by the application of an existing law.* (The contrast between the following two cases must be carefully noted.) In *Baily* v. *de Crespigny* (1869) a lessor, on leasing premises to the lessee, undertook not to build on land opposite that on which the premises leased stood. Later, by virtue of powers given to it by an Act of Parliament, a railway company compulsorily acquired the land opposite and built on it. It was held that the lessee was not entitled to damages, as the statute had discharged the lessor from his obligation under the lease.

> But in *Walton Harvey Ltd* v. *Walker and Homfrays Ltd* (1931 the plaintiffs agreed to erect and maintain an illuminated sign on the roof of the defendants' hotel for a fixed period. During the period of the agreement Manchester Corporation, exercising statutory powers which had been obtained before the agreement had been made, acquired the hotel and demolished it. It was held that the plaintiffs were entitled to damages in respect of the loss which they suffered as a result of the premature termination of the contract.

> *Where a contract is for personal services and the person concerned is unable to perform the services because of illness or death.* In *Robinson* v. *Davison* (1871) the defendant, a pianist, was unable to play at a concert on a particular day, as

agreed with the plaintiff, owing to illness. It was held that she was not liable for breach of contract.

Where, in the circumstances mentioned above, a contract is dissolved by frustration the following rules are provided by the Law Reform (Frustrated Contracts) Act 1943:

—As a general rule, any person who has paid any sum of money under a contract which has been frustrated shall be entitled to recover the money so paid, and if any sum was payable at the time of frustration it shall cease to be payable.

—If the party to whom the money was paid or payable has incurred any expenses in connection with the performance of the contract, the court may in its discretion allow him to retain or recover, as the case may be, an amount limited to the expenses paid or payable.

—Where a person has received any benefit other than payment of money under the contract before frustration, the court may order him to pay to the other party an amount not exceeding the value of the benefit which he has received.

These provisions do not apply:

—where special provisions regarding frustration are made by the terms of the contract;

—to certain charterparties and other contracts for the carriage of goods by sea;

—to contracts of insurance;

—to certain contracts governed by the Sale of Goods Act 1979.

7A4. Release The parties to a contract, having entered into it by mutual agreement, may similarly bring it to an end by mutual agreement. Where both parties still have obligations to perform under the contract, they may mutually agree to release each other from these obligations. This is known as waiver, and no particular formality is required to waive a contract; for example, the waiver may be oral even though the original contract was in writing. However, where a contract which must be evidenced by writing is merely changed, rather than waived, there must be written evidence of the alteration in the same way as there must be written evidence of the original contract.

Where one party has performed all his obligations under the contract and is entitled to performance by the other party, he may release the other party from his obligations, but, as there is no consideration to support such release, to be effective the release must be under seal, unless the rule of equitable estoppel applies.

The problem which arises when one party partially releases the other from his obligations, and in particular, when one party agrees to accept a smaller sum of money than is due under the contract, presents some difficulty. The general rule is that since such agreement is not supported by consideration it is not binding, and the creditor may later sue for the balance.

In *Richard's and Bartlet's Case* (1584) the defendant agreed to buy from the plaintiff a quantity of corn for £10. Before delivery, the corn was severely damaged in a storm, and the plaintiff then agreed to accept only £1/13/4d. It was held that there was no consideration to support the promise to accept the smaller amount as the risk had passed to the defendant before the storm and, therefore, that notwithstanding his promise the plaintiff was entitled to sue for the full amount. There are, however, exceptions to the rule, and in the following cases payment of a smaller amount will discharge a greater debt.

Where payment is made at a date earlier than it is due. In *Pinnel's Case* (1602) the defendant owed the plaintiff £8/10/– and paid him £5/2/3d before the due date. the plaintiff agreeing to accept this sum in full satisfaction. Later, the plaintiff sued for the balance and in fact succeeded on a technical point, but the court indicated quite clearly that but for this technicality the defendant would have succeeded, because payment before the due date is sufficient consideration to support an agreement to accept a lower sum.

Where an obligation to pay an unliquidated, that is, an uncertain, amount is discharged by payment of a smaller liquidated, that is, a certain amount. In *British Russian Gazette and Trade Outlook Ltd* v. *Associated Newspapers Ltd* (1933) the plaintiff commenced proceedings against the defendants in connection with an alleged libel, but later agreed to accept the sum of £1050 in full satisfaction of their claim. Before the money was paid the plaintiffs decided to go ahead with the libel proceedings, but it was held that they were bound by the terms of the settlement which they had negotiated with the defendants.

Where the creditor agrees to accept a smaller sum from a person other than the debtor. In *Welby* v. *Drake* (1825) the defendant owed the plaintiff £18/4/–. The plaintiff agreed that if the defendant's father would pay him £9, he would accept that amount in full satisfaction. After his father had paid the £9 the plaintiff sued the defendant for the balance, but it was held that he could not recover, as to do so would be a fraud on the father.

Where a debtor makes a composition with his creditors. This arises where a debtor is unable to pay all his debts, and the creditors enter into an agreement with him for part payment of their debts instead of instituting bankruptcy proceedings.

Where the doctrine of equitable estoppel can be applied.

7A5. Accord and satisfaction

When one party under a contract is under some obligation, for example, to pay money or to perform some service, towards the other, the parties may agree that something different should be done instead of discharging the original obligation. This is known as accord and satisfaction.

Novation is the substitution of a new contract for an existing one. For example, if A is by contract under an obligation to perform some service for B, A and B may agree that A's obligations shall be performed by C, provided, of course, that C also consents. Thus, the original agreement between A and B is extinguished, and there is a new contract between B and C.

Another example of novation is where a person agrees to accept a cheque in absolute discharge of a debt due to him. The accepting of the cheque extinguishes the original debt, but a new right of action arises on the cheque if it is not honoured. However, if a creditor accepts a cheque in conditional discharge (and it will be presumed that it has been accepted in conditional rather than absolute discharge unless there is clear evidence to the contrary), the creditor's right of action on the debt is not extinguished, but merely suspended. If the cheque is not duly honoured, the creditor has a right either to bring an action on the original debt or to sue on the cheque.

There is also accord and satisfaction where there is acceptance of an act different from that which was due under the contract in discharge of the obligation. For example, if one person is under an obligation to perform some service for the other, the other may agree instead to accept a sum of money.

7A6. Merger

Merger occurs when one contract is extinguished by being merged in another. The most important example is the merging of a simple contract into a specialty contract. If, for example, A owes B money under a simple contract and enters into a written and sealed agreement, known as a bond, to pay it, all rights under the original agreement are extinguished, becoming merged in the bond. In *Price* v. *Moulton* (1851) the defendant owed the plaintiff £3000, and entered into an agreement under seal to repay it with interest on 21 December 1851. Before that date, the plaintiff sued the defendant in respect of the amount due, but it was held that he could not recover it, as the original contract had become merged in the contract under seal and under the latter no amount was due before 21 December 1851.

Another example of merger is where an action is brought under a contract and decided by the court. The decision of the court, as mentioned earlier, is known as a contract of record, and the right of action becomes merged in this contract. The result is that once a case has been brought and decided no further action can be brought on the same facts, but if judgment is not satisfied, that is, if a party against whom damages are awarded does not pay them, the judgment creditor may take proceedings to secure payment of the damages awarded.

7B. Remedies
7B1. Damages

The common law remedy for breach of contract is an award of damages. In appropriate circumstances, the equitable remedies of specific performance and injunction may be granted instead of or in addition to damages.

Liability in contract is strict. This means that the plaintiff is entitled to damages if he can simply prove that there has been a breach of contract; he does not have to go further, as is usually the case in tort, and show that the defendant has been in some way at fault.

The general purpose of an award of damages is to compensate a party for the monetary loss which he has suffered as a result of breach of contract by the other party, and the amount of damages awarded is therefore normally the monetary value of the loss. There are some exceptions to this rule, as will be seen later. Where there has been a breach of contract, but in fact no pecuniary loss has been suffered, the successful party is entitled to nominal damages of, say, £2.

In *Marzetti* v. *Williams* (1830) the customer of a bank drew a cheque for an amount which was well within the amount standing to his credit at the bank, but the bank nevertheless refused to pay the sum for which the cheque was drawn. It was held that the customer, although he had not suffered any actual pecuniary loss as a result of the breach of contract by the bank, was entitled to nominal damages. If the customer had been a trader, on the other hand, he might well have been entitled to substantial damages for loss of credit.

Real damages, as distinct from nominal damages, are an award of damages intended to compensate an injured party for actual pecuniary loss which he has suffered. The aim is to put the aggrieved party in the same financial position as he would have been if the contract had been performed.

The following cases illustrate the general principle that damages are a measure of the pecuniary loss suffered by the plaintiff.

In *Robinson* v. *Harman* (1848) the defendant agreed to lease to the plaintiff premises to which he had no title. The plaintiff was held entitled to damages and it was said that the general principle was that 'where a party sustains a loss by reason of a breach of contact he is, as far as money can do it, to be placed in the same situation with respect to damages as if the contract had been performed'.

In *Interoffice Telephones Ltd* v. *Robert Freeman Co. Ltd* (1957) the defendants agreed to hire from the plaintiffs a telephone installation for twelve years, but repudiated the agreement after six years. The plaintiffs retook possession of their equipment and also sued for damages. The plaintiffs were able to show that they had sufficient equipment to meet all demands without using that retaken from the defendants and it could not therefore be said that they could reduce their loss by rehiring that equipment. They were accordingly awarded as damages the amount of the rental for the unexpired period of six years, less certain reductions in respect of expenses which, as a result of the termination of the hire, they would not incur.

In *Pilkington* v. *Wood* (1955) the plaintiff engaged the defendant, a solicitor, to act for him in the purchase of a house. Later, when the plaintiff wished to sell the house, it was discovered that the title was defective, a matter which the defendant ought to have discovered at the time of the original purchase. The plaintiff therefore sued the defendant for the difference between the value of the house with a good title and its value with a defective title and also for travelling, hotel, and telephone expenses, and interest on a bank overdraft, all said to be caused as a result of delay in selling the house. It was held that he could recover the difference in value, but not the extra expenses, as they did not arise as a natural result of the breach of contract.

It is now well established that damages can be recovered, not only for financial loss, but also for inconvenience or injured feelings. Damages under these headings have been awarded in the context of contracts for holidays and entertainment, and also in cases of wrongful dismissal of employees and for other breaches of contracts of employment.

7B1A. Income tax

Income tax must be taken into account in an award of damages, if damages are not taxable in the hands of the recipient. For example, if a person is injured as a result of a breach of contract and claims in respect of loss of earnings, the gross amount of his loss must be reduced by the amount of income tax which he would have paid on those earnings.

In *Beach* v. *Reed Corrugated Cases Ltd* (1956) the defendants wrongfully dismissed the plaintiff from their service. He was held entitled to damages for loss of earnings, but the amount was reduced to take account of the incidence of income tax. Similarly, in *re Houghton Main Colliery Ltd* (1956) a company which was under obligation to pay pensions to two men went into liquidation and therefore was unable to continue payment of the pensions, and was thus held in breach of contract. It was held in assessing damages that the lump sum to be awarded to the men should be reduced to take account of the fact that they would have had to pay income tax on their pensions.

If, however, the damages will rank as income in the hands of the plaintiff, so that he has to pay tax on them, they must be paid gross. Thus, if a trader suffers loss of trade through the breach of contract of the defendant, any damages paid will rank as trading income and tax will be payable on them.

7B1B. Minimisation of loss

Where a person suffers loss as a result of a breach of contract he must take all reasonable steps to minimise the loss. If he does not do so he will not be entitled to recover the additional loss incurred by his failure to take such steps.

For example, in *Brace* v. *Calder* (1895) the plaintiff, who was employed as a manager of a business for two years, was wrongfully dismissed after five months, but was offered other employment at the same pay, which he refused. It was held that he was entitled only for nominal damages for breach of contract, as he had failed to mitigate his loss by taking the other employment.

In *Luker* v. *Chapman* (1970) the plaintiff was injured in a road accident caused partly by the negligence of the defendant, and was unable to continue as a telephone engineer. He was offered a clerical job, but instead elected to take up a course of teacher training. It was held that the defendant was not liable for the loss of income involved during the course of teacher training, as the plaintiff could have mitigated the loss by accepting the clerical job.

7B1C. Remoteness of damage

Damages cannot be recovered in respect of loss arising from a breach of contract which is too remote. It is possible to conceive an almost endless chain of consequences arising from a breach of contract, and it would be neither just nor practicable to hold a party liable for all the consequences of his breach of contract, however remote. Damages are, therefore, limited to consequences which are such as can either:

—reasonably be considered to be the natural consequences of the breach; or

—reasonably be supposed to have been in the contemplation of both parties at the time of the contract. This is known as the rule in *Hadley* v. *Baxendale.*

In *Hadley* v. *Baxendale* (1854) the crankshaft of the plaintiff's steam engine was broken. They gave it to the defendants, who were carriers, to be taken to a foundry where it was to be used as a pattern for a replacement crankshaft. Although the defendants promised to deliver the crankshaft at the foundry the following day they did, in fact, take a week to deliver it, with the result that production at the plaintiff's mill was held up and they lost a particularly valuable contract. The plaintiffs sued for the loss of profits thus arising, but their claim failed on the grounds that the loss could not be considered to be a consequence which could reasonably have been contemplated by both parties when they entered into the contract of carriage.

Another case which exemplified the rule is that of *Victoria Laundries (Windsor) Ltd* v. *Newman Industries, Ltd,* (1949). The plaintiffs agreed to buy a boiler from the defendants. The defendants knew that the plaintiffs required the boiler for immediate use, but, nevertheless, delivery was delayed for five months. The plaintiffs sued for loss of profits in respect of the ordinary use of the boiler and an additional amount in respect of some exceptionally profitable contracts which they would have obtained had they had the use of the boiler. It was held that they were entitled to recover in respect of the profits they would have made from normal use of the boiler during the five months, on the grounds that persons must be deemed to foresee that loss of profits will result from failure to deliver profit-making plant; but that they could not recover in respect of the exceptionally profitable contracts which they had lost, as this loss could not be considered to be within the contemplation of the parties at the time of the contract.

In recent years, however, the courts have tended to adopt a generous attitude as to what might be considered to be natural consequences. In *Cox* v. *Philips Industries Ltd* (1976) where an employee was demoted and eventually persuaded to leave his employment in circumstances which constituted a breach of contract by his employer, he was held entitled to damages for mental distress although his salary had not been reduced as a result of the demotion. In *Parsons (H) (Livestock) Ltd* v. *Uttley Ingham and Co. Ltd* (1977) the defendant supplied and erected a pig hopper for the plaintiff but, in breach of contract, left a ventilator on the hopper in a closed position. The result was that the nuts in the hopper became mouldy, and a number of pigs who ate the mouldy nuts took ill and died. It was held that it was within the contemplation of the defendant that if food affected by bad storage conditions was fed to pigs it would cause illness or death, and that they were therefore liable.

Damage is too remote when there is a *novus actus interveniens*, that is, when the real cause of the damage is not directly the breach of contract but some new intervening cause. The *novus actus interveniens* may be the action of a third-party or of the person suffering the breach of contract. For example, if a person suffers personal injuries as a result of another's breach of contract, and on his way to hospital to have injuries attended to is involved in another accident and sustains further injuries, such further injuries are caused by a *novus actus interveniens* and the plaintiff cannot be heard to say that they would not have been sustained but for the original breach of contract.

Again, if a person suffers some loss as a result of a breach of contract, but the loss becomes exaggerated by his own failure to take steps to minimise it, such failure is a *novus actus interveniens* and he will not be able to recover in respect of such loss as is caused by his own default.

7B1D. Pre-contract expenditure

Expenditure incurred before the date of a contract may in a suitable case be recovered if it was in the contemplation of the parties. For example, in *Anglia Television Ltd* v. *Reed* 1971) the defendant agreed to appear in a film, as a result of which the plaintiffs spent £2750 in employing a director and a designer. Before filming commenced, the defendant repudiated the contract, and it was held that the plaintiffs could recover damages from him.

7B1E. Prospective loss

A plaintiff is entitled to recover not only in respect of loss which he can show that he has suffered, but also in respect of prospective loss, that is, loss which he will suffer in future as a result of the breach, provided that such loss is not too remote. It may be difficult to assess prospective loss but this will not prevent the court making as accurate an assessment as possible.

7B1F. Liquidated damages and penalties

An action for breach of contract is usually an action for unliquidated damages, that is, the amount to be awarded is fixed by the court. Sometimes, however, contracts mention an amount or amounts which are to be payable in the event of specified breaches of contract, or contain a formula for the assessment of the amount to be paid in the event of a breach. If such amounts or formulae are a genuine attempt by the parties to assess in advance the damage likely to be suffered as a result of a breach of contract, they will be treated as liquidated damages and enforced by the court.

If, on the other hand, such amounts or formulae are not a genuine pre-estimate of damages, but are inserted as a penalty to discourage breach of the contract, they will not be enforced by the court, which instead will assess damages on the usual principles.

Whether an amount represents liquidated damages or a penalty is in general a matter to be decided by the court in the light of the circumstances existing at the time the particular contract was formed. Certain general principles, however, have been evolved and are exemplified by the following cases.

If it can be shown that a genuine attempt was made to estimate in advance the loss likely to accrue, the sum stated will not be treated as a penalty, irrespective of whether it is called a penalty or not. In *Cellulose Acetate Silk Co. Ltd* v. *Widnes Foundry Ltd* (1933) the defendants, makers of machinery, agreed to pay a penalty of £20 a week for every week in excess of eighteen weeks which it took to make a machine. There was delay and the plaintiffs sued for damages in excess of £20 a week. It was held that £20 a week was agreed damages, and therefore no more and no less should be awarded.

If the same amount is to be payable on the occurrence of any of several events, some of which may cause serious loss and others only trifling loss, there is a presumption, which may be rebutted, that the sum is a penalty. In *Cooden Engineering Co. Ltd* v. *Stanford* (1952) the plaintiffs hired a car to the defendant under a hire-purchase agreement. The agreement provided that if any instalment was not paid on the due date the full amount was at once payable together with interest at ten per cent. When the defendant fell into arrears the plaintiffs repossessed the car and sued for the unexpired balance. The court held that this was an attempt to enforce a penalty and was no reasonable assessment of damages; hence it was unenforceable.

If the sum stated in the contract is excessive having regard to the maximum loss which could be suffered as a result of a breach of contract, it will be treated as a penalty. (The case of *Cooden Engineering Co. Ltd* v. *Stanford (supra)* is also an example of this point.)

If payment of a smaller sum is secured by payment of a larger sum, the latter will be treated as a penalty.

The fact that damages would be difficult to assess does not make a sum a penalty, and indeed if the intention of the parties is to fix a sum in order that possible litigation as to the amount shall be avoided with a view to saving expense, the amount will be treated as liquidated damages. In *English Hop Growers Ltd* v. *Dering* (1928) the defendants agreed to deliver to the plaintiffs all the hops which he should grow on his sixty-three acres of land during 1926. The agreement contained a condition that if he did not deliver the whole of his crop he should pay damages at the rate of £100 an acre. The defendant made no deliveries at all and the plaintiffs claimed £6300. It was held that the plaintiffs were entitled to succeed on the grounds that the figure of £100 an acre was a genuine attempt to fix a reasonable sum, and it was a convenient way of circumventing the difficulties which would arise in proving the actual amount of loss.

The fact that the sum stated in a contract is referred to as 'damages' or 'liquidated damages' will not prevent the court in an appropriate case from holding it to be a penalty.

7B1G. Interest

The rules regarding payment of interest are as follows:
— It is payable if so stipulated by the contract.
— It may be implied from the course of dealings between the parties.
— Overdue bills of exchange and promissory notes bear interest.
— The court has a discretion to allow interest on claims for debt or special damages from the date when the claim arose to the date of judgment.
— Interest must be awarded on damages in personal injury cases.
— Once a judgment has been given, unless it is immediately satisfied, interest begins to accrue.

7B2. Quantum meruit

The remedy of *quantum meruit* means that, where there has been a breach of contract, a person will be awarded as much as he has earned up to the time of the breach. For example, in *Craven-Ellis* v. *Canon Ltd* (1936) the plaintiff was employed as managing director of a company, but did not comply with a requirement of the Articles of Association of the company that he should take up a number of shares. It was held that he was nevertheless entitled to a reasonable sum for the work which he had done for the company.

7B3. Specific performance

The equitable remedy of specific performance is available as a remedy for breach of contract when an award of damages would be inadequate and justice can only be done by ordering the party in breach to carry out his obligations under the contract.

In *Carpenters Estates Ltd* v. *Davies* (1940) the defendant, in selling some land to the plaintiffs, covenanted to construct sewers on the land, but neglected to do so. It was held that the plaintiffs were entitled to a decree of specific performance, as an award of damages would not be a sufficient remedy in the circumstances.

A grant of specific performance is always at the discretion of the court. It can never be claimed as of right.

Specific performance will not be granted in any of the following circumstances:
— where there has been fraud, mistake, or accident on the part of the plaintiff;
— where the plaintiff has been responsible for delay in seeking the remedy;
— where it would cause undue hardship to the defendant;
— where damages would be an adequate remedy; therefore, an order to deliver specific goods will not be made unless they are unique, but on the other hand an award of specific performance of a contract for the sale of land is common;
— in favour of a plaintiff against whom, were the circumstances reversed, specific performance could not be awarded; for example, specific performance will not be awarded in favour of a minor as it could not be awarded against him;
— where the court could not superintend performance; therefore, for example, specific performance of a contract of personal service will not be awarded;
— where the loss which the plaintiff has suffered is trivial.

In *Lumley* v. *Wagner* (1852) the defendant agreed to sing at the plaintiff's theatre for a certain period and not to sing elsewhere without his written permission. It was held that no grant of specific performance could be made to compel the defendant to sing for the plaintiff, although an injunction (see below) would be granted to prevent her singing for a third party.

Failure by the defendant to comply with a grant of specific performance constitutes contempt of court.

7B4. Injunctions

Injunction is an equitable remedy, similar in nature to specific performance, and is an order of the court restraining the defendant from breaking his contract, whereas specific performance is a positive order that he should carry out his obligations under the contract. The case of *Lumley* v. *Wagner (supra)* illustrates the similarity between the two remedies. Like specific performance, injunction is always a discretionary remedy and will be granted or refused on the same conditions as those mentioned above in connection with specific performance.

Injunctions are of two types, prohibitory and mandatory. A prohibitory injunction prevents a person from doing, continuing to do, or repeating a wrongful act. A mandatory injunction is an order to the defendant to do something in order to end a wrongful state of affairs which he has brought about.

Instead of granting an injunction the court may award damages, not only in a case where there has actually been a breach of contract, but also in a case where a breach of contract has merely been threatened.

The following two cases are typical of the circumstances in which the court will or will not, as the case may be, grant an injunction.

In *Warner Brothers Pictures Inc.* v. *Nelson* (1936) a film star, Miss Bette Davis, entered into an agreement to work for the plaintiffs and not accept any other engagements without their written consent. An injunction was granted in favour of the plaintiffs to prevent her from breaking the agreement.

In *Provident Clothing and Supply Co. Ltd* v. *Mason* (1913) the defendant, a collector and canvasser for the plaintiffs, agreed that if he terminated his employment with the plaintiffs he would not do any work similar to theirs for a period of three years within twenty-five miles of London. The defendant broke this agreement, but the House of Lords refused the plaintiffs an injunction to restrain him from violating the contract on the grounds that, having regard to all the circumstances, this term of the contract was in restraint of trade and was too harsh.

A type of injunction which has come into fairly common use in recent years is a Mareva injunction. Such an injunction is granted where the defendant is a foreign national and there is a real risk that he will remove assets outside the jurisdiction, and so frustrate the courts if they award damages against him. The injunction restrains the removal of his assets until the case has been heard.

7C.Limitation Where a person suffers a breach of contract he must begin proceedings within a prescribed period, for otherwise his right of action will be lost.

The periods of limitation and the rules relating to them are laid down in the Limitation Act 1980, a consolidating Act which brings together the provisions of a number of previous Acts and court decisions. The most important provisions, so far as they affect the law of contract, are summarised below:

— An action founded on a simple contract must be brought within six years from the date on which the cause of action accrued.

— An exception to this is that where a breach of contract gives rise to a claim in respect of personal injuries, such claim must generally be brought within three years.

— An action founded on a specialty contract must be brought within twelve years from the date on which the cause of action accrued.

— If at the time of accrual of a right of action the person to whom it accrued was under a disability, for example, was a minor or insane, the period of limitation does not begin to run until either the disability ceases or the person under disability dies, whichever occurs first.

— Once time begins to run, subsequent disability is of no effect.

— Where a right of action in respect of personal injuries accrues to a minor, the period of limitation will, notwithstanding what has been said above, run from the time of accrual of the cause of action, unless it can be proved that he was not, at that time, in the custody of a parent.

— Where a right of action has accrued to recover any debt or other fixed sum and the person liable to pay that sum acknowledges his obligation or makes a part payment in respect of it, the right of action is deemed to have accrued from the date of acknowledgement or part payment, even though the action would have been barred had the acknowledgement or part payment not been made. Thus, a right of action which has become barred by reason of the Limitation Acts can be revived. However, a right of action can only be thus revived if the acknowledgement is in writing, signed by the person making the acknowledgement or his agent, and made to the person, or the agent of the person, whose claim is being acknowledged.

— An acknowledgement or part payment made by one of two or more joint debtors after the period of limitation has expired is binding on the person making it, but not on his co-debtors unless he is acting as their agent.

— Where an action is based on the fraud of the defendant, or where the existence of a right of action has been fraudulently concealed by the defendant, or where the action is for relief from the consequences of a mistake, the period of limitation does not begin to run until the plaintiff has discovered the fraud or the mistake, or could with reasonable diligence have discovered it. For example, in *Lynn* v. *Bamber* (1930), the plaintiff purchased plum trees from the defendant and was given a warranty that the trees were 'Purple Pershores'. Seven years later he discovered that the trees were not Purple Pershores. The plaintiff sued for damages and it was held that his claim was not statute barred, as the defendant had made a fraudulent misrepresentation and had fraudulently concealed the breach of warranty.

The periods of limitation mentioned above do not affect the right of the court to refuse equitable relief on the grounds that the plaintiff has been guilty of unreasonable delay in seeking a remedy.

In *Leaf* v. *International Galleries* (1950) the plaintiff bought an oil painting, the defendants representing that it was a genuine Constable. Five years later the plaintiff discovered that the painting was not a genuine Constable and claimed rescission of the contract on the grounds of innocent misrepresentation. It was held by the court that he was not entitled to this remedy as the action had not been started within a reasonable time.

7D.Interpretation of contracts It is sometimes necessary to have recourse to the courts to determine precisely the meaning of terms used in a contract. The courts in such circumstances follow certain rules of interpretation (sometimes referred to as rules for construction – an ambiguous word derived, in this context, from the verb 'to construe', not 'to construct'). The main rules of interpretation are:

— The intention of the parties must prevail. This rule is, however, subject to the important qualification that the intention must be deduced from the written agreement, and is significant only when the writing is not clear. It is not open to either party to say that his intentions were different from what is clearly expressed in the written agreement.

— Where a contract is expressed in a standard printed form, to which has been added any typewritten or handwritten wording, then if there is any conflict between the printed and written wording, that latter will prevail as it is construed as representing the adaptation of a general form to meet the needs of the particular case.

—A written document must be construed as a whole, and words and phrases must not be construed in isolation. For example, where a word or phrase is given a specific meaning in one part of a document, it is deemed to have the same meaning throughout the document.

—An express term overrides an implied term where they are inconsistent.

—The ordinary rules of grammar are to prevail if there is any ambiguity or lack of clarity.

—Generally, words are construed in their plain and normal sense, but where a technical term is used, it will be given throughout the technical meaning normally assigned to it.

—The significance of a word must be determined by its context. This is what is known as the *ejusdem generis* rule.

—Words must be construed literally. If such literal construction is ambiguous, and on one construction would favour the party responsible for drawing up the contract, and on another would favour the other party, then the meaning which favours the other party is taken. This is known as the *contra proferentem* rule.

These rules apply to insurance contracts in the same way as they apply to others. For example:

—If a policy is issued in standard printed form and a typewritten endorsement is attached, the wording of the endorsement overrules that of the printed policy in so far as the wordings may be inconsistent.

—Technical terms, such as the phrase 'subject to average' in a property policy, are construed by the courts as having the meaning associated with them in the normal course of business dealings.

—In a phrase such as 'jewelry, works of art and other similar articles', the *ejusdem generis* rule would require the words 'and other similar articles' to be confined to items of high monetary value in comparatively small bulk (although it is obviously preferable to avoid the use of such vague words entirely).

—If a phrase in an insurance policy is ambiguous, the meaning more favourable to the insured is taken under the *contra proferentem* rule, as it is the insurers who prepare the policy and ought therefore in equity to suffer the consequences of any ambiguity.

An exception to this is that sometimes the wordings of certain clauses and endorsements in policies are prepared by brokers to meet the particular needs of their clients, and are incorporated in the policy with the agreement of the insurers. In such circumstances, the brokers' wording would be construed against the insured in the event of ambiguity, as the wording is that of his agent and not of the insurers.

8. Agency

8A.Creation of agency	8C.Rights of an agent
8A1.Consent	8C1.Indemnity
8A2.Apparent authority	8C2.Remuneration
8A3.Necessity	8C3.Lien
8A4.Ratification	8D.Authority of an agent
8A5.Undisclosed principal	8D1.Express authority
8B.Duties of an agent	8D2.Implied authority
8B1.Obedience	8D3.Usual authority
8B2.Care and skill	8D4.Apparent authority
8B3.Personal performance	8E.Relationship between princi-
8B4.Good faith	pal and third party
8B5.Accounting for money received	8F.Relationship between agent and
8B6.Remedies for agent's breach	third party
of duty	8G.Termination of agency

In the ordinary sense of the word, an agent is a person who is employed to do something in the place of another. The person who employs him is called the principal. In law, however, the term 'agent' has a more restricted meaning. It was defined in *Towle and Co.* v. *White* (1873) as 'a person invested with a legal power to alter the principal's legal relations with third parties'.

The law of agency is based on the maxim *qui facit per alium facit per se* (he who employs another to do something is deemed to have done it himself). Any person who himself has contractual capacity may employ an agent, and if he does so he is, with minor exceptions mentioned later, bound by what the agent does on his behalf. On the other hand, if a person lacks contractual capacity, as does, for example, a person of unsound mind, any purported authority which he may give to an agent is of no effect.

Most often, a person may have the choice whether he performs an act himself or deals through an agent; for example, a person may place his insurances directly with an insurance company or may employ a broker. A company registered under the Companies Acts, however, although a legal person, has no physical existence and must always therefore act through an agent or agents — for example, the directors. With a partnership, any partner may enter into contracts on behalf of the firm as a whole.

The most important function of an agent is the making of contracts on behalf of his principal, although he may also have authority to dispose of his principal's property. This latter function is outside the scope of this book. Three sets of relationships must be considered in connection with agency:
—the relationship between principal and agent;
—the relationship between principal and third party; and
—the relationship between agent and third party.
These relationships are dealt with fully in this chapter.

Because a person is called an agent, that does not mean that he is in law an agent. For example, a motor manufacturer may give a dealer a 'sole agency' for the sale of his cars. In such a case, the dealer buys the cars from the manufacturer and in turn sells them to the public. In so doing, he is acting as a principal, and not as an agent.

In *W. T. Lamb & Sons* v. *Goring Brick Co. Ltd* (1932) the defendants appointed the plaintiffs 'sole agents' for the sale of their goods for a fixed period. Before the end of the period the defendants gave notice to the plaintiffs that they intended immediately to start selling the goods to the public themselves. If the plaintiffs were in fact merely agents it would not have been necessary for the defendants to give such notice. It was held that by their conduct the defendants had recognised that the plaintiffs were principals and not agents, and that the action therefore constituted a breach of contract.

The position of an agent has something in common with that of a trustee, a servant, or an independent contractor. An agent, like a trustee, must not make a secret profit and must not allow his own interest to conflict with his duty to his principal, and if he misappropriates his principal's property he can be treated as a trustee of the property. An agent differs from a trustee, however, in that he is not the legal owner of his principal's property, although he may have a right to dispose of it: and an agent represents his principal, whereas a trustee does not represent the beneficiaries under a trust.

The distinction between an agent on the one hand and a servant or independent contractor on the other is that, as mentioned above, an agent is employed to make contracts and to dispose of property, whereas servants and independent contractors may perform various duties. The distinction is therefore one of function. Generally, an agent is a person who has greater freedom from control than has a servant. But a servant may for some purposes be an agent of his employer, as also may be an independent contractor; many servants of a company, such as salesmen (including, for example, so-called agents of industrial life assurance companies) are in the performance of their duties to some extent acting as agents of the company.

8A.Creation of agency

The relationship of principal and agent can arise in any one of five ways:

—by consent;
—by the application of the doctrine of apparent authority;
—by necessity;
—by ratification;
—by the application of the 'undisclosed principal' rule.

8A1.Consent

The most common way of creating the relationship of principal and agent is by consent, the agent being authorised by the principal to act on his behalf. The agent may be appointed:

—by deed;
—in writing not under seal;
—orally, that is, by word of mouth.

Generally, it is of no consequence which method is adopted, but there are exceptions. An agent appointed to execute a deed on behalf of his principal must himself be appointed by a deed, this deed being known as a power of attorney. Further, an interest in land cannot be granted or disposed of except in writing and therefore an agent engaged in such a transaction must do so in writing.

The authority of a minor or of a person of unsound mind to appoint another to act as his agent is not free from doubt, as the decided cases are conflicting. It is logical, however, and probably represents the consensus of legal opinion, to say that a minor can appoint an agent to enter into any contract which he could have made personally (except that he cannot grant a valid power of attorney); and that a person who is of unsound mind cannot appoint another person to act as his agent.

A person who himself does not have full contractual capacity may nevertheless act as agent, and on behalf of his principal enter into any contracts which the principal himself had capacity to make personally.

8A2.Apparent authority

When a third party deals with an agent, he cannot know, nor can he be expected to know, the precise limits of the agent's authority. For example, a member of the public cannot be expected to know the extent, if any, to which an insurance broker is entitled to give temporary cover. He must therefore rely on what appears to be the authority of the agent. This is recognised by law, in the existence of what is termed apparent authority. Thus, a principal is bound, not only by acts which are within the express authority of the agent, but also by acts which are within his apparent authority, that is, where he has no authority but the third party is justified in presuming that he has. In these circumstances the principal is said to be estopped from denying the existence of the agency.

The principle of apparent authority is of very wide application. For example, a wife very often acts as agent for her husband, and the husband will be estopped from denying that his wife is his agent unless clear notice that the wife was acting without authority has been given.

A different application would be in the case of a person such as a company secretary, who by the nature of his office, has apparent authority to act on behalf of the company. Within the company, it will be known that there are limits to the authority of the secretary, but outsiders cannot be expected to know what these limits are, and so the company will be bound by any acts within the apparent authority of the secretary.

8A3.Necessity

Agency by necessity arises where a person is entrusted with the goods of another and it becomes necessary to do something to preserve the property in an emergency. It originated with masters of ships having to take certain action in an emergency, particularly with regard to the disposal of perishable goods, without having the opportunity to seek instructions from the owners of the goods.

8A4.Ratification

Ratification occurs where an agent performs an act which is not within his actual authority, but which later becomes binding on the principal because the principal agrees to accept the act as having been done on his behalf. Ratification may be express or it may be implied from conduct, as where the principal takes the benefit of the act with the knowledge of the circumstances in which it was done. To constitute valid ratification, the following conditions must be fulfilled:

—The person doing the act must purport to do it as agent and not on his own behalf.
—The principal must be the person whom the agent had in mind at the time he performed the act, although it is not necessary that the principal should actually be named.
—At the time of ratifying the act, the principal must have full knowledge of the circumstances relevant to the act, or must at least have waived further enquiry.
—The principal must have been in existence at the time when the unauthorised act was done.

—The principal must have had the capacity to do the act at the time when it was done. Thus, an act done on behalf of a company cannot be ratified if it was *ultra vires*.

—Ratification must take place within a reasonable time.

—The whole contract must be ratified.

A valid ratification is generally retrospective to the date of the original act. This is however subject to the rule that ratification cannot operate so as to divest a person of rights already vested in him. In *Bird* v. *Brown* (1850) P sent goods to T. P's agent, A, while the goods were in transit, gave notice to the carrier to stop the goods; in doing so he was acting without authority. Later, P purported to ratify A's act, but meanwhile T's trustee in bankruptcy had already seized the goods. It was held that P's purported ratification was too late, as the trustee in bankruptcy already had an interest in the goods.

Sometimes, an agent may make an offer in respect of something which is outside the scope of his authority 'subject to ratification' by the principal whom he has in mind. Even if the offer is accepted, the principal still has the right not to ratify the act, and if he does not do so there is no valid contract.

8A5.Undisclosed principal

The doctrine of the 'undisclosed principal' must be distinguished from that of ratification. In the case of ratification, the agent must contract as agent and have a named principal in mind. English law, however, permits an agent to act for an undisclosed principal, whilst purporting to act on his own behalf, and unless the terms of the contract otherwise provide, the undisclosed principal may sue and be sued under it. Where a contract is made on behalf of an undisclosed principal the agent must have authority to act at the time when the contract was made.

8B.Duties of an agent

An agent has the following duties:

—to obey his principal's instructions;

—to exercise care and skill;

—with exceptions, to perform his duties personally;

—to act in good faith towards his principal;

—to account for money received on behalf of his principal.

8B1.Obedience

Where the relationship between the principal and agent is contractual, as it normally is, the agent is liable in damages for breach if he does not carry out the terms of his contract, although he is under no obligation to perform an act which is either illegal or void. If the agency is non-contractual, that is, gratuitous, the agent is under no obligation to commence the performance of any act, but if he does so he has the same duties as a paid agent.

An agent must keep within his authority, express or implied, and has no right to exceed his authority even if to do so would be for the benefit of his principal.

8B2.Care and skill

An agent must exercise due care and skill in the performance of all acts done in the course of his duty as agent. The basic principle is that a person professing a particular calling must show the degree of care and skill appropriate to that calling. For example, in the arranging of insurances on behalf of a client, a registered insurance broker is expected to exercise a higher degree of care and skill than is, say, a solicitor who acts as a part-time agent.

There is conflict in the decided cases on the question whether a paid agent must exercise a higher degree of care and skill than a gratuitous agent, but the balance of legal opinion favours the view that no distinction should be made.

8B3.Personal performance

There is a legal maxim *delegatus non potest delegare* — an agent may not delegate his duties. Although this may be stated as a general rule, there are important exceptions to it. Where the personal qualities and skill of the agent are essential to the transaction, delegation is not permissible, but the agent may delegate his duties in the three following sets of circumstances:

—where the principal expressly authorises the agent to delegate all or some of his functions;

—where the delegation is to be implied from the circumstances of the case, as in many business transactions where it is the recognised practice that the agent will delegate all or part of his work to, say, his employees;

—where the delegation relates to some purely administrative act where no special skill or discretion is required.

In all the circumstances just mentioned, the agent is liable to the principal for the work delegated, for any personal fault of his, and for any fault on the part of the person or persons to whom he has delegated the duty.

8B4.Good faith

An agent has a fiduciary relationship with his principal, and therefore must not allow his own interest to conflict with his duties towards his principal. He is entitled to accept normal remuneration, such as the commission which an insurance broker receives by custom from insurers, but if he receives a bribe or a secret commission from a third party, he is liable to prosecution under the Prevention of Corruption Acts 1889–1916, he forfeits his rights to indemnity and remuneration, and is liable to instant dismissal. The principal can also repudiate any contract made by an agent who was bribed, recover the amount of the bribe from the agent, and bring an action against the agent and the third party in respect of any loss which he has suffered.

Because of the duty of good faith, an agent employed to sell something on behalf of his principal cannot buy the thing himself in the absence of full disclosure of the circumstances, and similarly if he is employed to buy he cannot buy from himself without full disclosure. He must not make use of confidential information which comes to him as agent for the purpose of obtaining some personal benefit. Even after the termination of the agency the agent is not entitled to make use of the confidential information.

8B5.Accounting for money received

An agent must pay to the principal all money received by him on behalf of the principal. Supplementary to this basic duty is the duty of the agent to keep his principal's property distinct from his own, to keep an account of transactions entered into on behalf of the principal, and to produce the account to the principal on request or as agreed.

An agent must not deny the title of his principal to any property or money which is the subject-matter of the agency. There is however an exception to this rule where the agent is in possession of goods as bailee for his principal; in this case he can set up a third party's title if he defends the action with the authority of the third party.

8B6.Remedies for agent's breach of duty

Where an agent is in breach of duty, the remedies of the principal can be summarised as follows:
— he can sue the agent for damages for breach of contract;
— in some circumstances, for example, where the agent has refused to return the principal's property, he can sue the agent in tort;
— he can sue the agent to recover a bribe, a secret profit, or any money received by the agent on behalf of the principal;
— he can sue for an account if the agent fails to keep proper accounts of the agency transactions;
— he can dismiss the agent without compensation.

8C.Rights of an agent
8C1.Indemnity

If an agent incurs liability or pays out money in the performance of his duties as an agent, he has a right to be indemnified by the principal unless the agency agreement provides otherwise. He loses his right to an indemnity:
— if his act is not authorised or ratified by the principal;
— if he is in breach of his duties as an agent;
— if he incurs liability or expends money solely as a result of his own fault;
— if the act in respect of which he claims indemnity is illegal, unless he can show that he was unaware of the illegality.

8C2.Remuneration

By definition, a gratuitous agent is not entitled to remuneration. Apart from this, the entitlement to and amount of remuneration depends on express or implied agreement. Agreement is implied where the circumstances are such that it would have been reasonable for the agent to presume that he would be paid for his work, as in any normal commercial transaction.

If the amount to be paid is an express term of the contract, no particular problem is likely to arise. Otherwise the agent is entitled to receive the amount fixed by any relevant trade usage, or in default of such guidance, a sum which is reasonable in the particular circumstances.

Disputes have often come before the courts on the question whether in a particular case the agent has done all that was necessary to entitle him to remuneration. In deciding whether the remuneration has been earned, two main questions have to be answered:
— Has the event on which the payment of remuneration depended actually happened?
— Has the agent been the effective cause of the happening of the event?
Most of the cases which have come before the courts relate to the entitlement of estate agents to commission, but the same principles apply to the remuneration of other types of agent.

Often an estate agent, acting on behalf of the vendor of property, easily finds a buyer. It is settled law, however, that he is entitled to full commission even if he has had comparatively little work to do. On another occasion he may go to a great deal of trouble before he finds a person who agrees to buy 'subject to contract', but later the sale falls through with no fault on the part of the agent. Despite the expense and trouble which the agent has incurred, he is nevertheless not entitled to any commission unless otherwise expressly agreed. It is common for an estate agent to accept the duties of agent on condition that his commission will be payable when he has found a buyer 'ready, willing and able' to purchase. In such a case, he is entitled to his commission only on completion of the sale, and not when contracts are exchanged. If, on the other hand, the agreement is that the agent will be entitled to commission when he has found a person 'who signs a legally binding contract', he is entitled to commission when contracts are exchanged, even if the sale later falls through. There are various other possible wordings, and naturally the position in any particular case depends on the exact terms of the agreement between vendor and agent.

Even if the event intended to give rise to remuneration happens, there still remains the question whether the agent was the effective cause of the happening. Again, the problem is likely to arise frequently, but not exclusively, in connection with estate agents.

In *E. P. Nelson Ltd* v. *Rolfe* (1950) a seller appointed several agents to secure a person 'ready, able and willing' to buy his bungalow. One agent introduced a person who was given an option on the bungalow, and another later introduced a person who was willing to purchase, but the seller refused because of the option which had already been granted. It was held that the second agent was entitled to commission because he had introduced a person who was 'ready, able and willing' to buy, whereas the first agent had merely introduced a person who at that moment was only interested in an option for which no consideration had been given and which therefore was not a legally binding contract.

An agent who insists on a 'sole agency' is in a stronger position than that when he is one of several, but even a sole agency does not prevent the seller from selling direct, thus depriving the agent of his commission.

Another question arises regarding remuneration, and that is whether an agent may be entitled to his commission after his agency has been terminated. A typical example is where a salesman brings in an order for which he is paid commission, the agency is terminated, and later repeat orders are received from the same source. Again, the answer depends on the exact terms of the agency, and it is impossible to lay down a general rule. The most common practice is for the parties to agree that commission will not be payable in respect of repeat orders received after the termination of the agency.

8C3.Lien

A lien is the right to retain the goods of another as security for payment of a debt. In terms of agency, a lien may be particular, that is, limited to money outstanding in a particular transaction, or general, where it extends to a general balance of account. Thus, if a person has both a current account and a deposit account at a bank, and the current account becomes overdrawn, the banker has a particular lien if his right is restricted to possession of any amounts which may be paid into the current account, and a general lien if it extends over both current and deposit accounts. (In practice, by usage of their trade, bankers are deemed to have a general lien, but the court will consider a lien to be a particular lien unless there is clear evidence to the contrary.)

An agent can claim a lien only if he has lawful possession of the property concerned. If he voluntarily parts with possession he loses his lien, but not if he loses possession of the property by fraud. Naturally, the lien comes to an end when the principal pays or tenders the sum due.

8D.Authority of an agent

It has already been mentioned that an agent's authority may be express, implied, or apparent. It is necessary now to go further into this subject, and also to refer to what is known as usual authority. The following must therefore be considered: express authority, implied authority, usual authority and apparent authority.

8D1.Express authority

Express authority may be given to an agent orally or in writing, and in the latter case the writing may or may not be under seal. If the writing is ambiguous, no liability can fall on the agent provided that he interprets the ambiguous words in a way in which they can reasonably be construed, even if it was not the way the principal intended. As a matter of practice, however, it is obviously desirable for an agent to seek clarification of an ambiguity from his principal.

8D2.Implied authority

In order to carry out acts which are within the terms of his express authority, the agent has authority to do anything which is necessary for, or incidental to, the carrying out of his express authority. This is known as implied authority.

8D3.Usual authority

When an agent carries on a particular trade or profession, his express and implied authority carry with them a usual authority, that is, the authority to perform such acts as are usual in the particular trade or profession. If there are certain customs of a trade, the agent has a usual authority to comply with such customs. The following three examples may make clear the nature of usual authority:

Firstly, an auctioneer with authority to sell has a usual authority to sign a memorandum of the contract of sale on behalf of the vendor and also, in accordance with the custom of the profession, on behalf of the purchaser.

Secondly, an estate agent who has authority to sell on behalf of his principal (not merely authority to find a purchaser) has a usual authority to sign a contract on behalf of the vendor.

Thirdly, a *del credere* agent, that is, an agent appointed to sell, who guarantees payment of the price in return for a commission, even if, because of insolvency or any other cause, he does not receive the money from the purchaser. He has the usual authority to make contracts on the principal's behalf.

A principal may restrict the usual authority of an agent, but this restriction does not affect any third party who may be unaware of it.

In *Watteau* v. *Fenwick* (1893) the defendant appointed a manager of his public house. The licence was taken out in the name of the manager, whose name appeared over the door. The manager bought cigars on credit from the plaintiff, a transaction which was within the usual authority of the manager in such circumstances, but in fact the defendant had forbidden the manager to do such a thing. The plaintiff sued the defendant for the cost of the cigars. It was held that he was entitled to succeed, as he had no knowledge that the usual authority of the agent had been restricted.

8D4.Apparent authority

A principal is responsible for acts which are within the apparent authority of the agent, even if they are not within his actual authority. Any representation made by the principal which induces a third party reasonably to believe that a particular person is an agent of the principal makes the principal liable. The representation may be by words or by conduct, it must clearly indicate that the agent has authority to do a particular act on behalf of his principal, and the representation must be made to the person seeking to hold the principal liable. Since a plea of apparent authority is based on a belief that the agent had authority, it follows that a third party cannot rely on the plea if he had actual or constructive notice that in fact the agent had no authority or if the circumstances should have aroused his suspicions.

A principal can be held liable on the grounds of apparent authority even if the agent acted fraudulently and for his own benefit.

8E.Relationship between principal and third party

Where a contract has been made by an agent on behalf of a principal, the relationship between principal and third party depends on whether the principal was named, disclosed, or undisclosed.

If an agent makes a contract on behalf of a named principal, the agent, having performed his duties, is generally no longer concerned with the contract, the partners to which are the principal and the third party. The principal is liable if the agent had authority of any of the forms mentioned earlier, or if he has ratified the act of the agent, and similarly the third party is liable to the principal under the contract.

There is, however, an exception to this rule. A principal cannot be sued on a deed made by an agent unless the principal is described in the deed as a party and the deed is executed in his name. But if the agent enters into the deed as trustee for his principal, the principal can sue by joining the agent as a party to the action. Furthermore, if an agent executes a deed in pursuance of a power of attorney, the Law of Property Act 1925 s. 123(i) provides that the agent may sign and seal any instrument with the authority of the principal, and if he does so the execution is as effective as if the agent had executed it in the name of the principal.

If an agent discloses to a third party that he is acting on behalf of a principal, but does not disclose the name of the principal, the legal rights and liabilities of the principal and the third party are the same as if the name of the principal had been disclosed but, as will be seen later, the position of the agent is different.

The doctrine of the undisclosed principal has already been mentioned. When the third party discovers the identity of the principal, he generally has the same rights as if the principal had been named. There are, however, three cases in which an undisclosed principal cannot sue or be sued by the third party:

Firstly, if the contract expressly provides that the agent is the sole principal.

Secondly, if the terms of the contract are inconsistent with agency. In *Humble* v. *Hunter* (1848) an agent signed a charterparty in his own name and described himself as owner of the ship; it was held that his undisclosed principal could not sue.

Thirdly, if the identity of the principal is material to the third party. This applies if the contract is of a personal nature, such as a contract for personal services or most contracts of insurance. But if the contract was not of a personal nature, the undisclosed principal can sue even if the third party would not have dealt with him directly had he known who he was, unless the agent has misrepresented the existence or identity of his principal.

If a principal owes a debt to the third party and pays his agent, he is nevertheless generally liable to the third party if the agent fails to pay over the money. However, there are two exceptions to this rule. The first is that the principal is not liable to pay twice where it would be inequitable to expect him to do so. This applies where the third party by his own conduct leads the principal to settle with the agent, for example, by representing to the principal that the third party had already been paid. The second is that where an undisclosed principal has paid an agent before the third party has discovered the existence of the principal, the principal cannot be asked to pay again. (It may be noted that this rule has been severely criticised by judges, and may well be overruled in some future case.)

A third party who owes a debt to a principal is generally still liable to the principal if he pays the agent and the agent does not pay over the money to the principal, unless the agent has actual, usual, or apparent authority to receive payment (which in many cases he has).

Where the agent does not disclose the existence or identity of his principal, the general rule is that payment by a third party to an agent is equivalent to payment to the principal.

If an agent owes a debt to a third party, who in turn owes a debt to a disclosed principal, the general rule is that the third party cannot set off the debt which he owes to the principal against the debt which the agent owes him, but must pay it in full. Set-off may, however, be expressly allowed by the principal.

The position is different, however, if the principal is undisclosed. If a third party deals with an agent believing him to be the principal, the third party obviously has a right to set off any amount which he owes to the agent against any amount which the agent owes him. It would be inequitable if this right could be defeated by the later appearance of the undisclosed principal; the principal is therefore bound by the third party's right of set-off.

Yet another complication must be considered. If a principal expressly instructs his agent to contract on behalf of him (the principal) but the agent in fact contracts in his own name, the principal may find himself involved in a set-off by the third party against the agent, whereas if the agent had acted in accordance with his instructions, no set-off would have been possible. In such a case, the rule is that the principal is bound by the third party's right of set-off if, and only if, the agent had actual or apparent authority to contract as principal.

Although the general rule, as stated above, is that where an agent has brought his principal into a contractual relationship with a third party, he then has no further standing in connection with the contract, exceptions to this rule occur where the agent contracts personally as a contracting party, and where the principal is undisclosed. In the latter case the reason for the exception is obvious; the third party believes that he has contracted with a principal, and his rights against the person with whom he has contracted cannot be destroyed by the emergence of an undisclosed principal.

In both cases mentioned, the third party has what is known as a right of election; he can elect whether to sue the principal or the agent, but once having made the election, the party against whom he has not made the election is free from liability. Thus, if he elects to look upon the agent as the other party to the contract, the principal is free from liability, and even if the third party sues the agent and obtains judgment against him which is not satisfied, he still has no right to proceed against the principal.

Where an agent is acting within the scope of his authority, there is the possibility, comparatively rare, that the principal may be liable in tort rather than for breach of contract. Where an agent is liable for the tort of deceit, the principal is also liable, whether the agent acted for his own benefit or for the supposed benefit of the principal.

There are three rules which govern the position when the agent makes a statement which he believes to be true, while the principal knows that the statement is untrue:

Firstly, if the principal deliberately keeps the agent in ignorance of the true facts, the principal is liable in tort for fraud.

Secondly, if either the agent or the principal makes the statement on the basis of information passed on by another agent who knows that it is untrue and that it is going to be passed on to a third party, again the principal is liable for fraud.

Thirdly, if the agent makes the statement believing it to be true, and the principal, knowing the true facts, nevertheless does not know that the statement has been made, the principal is not liable for fraud.

In many cases where disputes arise because the agent has disposed of the property of his principal, the essence of the matter is that the agent has acted fraudulently and for his own benefit, but nevertheless the position as between the principal and the third party is unaffected and the principal is bound by the disposition of the property.

In *Rimmer* v. *Webster* (1902) an agent by fraud induced his principal to transfer certain bonds into the agent's name. The agent pledged the bonds with a third party. It was held that the principal was bound by the disposition of the property.

8F. Relationship between agent and third party

As the general rule is that an agent can neither sue nor be sued under a contract to which the only parties are the principal and the third party, it is only necessary to consider the exceptions to the rule.

If the agent is in fact the principal, although described in the contract as agent, then he is obviously liable as principal. An agent is also liable where he contracts for a principal not yet in existence, as where he contracts on behalf of a company still to be formed.

An agent is also liable under a contract if it is made in such a way as to indicate that he has assumed personal responsibility, as in a contract made on behalf of an undisclosed principal. Generally in such cases, evidence is admissible that the undisclosed principal is liable as well as (not instead of) the agent.

An agent who appears to be a contracting party cannot relieve himself of liability by proving that he was merely acting as agent for another party.

The question of the agent's personal liability is in every case a matter of the construction of the contract, having regard to the contents of the contract as well as to its signature. Sometimes it is the custom of a particular trade that an agent is personally liable, and the courts will take note of and give effect to the custom, providing that it is not contrary to the express terms of the contract.

Finally, an agent is personally liable where he acts in a dual capacity. A common example of this arises in connection with hire-purchase contracts. In the course of negotiating with a buyer, a dealer may make certain representations to the buyer, and if the sale is agreed a hire-purchase contract (under which the finance company becomes the owner of the goods and the so-called purchaser is merely a hirer) is arranged. In such a case, the representations are made by the dealer both as agent for the finance company and in his personal capacity as seller of the goods.

Although thus far the liability of the agent has been considered, it must be emphasised that in such cases the principal is also liable. In these cases the third party may elect unequivocally to pursue his rights against the principal, in which event the agent is relieved of liability.

If an agent in fact has no authority, but warrants that he has, a third party who relies on the warranty can sue the agent for breach of warranty of authority. The third party cannot, however, sue the agent if he knew that the agent was not warranting his authority, or ought to have known of the position from the circumstances of the case.

8G. Termination of agency

An agency may be terminated in any one of the following ways:
—by agreement between the parties;
—by revocation on the part of the principal of the agent's authority;
—by renunciation by the agent;
—by performance of the duties and obligations by the parties to the agency agreement;
—by lapse of time, where the agency has been created for a specified period of time;
—by the death of either the principal or the agent;
—by the bankruptcy of the principal, and also by the bankruptcy of the agent if, as is usual, the bankruptcy prevents the agent from carrying out his duties;
—by frustration, where the subject-matter of the agency has been destroyed or become impossible of fulfilment, or where the objects of the agency have become illegal;
—by the insanity of either party if the insanity is such as to prevent his entering into a contract.

Not all the consequences flowing from the principal/agent relationship cease immediately the agency is terminated. For example, if at the time of termination the agent has a right to commission or indemnity, these vested rights do not cease to exist. Conversely, if the agent has been guilty of a breach of duty and on that account the principal dismisses him, thus bringing the agency to an end, the principal's right to sue the agent in respect of the breach still remains.

An agency coupled with an interest cannot be revoked. This requires some explanation. The situation usually arises where a principal owes money to an agent and the agent's authority is given to him (the agent) as security for the debt.

In *Raleigh* v. *Atkinson* (1840) it was the practice from time to time for the agent to advance money to the principal, and the principal entrusted the agent with goods for sale which the agent then sold, repaying himself the advances which he had made to the principal out of the proceeds. It was held that this was an agency coupled with an interest, and could not therefore be revoked. In such a case, the authority is not terminated by the bankruptcy, death, or insanity of the principal. But it is important to note that it is not enough that an agent has both an authority and an interest; the authority must be given as security for the interest.

In connection with the revocation of an agency where the agent has been appointed by a power of attorney, there are two important sections of the Law of Property Act 1925:

—under s. 126 a power of attorney given for valuable consideration and expressed as irrevocable cannot be revoked by the act of the principal unless the agent consents, nor is it revoked by the death, disability, or bankruptcy of the principal;

—under s. 127, even if the power of attorney is not given for valuable consideration but is nevertheless expressed to be irrevocable for a period not exceeding one year, it cannot be revoked during that period except with the consent of the agent.

With the exceptions mentioned above, the termination of an agency is effective for the future as between principal and agent, but the problem is considerably more complicated as regards third parties. The termination of an agency may divest the agent of his actual authority, but it does not necessarily deprive him of his apparent authority. If the principal has held out the agent as having authority he remains liable, so far as a third party is concerned, until the third party has had notice that the agency is at an end. This is so if the termination of the agency is the voluntary act of the principal, or even if the agency is terminated because of the insanity of the principal. On the other hand, where the agency is terminated by the death of the principal, his personal representatives are not liable on contracts made by the agent after the death of the principal.

The question further arises whether the agent is liable to the third party where he acts as agent after the agency has been terminated. In *Yonge* v. *Toynbee* (1910) solicitors acting for a client took certain steps in defence of an action at a time when, unknown to them, their client was insane. On learning of the insanity, the plaintiff applied successfully to have the proceedings terminated. He then sued the solicitors personally for the payment of the costs which he had incurred in connection with the action up to the date at which it was terminated. It was held that he was entitled to recover his costs from the solicitors.

This case is authority for the proposition that a person who has not been held out as an agent but who nevertheless acts as agent is liable to the third party. But on the other hand, if a person of sound mind holds another out as his agent and later becomes insane, the agent is not personally liable. The reason why the agent was held liable in *Yonge* v. *Toynbee* was that in fact he had no authority to bind his principal, and thus was liable for breach of warranty of authority.

9. Torts – 1

9A. The nature of tortious liability	9D. Parties to an action
9B. General conditions of tortious liability	9D1. Diplomatic immunity
	9D2. Unborn children
9C. General defences in tort	9D3. Minors
9C1. Contributory negligence	9D4. Husband and wife
9C2. Self-defence	9D5. Persons suffering from mental disorder
9C3. Volenti non fit injuria	
9C4. Inevitable accident	9E. Joint torts
9C5. Act of God	9F. Vicarious liability
9C6. Necessity	9G. Survival of actions
9C7. Statutory authority	9H. Remedies in tort
9C8. Mistake	9H1. Damages
9C9. Illegality	9H2. Specific restitution
9C10. Limitation	9H3. Injunction

9A. The nature of tortious liability

The most commonly accepted definition of tort is that of the late Professor Winfield:

> Tortious liability arises from the breach of a duty primarily fixed by the law: such duty is towards persons generally and its breach is redressible by an action for unliquidated damages.

Torts must be distinguished from crimes on the one hand, and from breaches of contract on the other.

Although, as has been seen earlier, the same act may constitute both a crime and a tort, the essence of a tort is that it is a breach of a civil duty, which entitles a person who has suffered damage or injury to compensation, usually in the form of a sum of money fixed by the court. The amount awarded is intended to place the plaintiff in the same position as he was before the tort occurred, so far as this can be done purely in terms of money. Very occasionally exemplary damages, that is, damages in excess of the amount required to compensate the plaintiff, are awarded in order to punish the defendant. This only arises, however, where an award of compensatory damages would be insufficient to deter the tortfeasor (the person who commits the tort) from repeating his wrongdoing.

Another distinction between a crime and a tort is that criminal proceedings are almost invariably brought in the name of the Crown, irrespective of the wishes of the victim of the crime, and once started can be stopped only by the intervention of the Attorney-General, something which rarely happens. Whether an action in tort is brought, on the other hand, depends entirely on the plaintiff, and even after proceedings have begun, the action can be withdrawn, perhaps as a result of an out-of-court settlement, before or during the course of the trial.

A tort differs from a breach of contract in various ways. The basic distinction is that a breach of contract is a breach of a duty which a person has voluntarily assumed under an agreement and, therefore, only the parties to the contract can be affected, whereas a tort is a breach of a duty which a person owes to his fellow-men in general.

In tort, the plaintiff has a legal right only to unliquidated damages, that is, the amount of damages is fixed by the court, although forms of equitable relief may be allowed alternatively or additionally, whereas damages for breach of contract may be liquidated or unliquidated.

As a general rule, liability in contract is strict; if there is a breach of contract, the party in breach is, except in some special circumstances, liable in damages irrespective of any fault on his part. In tort, on the other hand, liability as a general rule is based on fault; the tortfeasor has done or omitted to do something intentionally or negligently, but the mere occurrence of an act does not make him liable unless the act or omission causes damage or injury. There are, however, some cases in tort where liability is strict. These will be dealt with in more detail later.

Despite the general differences, a particular act or omission may simultaneously be both a breach of contract and a tort. For example, a person may hire a taxi to take him to a particular destination and in the course of the journey the driver may drive negligently, with the result that there is an accident in which the passenger is injured. In those circumstances the passenger may sue the driver for breach of an implied contractual condition to take him to his destination with due care; or he may sue in tort for negligence. In such a case, it makes little significant practical differences whether the action is brought in contract or in tort.

9B. General conditions of tortious liability

There is no single general principle of tortious liability. In very broad terms, it may be said that a person has rights of protection for his person, his property and his reputation, and that any infringement of these rights is a tort. He only has such rights, however, as are specifically recognised by the courts, so that, for example, he has a right of action if he suffers assault and battery, but English law does not recognise a right of privacy. Thus, this branch of law deals with a heterogeneous collection of torts rather than a general principle of tortious liability.

In *Hargreaves* v. *Bretherton* (1958) the plaintiff pleaded that the defendant had committed perjury, as a result of which he (the plaintiff) had been convicted and sentenced to imprisonment. It was held that the plaintiff had no right of action, as the law knows of no tort of perjury (although perjury is, of course, a crime).

Where a person suffers loss from a cause which is not recognised by law as giving rise to an action in tort, as, for example, where a tradesman loses custom as the result of the competitive action of neighbouring tradesmen, there is said to be *damnum sine injuria* – loss without any means of redress. On the other hand, there are a number of cases in the law of torts, for example, nuisance, trespass, and defamation, where if a person's right has been infringed he is entitled to damages, albeit of a nominal amount, even if no pecuniary loss has been suffered. In other words, in these cases there is said to be *injuria sine damno* – a right of action without any pecuniary loss having been suffered. It should, however, be mentioned that such cases are exceptional; to succeed in an action for tort it is generally necessary to show, among other things, that some loss which can be compensated for in monetary terms has been suffered.

Where a person is liable in tort, he may have acted intentionally (or deliberately), or negligently, or, in some cases, quite innocently. For example, if a person in the course of a live television interview makes defamatory remarks relating to another, he may do so deliberately, or negligently in the sense that he had not taken sufficient care to check whether his remarks were true (and thus not defamatory) or false. The broadcasting authority would also be liable even though they could not have known that the defamatory remarks would be made.

Negligence may be an ingredient of a number of torts – a person may, for example, commit trespass or nuisance negligently as distinct from deliberately. But negligence, in a sense which will be defined later, is in itself a tort; it is indeed, in terms of the number of cases which come before the courts, the most important tort at the present day.

Where a person is liable in tort even when he has not been in any way at fault, liability is said to be strict. The classic case of strict liability is the rule in *Rylands* v. *Fletcher* (1868) which, to quote a passage from the judgment in the case, is that '. . . the person who for his own purposes brings on his land and collects and keeps there anything likely to do mischief if it escapes, must keep it in at his peril, and, if he does not do so, is *prima facie* answerable for all the damage which is the natural consequence of its escape.'

As a general rule, motive is not relevant in deciding whether or not a person is liable in tort. A person may act with the best intentions in given circumstances, but this will not avail him if his action is unlawful.

On the other hand, if a person maliciously does something which causes loss to another, he is nevertheless not liable if what he has done is not unlawful. For example, in *Bradford Corporation* v. *Pickles* (1895) the defendant wished to sell his land to the corporation at an excessively high price, and when they refused to buy he made excavations on his land and abstracted some of the water which would normally have flowed into the corporation's reservoir. It was held that his action was lawful – a person is entitled to make excavations on his land – and the fact that he acted out of spite did not make his action unlawful.

The exceptional cases, where malice is relevant in tort, are as follows:
—Malice is of the essence of the torts of malicious prosecution and malicious falsehood. For example, in malicious prosecution, the plaintiff must show that the defendant had no reasonable cause for instituting the prosecution.
—In the tort of defamation, certain statements and documents are protected by the defences of qualified privilege or fair comment, but this defence is destroyed if there is malice. For example, a reference given by a former employer in respect of an employee is generally privileged, but the employee will have a right of action if he can show that the employer's statements were actuated by malice.
—In the tort of nuisance, some actions which are normally lawful are rendered unlawful and therefore actionable if they are actuated by malice. For example, it is generally lawful if a person shoots on his own land, but in *Hollywood Silver Fox Farm Ltd* v. *Emmett* (1936) the defendant, following a dispute with the plaintiff, deliberately arranged for guns to be fired on his own land but near the plaintiff's land during the foxes' breeding season, with a view to preventing their breeding. It was held that he was liable in nuisance.

9C. General defences in tort

There are a number of general defences to an action in tort.

9C1. Contributory negligence

Strictly, contributory negligence is not now a defence, but it is convenient to treat it under this heading, because it is of wide application, and is not specifically connected with a particular tort.

At common law contributory negligence was until 1945 a complete defence; if a defendant could show that a plaintiff had, to even the slightest degree, been himself responsible for the loss or damage which he had suffered, the defendant was not liable. This commonly happened, and still happens, in connection with some road accidents; injury or damage is caused partly by the fault of the defendant, and partly by the fault of the plaintiff.

In 1945 Parliament decided that the defence of contributory negligence was inequitable, particularly where the plaintiff's share of blame was minor. The Law Reform (Contributory Negligence) Act 1945 therefore provides as follows: 'Where any person suffers damage as the result partly of his own fault and partly of the fault of any other person or persons, a claim in respect of that damage shall not be defeated by reason of the fault of the person suffering the damage, but the damages recoverable in respect thereof shall be reduced to such extent as the court thinks just or equitable having regard to the claimant's share in the responsibility for the damage. . . .'

A typical case of contributory negligence was *Baker* v. *Willoughby* (1969). A pedestrian had a clear view of the road for at least 200 yards, and, similarly, the driver had plenty of warning of pedestrians attempting to cross the road. Nevertheless, the pedestrian stepped out into the road and was struck and injured by the car. In an action brought by the injured pedestrian, the Court of Appeal held that driver and pedestrian were equally to blame, and that the plaintiff's damages should be reduced to half the amount which he would have received had he been without fault.

Where damages are reduced as a result of contributory negligence, the court is required to assess the full amount of damages, and then indicate the percentage by which they are to be reduced as a result of the contributory negligence. One reason for this is that a possible ground of appeal lies in the assertion that the percentage reduction is either too great or too small. In *Baker* v. *Willoughby* (*supra*), for example, the court of first instance had held that the motorist was 75% to blame, but this figure was reduced to 50% on appeal.

There is, in truth, no precise manner in which the courts can express degrees of blame in percentage terms – it is impossible to prove, for example, that a person was 25%, rather than 20% or 30%, to blame. What can be said is that the present law works well in practice, and is generally accepted to be a great improvement on the pre-1945 common law position.

Apart from the obvious cases of contributory negligence, it has been held that a person is partly to blame if he accepts a lift from a driver whom he knows to be drunk, and it was decided in *Owens* v. *Brimmell* (1976) that there is contributory negligence, not only if the passenger knows that the driver is drunk, but also where the passenger himself goes drinking with the driver knowing that later the drinking will deprive him of his own capacity to appreciate the danger.

Recent case law has established the fact that there are two types of contributory negligence. The first is where the plaintiff is partly at fault in causing the accident, as already explained. The second is where the plaintiff has not been involved in causing the accident, but where his injuries are greater than they would have been if he had taken precautions for his own safety. Thus, it is now firmly established that a motorcyclist who does not wear a crash helmet, or a person in the front seat of a car who does not wear a seat-belt, will have his damages reduced if as a result his injuries are more severe than they would otherwise have been. So far as seat-belts are concerned, the law has developed with some precision:

—If failure to wear a seat-belt would have made no difference to the injuries caused, damages will not be reduced.

—If no injury at all would have been suffered if a seat-belt had been worn, damages will be reduced by 25 per cent.

—If injury would have been reduced if a seat-belt had been worn, damages will in general be reduced by 15 per cent unless there are special reasons justifying the failure to wear a seat-belt, as in the case of a woman in an advanced state of pregnancy.

In *Pasternak* v. *Poulton* (1973), however, the plaintiff was a front seat passenger who did not know that a seat-belt was available. It was held that, because the defendant had taken no steps to encourage her to wear a seat-belt, damages would be reduced by only five per cent. This case was unusual: minor contributory negligence justifying only a nominal reduction in damages is usually ignored. In any event the assessment of damages is not so exact a science as to make it possible to arrive at a precise sum, so that it is somewhat artificial to talk in terms of a reduction of five per cent. (As the wearing of seat-belts by front seat passengers is now generally compulsory, it is unlikely that in future the court would accept the argument that the plaintiff did not know that a seat-belt was available.)

9C2. Self-defence

A person is entitled to defend himself or members of his family, and he may also take any necessary action to protect his land and personal property. In every instance, the harm which he is entitled to cause in defence must be reasonable in relation to the harm which he would otherwise suffer. For example, he may prevent children from entering his orchard – the tort of trespass – and stealing his apples – the tort of conversion – by, say, erecting a high wall, to climb which would be dangerous, but he would not be entitled to lay some hidden and dangerous trap to prevent their entry.

9C3. Volenti non fit injuria

The defence of *volenti non fit injuria* (a person who consents has no right of action) or assumption of risk, as it is sometimes called, needs detailed explanation. The general rule is that a person who knows of a risk and willingly consents to run that risk has no right of action if he is injured as a result. Thus a footballer, by agreeing to participate in a game, impliedly undertakes to run the risk of injury which is necessarily incidental to playing (but not the risk that he may be deliberately injured by an opponent); and a spectator at a cricket match knowingly undertakes the risk that he may be injured by a cricket-ball and, by attending the match, may be taken to have agreed to run the risk.

There are a number of limitations to this defence. For example, there are many situations where a person may know of a risk, but cannot be said to have run the risk willingly. Three examples follow.

The first comes from a series of cases in which the courts have held that an employee may know of a risk, but cannot be taken to have willingly run it, if the alternative might be to lose his job. In *Smith* v. *Baker* (1891) the plaintiff was employed to drill holes in rock. To the knowledge of his employer, some of his fellow-employees worked on a crane in which stones were swung over the plaintiff's head, although he had complained of this practice. The plaintiff was injured when a stone fell on him, and it was held that he was entitled to succeed in an action which he brought against his employer; he knew of the risk, but had not consented.

It is otherwise if the employment by its nature involves obvious risks, and the employee is engaged on the footing that he will run the risks and be paid accordingly; a National Hunt jockey, for example, cannot complain if he is injured in a fall from his horse, as the risk is part and parcel of his normal obligation.

The second illustrates the legal principle that a person cannot be said to be 'willing' if the law imposes on him a duty to run a risk. In *Haynes* v. *Harwood* (1935) a horse and cart were left unattended in a busy street. The horse bolted and the plaintiff, a policeman, was injured in his attempts to catch the horse. It was held that he was entitled to succeed in action against the owner of the horse, as in the circumstances he had a legal duty to act as he did in order to protect the public. On the other hand, in *Cutler* v. *United Dairies Ltd* (1933) the plaintiff was inured when he tried to stop a runaway horse on a quiet country road. In this case the defence of *volenti* succeeded, as there was little danger to life or property, and therefore the plaintiff had no duty to try to stop the horse.

The third example indicates that the duty imposed on a person may be a mere moral duty, not a legal duty as in *Haynes* v. *Harwood* (*supra*). In *Chadwick* v. *British Railways Board* (1967), a railway accident was caused by the negligence of the defendants, and the husband of the plaintiff spent many hours assisting in rescue operations, as a result of which he suffered severe nervous shock. The defendants were held liable despite the fact that the plaintiff's husband was under no legal obligation to help with the rescue work.

The defence is not available where it is alleged that there has been a breach of statutory duty. This applies particularly in actions brought by employees against employers, and in practice the defence is rarely pleaded in any type of employer/employee case.

The defence is available, not only if the plaintiff agrees to run a risk, but also if he agrees to somebody doing something to him which would otherwise be a tort. Thus, a person may agree that a surgeon should perform an operation on him; in the absence of his consent, except, perhaps, in an emergency, performing the operation would amount to the tort of battery.

9C4. Inevitable accident

The defence of inevitable accident is that an accident has occurred which could not have been avoided by any precautions which a reasonable man could be expected to take. An example was *Stanley* v. *Powell* (1891). The defendant, a member of a shooting party, fired at a pheasant, but his shot glanced off an oak tree and injured the plaintiff. It was held that the defendant had taken all reasonable precautions, and the plaintiff's action therefore failed. (In a case like this, it is arguable that no special defence of 'inevitable accident' need be available; in effect, the 'defence' is simply the production of evidence to indicate that in the circumstances the defendant had not been negligent.)

9C5.Act of God The defence of Act of God is somewhat similar to that of inevitable accident. It was defined in *Greenock Corporation* v. *Caledonian Railway Co.* (1917) as 'circumstances which no human foresight can provide against, and of which human prudence is not bound to recognise the possibility'. A good example was *Nichols* v. *Marsland* (1876). The defendant had on her land several artificial lakes and on one occasion there was exceptionally heavy rainfall, 'greater and more violent than any within the memory of witnesses', which burst the banks of the artificial lakes so that water escaped and carried away four bridges belonging to the county council. The action brought by the council failed because, it was held, the defendant could not have been expected to take precautions against something which she could not reasonably have been expected to anticipate.

The essential difference between inevitable accident and Act of God is that the former involves some human agency, whereas the latter involves natural forces alone without any human intervention.

The defence of Act of God is now rarely brought, and is unlikely to succeed. There is much greater knowledge now of natural hazards than there was when *Nichols* v. *Marsland* was decided, and technological developments make it much more feasible to take proper precautions against such hazards.

9C6.Necessity Necessity is the defence that the defendant's acts where forced upon him by the need to take steps to protect person or property from imminent danger. He must show that in the circumstances of the case the steps which he took were reasonable.

So, in *Cope* v. *Sharp* (1912) the defendant, a gamekeeper, deliberately burned heather on land adjoining that belonging to his employer in order to create a firebreak and so prevent the spread of a fire, which had started on the adjoining land, to his employer's land. Despite the fact that the fire stopped before it reached the fire-break, the defendant was held not liable for trespass to land, as in all the circumstances he had acted reasonably.

It has been held (*Leigh* v. *Gladstone* (1909)) that the force-feeding of a prisoner on hunger-strike (in this case a suffragette) constitutes a defence to an action for battery brought by the prisoner. This case is, however, of doubtful validity, as it is difficult to see what duty a prison officer has to keep a prisoner alive against his or her will.

9C7.Statutory authority It is a defence that the defendant had statutory authority to perform some act which, in the absence of such authority, would constitute a tort.

For example, it will be seen in chapter 10 that continual excessive noise or vibrations which cause inconvenience or discomfort to the occupier of land adjoining one's own in general constitutes the tort of nuisance. At common law, therefore, the operation of what are in modern society essential services, such as railways and airports, would always involve the possibility of actions for nuisance. The operators of such services are, therefore, by the statutes which bring them into existence, permitted to perform acts which, in the absence of statutory authority, would constitute torts. They maintain their immunity, however, only if they keep within their authorised limits so that, for example, an aircraft may constitute a nuisance if it is flying faster or lower than in the circumstances it is permitted to do.

Sometimes, statutory authority is absolute, in which case there is a complete defence, although even here, if the defendant has alternative courses of action, he must choose the course which will cause least harm to others. In other cases, statutory authority is given conditionally, the condition being that the persons to whom it is given do not interfere with private rights. In this latter case, statutory authority is not a defence. Whether the authority is absolute or conditional depends on the precise wording of the statute.

The need to look at the wording of the statute is demonstrated in the case of *Marriage* v. *East Norfolk Rivers Catchment Board* (1950). In pursuance of their powers under the Land Drainage Act 1930, the Board deposited dredgings taken from the river on the south bank of the river, so raising its height. When the river next flooded, water, instead of escaping over the south bank, as it had always previously done, ran over the north bank, and swept away a bridge leading to a mill owned by the plaintiff. The Act provided that, in the event of injury or damage to any person by reason of the exercise by a drainage board of any of its powers, the board should make full compensation, and that if any dispute arose, the matter should be referred to arbitration. The plaintiff sued the board for nuisance, but it was held that he had no right of action in this respect: his only remedy was to claim compensation under the Act.

9C8.Mistake As in other branches of law, mistake of law is no defence in an action for tort. Similarly, it is generally true that mistake of fact is no defence, but there are exceptions.

For example, in defamation, by the provisions of the Defamation Act 1952, if the defendant did not intend to publish the words of and concerning the plaintiff, and did not know of the circumstances by virtue of which they might be understood to refer to him, he may make an offer to publish a suitable correction or apology. Such an offer constitutes a defence.

A further exception is if a policeman without a warrant arrests somebody who has not in fact committed an offence. He will not be liable to an action for false imprisonment if he can show that he acted reasonably and in good faith.

Similarly, it is a defence to an action for malicious prosecution for the defendant to show that he began the prosecution in good faith, with the mistaken but reasonable belief that the plaintiff was guilty.

9C9. Illegality

It is a defence that the plaintiff was committing an illegal act at the time when the alleged tort occurred. In *Ashton* v. *Turner* (1980) three men committed a burglary and tried to escape in a car owned by one of them. The car crashed and one of the passengers was injured. It was held that he had no case against the driver or the owner in negligence, because as a matter of public policy the law did not recognise a duty of care owed by one participant in a crime to another. It was also held that as the driver, to the knowledge of the passenger, had been drinking heavily, the defence of *volenti non fit injuria* would apply.

9C10. Limitation

It is a defence that the action is statute barred, that is, that the period which the law allows the plaintiff to bring his action has expired. The rules regarding limitation are now contained within the Limitation Act 1980. This is a consolidating Act, that is, it brings together all the previous statutes and some court decisions on individual cases into a single Act. The Act does not cover all causes of action, but those which are not dealt with are special cases such as under the Nuclear Installations Act or in relation to international carriage of goods.

The period of limitation depends upon whether the harm done to the potential plaintiff involved damage to his property, or bodily injury or death. If both bodily injury and damage are complained of then the action must normally be brought within the period for bodily injury, which is generally the shorter.

The basic rules are that the action must be begun by writ within:

(*a*) three years in the case of an action involving bodily injury or death;

(*b*) 12 years in the case of a dispute as to title to land;

(*c*) six years in other cases, usually actions relating to property damage.

The Crown is not bound by these time limits, but in practice observes them. The limits also do not apply in certain specific circumstances, for example, where there has been fraud.

It is the first category, claims for bodily injury or death, which causes most problems relating to limitation. Sections 11–14 of the 1980 Act deal with the basic rules for injury or death cases. When considering the actual period within which a plaintiff must bring his action, it is important also to consider how the time is measured, particularly the date from which the limitation period begins.

At first sight this might seem obvious: the relevant date will be the date upon which the injury occurs. In many cases this will be true, but sometimes the date will not be so obvious. The plaintiff may not find out until after the limitation period would have expired who was responsible for his injury. In the case of an industrial injury or illness caused by exposure to a toxic substance, the injury or illness may accrue over a period of months or even years. An injury which at first sight seems insignificant may later prove to be serious. To cover these and other similar circumstances, section 11 of the Act states that time begins to run from the date of accrual of the cause of action or, if later, the date of knowledge of the injured person.

The term 'date of knowledge' is defined in s. 14(1): 'references to a person's date of knowledge are references to the date on which he first had knowledge of the following facts:

(*a*) that the injury in question was significant; and

(*b*) that the injury was attributable in whole or in part to the act or omission which is alleged to constitute negligence, nuisance or breach of duty; and

(*c*) the identity of the defendant; and

(*d*) if it is alleged that the act or omission was that of a person other than the defendant, the identity of that person and the additional facts supporting the bringing of an action against the defendant;

and knowledge that any acts or omissions did or did not, as a matter of law, involve negligence, nuisance or breach of duty is irrelevant.'

The Act also clarifies what is intended by the word 'significant' in s. 14(1)(a): 'An injury is judged to be significant if the person whose date of knowledge is in question would reasonably have considered it sufficiently serious to justify instituting proceedings.'

A person cannot extend the date from which time begins to run against him simply by saying that he did not have knowledge of the right of action. The court must decide whether the plaintiff ought reasonably to have had knowledge of his right by reason of facts observable or ascertainable by him. If it is appropriate to obtain expert advice, for example, medical advice to ascertain the cause of an injury, then a person is assumed to have knowledge of facts which he would have discovered from taking such expert advice which the court deems it reasonable for him to have taken.

An important point is that although the person whose knowledge is in question will normally be the victim, this will not always be the case. It may be knowledge acquired by certain dependants of the victim who can have an independent right of action under the Fatal Accidents Acts.

There is also a further discretion given to the courts to extend the basic limitation periods where this would be equitable. The rules are contained in s. 33 of the 1980 Act. The court must 'have regard to the degree to which –

(a) the provisions of sections 11 or 12 of this Act prejudice the plaintiff or any person whom he represents and

(b) any decision of the court under the subsection would prejudice the defendant or any person whom he represents.'

The court is required to weigh the prejudice to the plaintiff in not being allowed to proceed against the prejudice to the defendant if the action were allowed to proceed. The wording of the Act appears to make the discretion unlimited, but to try to achieve a degree of consistency by the courts in exercising this discretion s. 33(3) of the Act provides that 'in acting under this section the court shall have regard to all the circumstances of the case and in particular to –

(a) the length of, and the reasons for, the delay on the part of the plaintiff;

(b) the extent to which, having regard to the delay, the evidence adduced, or likely to be adduced by the plaintiff or defendant is, or is likely to be, less cogent than if the action had been brought within the time allowed by s. 11 or (as the case may be) by s. 12;

(c) the conduct of the defendant after the cause of action arose, including the extent (if any) to which he responded to requests reasonably made by the plaintiff for information or inspection for the purpose of ascertaining facts which were, or might have been, relevant to the plaintiff's cause of action against the defendant;

(d) the duration of any disability of the plaintiff accruing after the date of accrual of the cause of action;

(e) the extent to which the plaintiff acted promptly and reasonably once he knew whether or not the act or omission of the defendant, to which the injury was attributable, might be capable at that time of giving rise to an action for damages;

(f) the steps, if any, taken by the plaintiff to obtain medical, legal or other expert advice and the nature of any advice he may have received.'

These are guidelines for the court to consider, and are neither exhaustive nor binding on the court.

A person who is under a disability cannot bring an action. Persons under a disability are minors, that is, persons under the age of eighteen, and persons suffering from mental illness. As such persons cannot sue for damages time does not begin to run against them until the disability ceases. In the case of minors, however, there is no extension in the period of limitation if when the cause of action arises they are in the custody of a parent. Although a person under disability cannot bring an action himself, it is possible for another person, known as his 'next friend', to bring an action on his behalf. The next friend is usually his father or mother, but there is no legal requirement that this should be so. A next friend who brings an action is personally liable for costs if the action fails.

The Limitation Act does not apply directly to claims for equitable relief. Such claims are liable instead to the doctrine of *laches*, which means that the court can refuse the remedy if it feels that there has been undue delay in bringing the case. An example is the case of *Allcard* v. *Skinner* (see chapter 6).

9D. Parties to an action

The general rule is that any person may sue or be sued in tort. It is the exceptional cases which must be dealt with here. The special position of the Queen, corporate bodies, partnerships, trade unions and employers associations, and other unincorporated associations in relation to, *inter alia*, the law of torts, has already been considered in chapter 4.

9D1. Diplomatic immunity

Foreign sovereigns, ambassadors of foreign powers, and their staffs may not be sued unless they voluntarily submit to the jurisdiction of the English courts. They are, however, entitled to bring civil proceedings, and in road accident cases they invariably consent to be sued.

In *Dickinson* v. *Del Solar* (1930) the plaintiff was injured by a car driven by the servant of the defendant, who was the first Secretary of the Peruvian Legation. The Head of the Legation instructed the defendant not to plead diplomatic immunity, and judgment was given in favour of the plaintiff. The defendant's insurers declined to indemnify him on the grounds that he could have pleaded diplomatic immunity. It was held that the defendant was entitled to be indemnified by the insurers, on the grounds that diplomatic immunity did not give immunity from liability for wrongful acts, but only from suit, and that the immunity could therefore be waived.

Diplomatic immunity lasts only so long as the person concerned occupies the post which gives him that immunity. For example, when an ambassador resigns or is recalled by his country, the Limitation Acts begin to run against him in respect of any torts which he may have committed during his term of office. In general, however, this is of little consolation to a would-be plaintiff, as he will normally leave the country and thus be outside the jurisdiction of the English courts.

9D2. Unborn children

English law does not give any rights to an unborn child as such, but once he is born, he may have rights in respect of something which happened to him before his birth. Under the Congenital Disabilities (Civil Liability) Act 1976, if a child is born disabled, abnormal, or unhealthy as a result of some breach of duty towards his parents whilst he was *en ventre sa mère* ('in his mother's womb') he has a right of action which accrues from the moment of his birth. A newly-born child has, however, no right against his mother in respect of a tort committed by her whilst he was *en ventre sa mère* with the important exception that 'a woman driving a motor vehicle when she knows, or ought reasonably to know, herself to be pregnant is to be regarded as under the same duty to take care for the safety of her unborn child as the law imposes on her with respect to the safety of other people'. Thus the law generally considers it unseemly that a child should sue its mother, but has no such qualms when, as where injury is caused by a motoring accident, the real defendant is not its mother but her insurance company.

9D3. Minors

There are no restrictions on the right of a minor to sue, except that he must do so through his 'next friend', and not personally.

In principle, a minor may be sued in tort in the same way as may an adult, but a number of reservations must be made.

The first of these reservations is that, as a matter of common sense rather than law, it is unlikely that a minor could pay any damages awarded against him, unless he is covered by insurance, so that in practical terms to bring an action against a minor may be to throw good money after bad. A successful plaintiff could not look to the minor's parents for redress, as they are not responsible for his torts.

A second reservation is that, in actions for negligence, a lower standard of care is expected of a child than of an adult; given the same circumstances, an action is less likely to succeed against a child than against an adult. Similarly, in torts which necessarily involve malice, the courts are slow to hold that a child could have had the necessary state of mind.

Although a parent is not liable for the negligence of a child, he may be personally liable in respect of some action involving the child. In *Bebee* v. *Sales* (1916) a father was held liable when his 15-year old son injured another boy, as it was negligent for him to allow his son to be put into a situation where he might cause injury. The father had allowed the son to retain a shot-gun which he knew had previously caused injury. In *Donaldson* v. *McNiven* (1952), however, a father showed his son how to use an air-rifle, warned him of its dangers, and told him not to use it outside the house. He was held not to be liable when his son injured another child, as he had taken all reasonable precautions to minimise the risk of injury.

The final reservation here considered follows on from the point noted in chapter 6 that, in general, a minor is not liable for breach of contract, and the courts will not allow this rule to be circumvented by the bringing in tort of an action which is essentially a breach of contract. Thus in *Jennings* v. *Rundall* (1799) a minor hired a horse, but rode it so hard that it was injured. It was held that he could not be sued in tort because essentially his action constituted a breach of contract for which, as a minor, he was not liable. On the other hand, if the minor does something which is quite outside the scope of the contract, he may be liable in tort. So in *Burnard* v. *Haggis* (1863), a minor hired a horse on the express condition that it was not to be used for jumping. He lent it to a friend who used it for jumping, as a result of which the horse was injured. It was held that the minor was liable in tort, as jumping was outside the scope of the contract, rather than a breach of contract.

9D4. Husband and wife

A husband is not liable in respect of a tort committed by his wife, nor vice versa.

At common law, a husband could not sue his wife in tort, and a wife could sue her husband only for the protection of her own property. However, the Law Reform (Husband and Wife) Act 1962 provides that husbands and wives may sue each other in tort, with the proviso that the court may stay the action if it appears that no substantial benefit would accrue to either party from a continuation of the proceedings. In practice, this means that the court is disinclined to get involved in quarrels between husbands and wives – 'the normal wear and tear of marriage', as it has been described – but a wife injured in a motor accident, for example, caused by the negligence of her husband, is allowed to bring an action against him because, as the husband's insurers will pay the claim, he will suffer no loss and his wife will reap a substantial benefit.

9D5. Persons suffering from mental disorder

A person suffering from mental disorder can be sued in tort, but as in the case of children the court will be slow to find that a mental patient has been negligent or has formed a particular mental state, such as malice.

However, in *Morris* v. *Marsden* (1952) the defendant violently attacked the plaintiff, who sued for damages for assault and battery. It was shown that the defendant did not know that what he was doing was wrong, but he was nevertheless held liable on the grounds that, although suffering from a disorder of the mind, he knew the nature and quality of his act.

Such a person may bring an action in tort, but it must be done through his guardian *ad litem*.

9E. Joint torts

It may be that two or more persons are liable to another in respect of the same injury or damage, as where two drivers, who are both negligent, cause injury to a pedestrian. A plaintiff can, in such circumstances, sue either of the defendants in respect of the full amount of his claim, but in practice he will tend to sue both and the court will have to consider not only the liability of the defendants to the plaintiff, but also the apportionment of damages as between the two (or more) defendants. This latter aspect is dealt with by the Civil Liability (Contribution) Act 1978.

By s. 1(1) of the Act, any person liable in respect of any damage suffered by another may recover contribution from any other person liable in respect of the same damage, and the Act provides that the amount of such contribution shall be 'such as may be found by the court to be just and equitable having regard to the extent of the person's responsibility for the damage in question'. The position is very much the same, therefore, as under the Law Reform (Contributory Negligence) Act 1945, except that it applies as between defendants rather than as between plaintiff and defendant.

If it is considered appropriate, the court may exempt a defendant from any liability to make contribution, or direct that the amount that he can recover shall amount to a complete indemnity. There is, however, an overriding principle that a defendant cannot, by way of contribution, be liable for a greater sum than could have been recovered from him by the plaintiff. For example, if a first defendant is liable to the plaintiff in tort, and a second defendant is liable in contract, subject to a contract term which limits liability to £500, the first defendant cannot by way of contribution recover from the second defendant more than £500, irrespective of the amount of damages recovered by the plaintiff, and irrespective also of the degree of blame of the second defendant.

Under the Act a defendant may seek contribution notwithstanding that he has ceased to be liable to the plaintiff since the damage occurred, provided that he was so liable immediately before the judgment or compromise in the plaintiff's favour, but his right to seek contribution is subject to a limitation period of two years from the time when it arises. The other party likewise is liable to make contribution notwithstanding that he has ceased to be liable in respect of the damage in question. For example, if there is negligence on the part of two defendants on 1 January 1982 and proceedings are brought against one of the defendants within the statutory limitation period, but not against the other, the other is nevertheless liable in an action for contribution provided that it is brought within two years of judgment being given in favour of the plaintiff.

The great majority of claims in tort are settled out of court and the law always encourages such settlements. Even where they are made without admission of liability it is felt that the defendant should not be deprived of any right of contribution which he might have had if the proceedings had come before the court. The 1978 Act therefore provides that a person who has *bona fide* settled a claim 'shall be entitled to contribution . . . without regard to whether or not he himself is, or ever was, liable in respect of the damage, provided, however, that he would have been liable assuming that the factual basis of the claim against him could be established.'

9F. Vicarious liability

Vicarious liability means that in simple terms one person may be held liable for a tort committed by another.

There are three main sets of relationships which may give rise to vicarious liability:
—Principal and agent.
—Partnership.
—Master and servant.

The relationships of principal and agent and of partnership are dealt with fully elsewhere in this book, and require no further mention here.

By far the most important case of vicarious liability, however, is that of master and servant. A master is liable for torts committed by his servant in the course of their employment. This gives rise to three difficult problems:
—Who is a servant?
—Who is a master?
—Where does the 'course of employment' begin and end?

It is important to determine whether those who are loosely called 'employees' are servants, for whose acts an employer is responsible, or independent contractors, for whose acts the employer is not responsible.

No help can be gained by looking at the nature of the work involved. A publishing-house may 'employ' one person to write a book and another to clean the office. It is likely, but by no means certain, that the writer is an independent contractor and the cleaner a servant. It is sometimes said that the master/servant relationship exists when the employer has the right to control not only what the employee does but also how he is to do it. With advances in science and technology over the years, this has become an increasingly unsatisfactory test. The staff of an insurance company may include a chief actuary, a data processing manager and a chief surveyor, all of whom may be servants of the company, but it is highly unlikely that the chief general manager could, even if he wished, tell even one of these officials how to do his work, and certainly not all three.

No statute nor any single legal decision indicates comprehensively when the master/servant relationship exists, but a series of decisions indicates that amongst the factors to be considered are the following:
—Is there a power to select or appoint?
—Is there a power of dismissal?
—Has the 'employee' the power to delegate the whole of the performance of his contract?
—Has the 'employer' the right to the exclusive services of the 'employee'?
—Upon whose premises is the work carried out?
—Who supplies the tools, if tools are used?
—What is the nature and method of payment?
—Who pays national insurance contributions?
—Is there any holiday entitlement?

Thus, if the work is carried out on the employer's premises with tools and equipment supplied by the employer, and the employee is paid a salary and/or commission with employer and employee sharing the cost of the national insurance contribution, and if the employee has a holiday entitlement, the master/servant relationship would certainly exist. But it is not necessary for all these circumstances to exist in every case; salesmen, for example, work away from the employer's premises, but the master/servant relationship usually exists.

On the other hand, if a person has an operation performed on him by a surgeon at a National Health Service hospital, he neither appoints nor has the power to dismiss the surgeon, and so the employer/employee relationship does not exist. Neither is a person an employee if he can delegate to another the whole of the work given to him, although partial delegation by employees is common. If a person has the right to the exclusive services of another the employer/employee relationship almost certainly exists, but many employees do not work exclusively for one employer.

It is not usually difficult to decide who is a master – he is, quite simply, the person who employs the servant. Difficulties have, however, arisen when a servant has been 'lent' by one employer to another. For example, in the classic case of *Mersey Docks and Harbour Board* v. *Coggins and Griffiths (Liverpool) Ltd* (1946) a craneman was employed and paid by A, but for a particular job was lent, with a crane, to B. While doing work for B, the craneman was negligent as a result of which C was injured. It was held that his usual employer, A, was liable. As Lord Parker said in giving judgment in the House of Lords: 'Where a man driving a mechanical device, such as a crane, is sent to perform a task, it is easier to infer that the general employer continues to control the method of employment since it is his crane and the driver remains responsible to him for its safe keeping'.

The term 'in the course of his employment' has been the subject of much litigation, and has generally been interpreted in a fairly wide sense, so that a master is responsible not only for any act which he has authorised, but also for an unauthorised mode of doing the type of act which he has authorised.

A consideration of the following cases will help to show the extent of and limits to the master's liability. In *Limpus* v. *London General Omnibus Co.* (1862) a bus driver who had been expressly forbidden to race other buses did so, and as a result of his reckless driving caused a collision. It was held that his employers were liable, as he was doing an authorised act (driving the bus) but in an unauthorised manner.

On the other hand, in *Beard* v. *London General Omnibus Co.* (1900) a bus conductor, at the end of a journey, attempted to turn the bus round and in doing so injured the plaintiff. It was held that his employers were not liable, as what he had done was not in the course of his employment; he was employed to conduct the bus, not to drive it.

The case of *Lloyd* v. *Grace Smith and Co.* (1912) gives some idea how far the employer's liability can extend. The defendants were a firm of solicitors, one of whose clerks defrauded a client by geting her to sign false documents. The clerk was acting illegally and entirely for his own benefit, but it was held nevertheless that his employers were liable.

On the other hand, in *Warren* v. *Henley's Ltd* (1948) an employer was held not liable when his employee, a petrol pump attendant, assaulted a customer following an argument regarding payment for petrol. (The position might have been different if a bouncer at a night club used excessive force in ejecting a customer.)

In *Morris* v. *C. W. Martin and Sons Ltd* (1965) the plaintiff sent a mink stole to a furrier's for cleaning. The furrier sub-contracted the work to the defendants, who were specialist cleaners, and it was stolen by one of the defendants' employees. It was held that the defendants were liable, as the employee was not acting outside the scope of his employment, and incidentally that the defendants were not protected by an exemption clause in the conditions on which they accepted business, as there was no contractual relationship between the plaintiff and the defendants.

In *Rose* v. *Plenty* (1976) a milkman employed a boy thirteen years of age to assist him with his milk round, contrary to the express instructions of his employer. The boy was injured when the milkman drove the float negligently, and it was held that he was entitled to recover damages against the milkman's employers.

A principal is not responsible for the actions of an independent contractor, but this general principle is subject to qualification.

Where a principal authorises or ratifies an unlawful act done by an independent contractor, both principal and contractor are liable. For example, in *Ellis* v. *Sheffield Gas Consumers Co.* (1853), the defendants employed a contractor to dig a trench in a street for the purpose of laying gas pipes, an action for which they had no authority. The contractor's employees left a pile of stones on the street and the plaintiff fell over them and was injured. It was held that the defendants were liable.

In *Tarry* v. *Ashton* (1876), the defendant employed a contractor to repair a lamp attached to his premises overhanging a path. The work was carried out incompetently, and the lamp fell and injured the plaintiff. It was held that the defendant was liable. He owed a duty to the plaintiff to ensure that the lamp was safe, and had failed to perform that duty.

In *Spicer* v. *Smee* (1946), a lessee employed a contractor to install electrical wiring in her bungalow. The work was done in such a way that the live wire was inadequately protected, as a result of which a fire was caused which spread to and destroyed the plaintiff's adjacent bungalow. It was held that the defendant's defective wiring constituted a nuisance, that the rule that a principal is not liable for the acts of his contractor does not apply to nuisance, and that therefore the defendant was liable.

The principal cannot escape liability in respect of 'extra-hazardous acts, that is, acts which, in their very nature, involve in the eyes of the law special danger to others'. In *H. & N. Emanuel Ltd* v. *Greater London Council* (1971), the defendants employed a contractor to clear a site and included in the contract a condition that the contractors were not to light fires or burn rubbish. Nevertheless, the contractors did light a fire, which spread and damaged nearby property. It was held that the defendants were liable notwithstanding the condition in the contract.

A principal is not liable for the casual negligence of an independent contractor, as distinct from negligence in the essential work delegated. This point is illustrated by the case of *Padbury* v. *Holliday & Greenwood Ltd* (1912). A sub-contractor was employed to put casements in the windows of a house which the defendants were building. While doing the work, an employee of the sub-contractor left a tool on the window sill, and the tool fell off and injured the plaintiff who was in the street below. It was held that the defendants, the main contractors, were not liable, as the leaving of the tool on the window sill was not an essential part of the work of installing the casement: it was merely casual or collateral negligence on the part of the employee of the sub-contractor.

As with the master/servant relationship, the fact that the principal is in some circumstances held liable does not mean that the contractor will escape liability, and in addition the terms of the contract may provide that, if the principal is liable, he is entitled to indemnity from the contractor.

9G. Survival of actions

At common law there was a maxim *actio personalis moritur cum persona* (a personal right of action dies with the person) but this rule has been much modified by statute, so that it is not now of general application.

The Law Reform (Miscellaneous Provisions) Act 1934 and subsequent legislation provide that, in general, rights of action in tort survive in favour of the estate of a deceased plaintiff and against the estate of a deceased defendant. There are, however, a number of exceptions and modifications:

—The common law rule still applies to actions for defamation, so that these do not survive death.

—Exemplary damages cannot be awarded in favour of the estate of a deceased plaintiff.

—In civil proceedings the death of a human being cannot be complained of as an injury. It has been said that 'it is cheaper to kill than to maim'. Thus, where a person has been killed, say, as a result of negligence, no action arises for the benefit of his estate, whereas had he been injured and later died from a different cause, the action would survive for the benefit of his estate.

The harshness of this rule has, however, been largely mitigated by legislative provisions first enacted in 1846 and now embodied in the Fatal Accidents Act 1976. Under the provisions of this Act, dependants of a deceased person can claim damages for loss arising by reason of his decease if the death was caused by some default on the part of the defendant which would have given the deceased person a right of action if he had been injured rather than killed. Dependants for this purpose are, where appropriate, a husband, wife, parent, child, grand-parent, grand-child, step-parent, step-child, brother, sister, uncle, and aunt. The amount of damages which can be recovered is measured by the pecuniary loss suffered by the dependant as a result of the death, and not by the amount which the deceased would have been awarded had he survived. No amount is awarded in respect of grief or mental suffering.

It may happen that two claims are brought in respect of the same fatal accident, one under the 1934 Act in respect of a cause of action arising before the death, and one under the 1976 Act by a dependant who has suffered as a result of the death. Although both actions are distinct, it is possible that the same person could receive a double benefit; a wife, for example, would probably benefit as a beneficiary under her husband's estate, and also as a dependant in the action brought under the 1976 Act. To avoid this, the 1976 Act provides that such circumstances must be taken into account in assessing damages, to ensure that no person receives a double benefit. However, the fact that the estate or a dependant may receive money from life assurance policies or pension payments is not taken into account to reduce the damages awarded.

9H. Remedies in tort

Remedies in the law of torts usually take the form of damages, but there are also the remedies of specific restitution and injunction, which may be awarded in addition to or instead of damages.

9H1. Damages

Contemptuous and exemplary damages have already been discussed, and need no further attention here.

For those torts which are actionable *per se*, nominal damages of, say, £2 may be awarded even though no pecuniary loss has been suffered.

The usual remedy in tort is, however, an award of what are called real or substantial damages. The prime object of an award of damages is to put the plaintiff in the same position after the commission of a tort as he occupied before, as far as this can be done in terms of money, while recognising that in many cases there must be a degree of arbitrariness because some things, such as pain and suffering, cannot be measured in terms of money.

Damages in tort are always unliquidated, that is, they cannot be determined beforehand but are at the discretion of the court. Even if, as sometimes happens, the parties agree on the measure of damages before the case is heard on the question of liability, damages are still unliquidated in that the court is not bound to accept the estimate of the parties.

Damages are divided into two different classes, special damages and general damages. Special damages are damages in respect of loss or expenditure which can be quantified at the time of the trial, and which relate to matters which are past. Thus, following a motor accident the plaintiff may present a claim for the cost of repairs to his vehicle, the cost of hire of another vehicle during the period when his own was being repaired, loss of income if he was injured, and damage to clothing. All these items are special damages which the parties will endeavour to agree before the trial. It may be that the claim is for special damages only, in which case the only substantial purpose of the trial will be to establish liability.

General damages are all other damages, that is, those which cannot be quantified before the trial. Thus, actual loss of earnings before the trial can be quantified and are therefore special damages; loss of future earnings cannot be quantified before the trial and so form one item of general damages. As well as loss of future earnings, general damages include such matters as compensation for pain and suffering, loss of amenity, loss of goodwill to a trader, and disturbance by noise. General damages are said to be 'at large', that is, they are at the discretion of the judge. For example, if the plaintiff at the date of trial can show that he is suffering a loss of earnings of £100 a month compared with his pre-accident average, and assuming the defendant to be liable, he is entitled to compensation for this. The judge must decide whether this loss is likely to continue, and if so, whether it will continue at the same rate and for how long. If it is likely to continue indefinitely he must award a lump sum; English law does not permit the award of an annuity.

The Administration of Justice Act 1969 provides that the court, when awarding damages, must in certain cases also award interest on the amount of the damages. In general, interest is awarded on amounts which relate to losses incurred by the plaintiff before the hearing, but not for amounts which relate to loss which the plaintiff will suffer in the future, such as future loss of earnings.

As a result of several decisions of the House of Lords, it is now settled that account must be taken of inflation occurring between the date of the cause of action and the date of judgment, but future inflation must be ignored. It would seem that the view of the courts is that the plaintiff should invest his damages in such a way as to mitigate the effects of inflation.

Damages under certain headings can be virtually impossible to assess. At one time it was the practice to award damages for 'loss of expectation of life' where the plaintiff's expectation of life was shortened as a result of injury, but this is no longer done. Because of the difficulty of assessment of damages, the law may fix an arbitrary figure. For example, a husband or wife may claim damages for the bereavement of the other, or parents may claim for bereavement of a deceased unmarried minor child, but the amount under this heading is fixed at £3500.

Another problem which arises with personal injury cases is that when a case comes before the courts the full extent of the injury may not be at all clear. The Administration of Justice Act 1982 therefore provides that a court may make an award of provisional damages where there is a chance that at a future stage the injured person may suffer some serious deterioration in his physical or mental condition. If such deterioration does occur, the plaintiff is entitled to have the case re-opened for the purpose of a revision of the amount of damages.

In tort, as in contract, a defendant is not liable for damage which is too remote, but the rules regarding remoteness of damage in tort do not follow exactly the same lines as those which apply in contract. The test to be applied in tort to decide whether damage is too remote was considered by the Judicial Committe of the Privy Council in *Overseas Tankship (U.K.) Ltd* v. *Mort's Dock and Engineering Co. Ltd* (1961) (usually referred to as *The Wagon Mound* from the name of the ship involved). This was an Australian case, but it is now generally accepted as representing English law as well.

The brief facts were that the defendants negligently spilt oil into Sydney Harbour. The oil spread to the plaintiffs' wharf where welding operators were causing sparks to fall into the water. The sparks caused the oil to ignite, setting fire to the plaintiffs' wharf.

The Judicial Committee held that the test to be applied was that of reasonable foreseeability – the defendants were liable for all the consequences of their act which a reasonable man could have foreseen, and on the facts of the case the Judicial Committee decided that the damage was not reasonably foreseeable, as it could not be expected that the oil would catch fire.

There is an exception to the *Wagon Mound* rule in what have come to be known as the 'eggshell skull' cases. It has always been a rule of English law that a defendant must take his victim as he finds him, and thus, for example, a person who deliberately pushes another to the ground may in fact kill him if he has an exceptionally thin skull, whereas a person with a normal-sized skull might only suffer comparatively minor injury. The 'eggshell skull' principle applies to any case where the victim suffers from some physical disability which is likely to cause him greater than normal harm if he is injured.

For example in *Smith* v. *Leech Brain and Co. Ltd* (1961) a workman was injured when, as a result of negligence on the part of a fellow-employee, a piece of molten metal fell on his lip. This would have caused only minor injury to a person in normal health, but in fact the victim was already pre-disposed to cancer, and the burn aggravated his condition and he died. It was held that the defendants were liable on the 'eggshell skull' principle, despite the fact that it could not reasonably have been foreseen that a comparatively minor burn would have caused death.

A defendant is not liable where damage results, not as a consequence of his original act, but from a *novus actus interveniens* (the intervention of a new act). The new act must, however, be such as to break the 'chain of causation'. The following cases illustrate the continuing causation and the break of causation respectively.

In *Davies* v. *Liverpool Corporation* (1949) a tram conductor negligently stayed on the top deck when the tram was at a stop. The plaintiff was injured when, as he was getting on the tram, the starting bell was rung by another passenger. It was held that the defendants were liable as the injury to the plaintiff resulted from the wrongful act of the conductor; the ringing of the bell by the passenger was not a *novus actus interveniens*.

Similarly, in *Weiland* v. *Cyril Lord Carpets* (1969) the plaintiff was injured as a result of the negligent driving of a bus by one of the defendants' servants. In consequence, she had to have a collar fitted to her neck, so that she could not use her bifocal spectacles with her usual skill, and this caused her to fall down some stairs, sustaining further injuries. It was held that her second injury was attributable to the original negligence of the bus driver, as it was a reasonably foreseeable consequence.

On the other hand, in *Hogan* v. *Bentinck Collieries Ltd* (1948) the plaintiff fractured his thumb at work and then, acting on bad advice, agreed to have it amputated. It was held that the amputation was a *novus actus interveniens*, for which therefore his employers were not liable.

9H2. Specific restitution

Specific restitution in tort is the counterpart of specific performance in contract and, like specific performance, is a discretionary equitable remedy. It is allowed where an award of damages would provide inadequate compensation. If, for example, the defendant has in his possession a unique object belonging to the plaintiff, the court may order that it be handed over; what the plaintiff requires in such a case is the return of his property, not monetary compensation for it. The court will not order specific restitution where damages are an adequate alternative or in circumstances in which the order could not be enforced; in particular, if the property has been removed to a country outside the jurisdiction of the court specific restitution will not be ordered, as the court would have no means of ensuring its return.

9H3. Injunction

Another equitable remedy which the court may award at its discretion, in addition to or as an alternative to damages, is an injunction. It is particularly appropriate as a remedy for nuisance; the plaintiff may ask for, and be granted, damages in respect of the disturbance which he has already suffered, but in addition he may wish the court to order the defendant to prevent the continuance of the nuisance.

An injunction is an order of the court restraining the defendant from committing, or continuing to commit, some act. There are various kinds of injunctions:

Interlocutory. An interlocutory injunction is one which is issued as a temporary expedient pending the trial of an action. For example, if the defendant intends to publish a book containing alleged defamatory statements, the plaintiff may obtain an injunction to prevent publication of the book until the action has been tried. The court, however, will not grant an interlocutory injunction lightly, as to do so may give the appearance of prejudging the case; it much prefers, for example, to allow the defendant, if he is so minded, so go ahead and publish the alleged defamatory book, leaving the plaintiff to pursue his action for damages at common law.

Perpetual. A perpetual injunction is granted at the end of a trial and binds the defendant for the future. It may be an injunction against the continuance of an injury, such as a nuisance, or against the repetition of an injury, such as a trespass, or it may restrain the defendant from committing an act which he intended to do in the future, in which case it is known as a *quia timet* injunction.

Prohibitory. A prohibitory injunction is one which prohibits a person from doing something, as in the examples just mentioned. The term is used in contrast to a mandatory injunction.

Mandatory. A mandatory injunction is one which orders the defendant to do something (rather than refrain from doing something) to redress a wrong which he has committed. For example, he may be ordered to dismantle a building which he has erected in defiance of the rights of his neighbour.

The court will not grant an injunction but will instead award damages:

—Where, if the positions were reversed, an injunction could not be granted. Thus, an injunction cannot be awarded against a minor, and so will not be awarded in his favour.

—If injury to the plaintiff's rights is small and is capable of being expressed in terms of money.

—If obedience to the order of the court would be impracticable.

—If the granting of the injunction would be unduly oppressive on the defendant.

In *Miller* v. *Jackson* (1977) it was held that the public interest, which requires young people to have the benefit of outdoor games, may be held to outweigh the private interests of neighbouring householders who are the victims of cricket balls landing in their gardens, so that it would be impossible to use the gardens when cricket is being played. Thus, although it was held that the sportsmen were liable both in nuisance and in negligence, the court refused to grant an injunction.

10. Torts – 2

10A. Negligence	10E. Trespass to land
10B. Breach of statutory duty	10F. Wrongful interference with goods
10B1. Employers' liability	10F1. Conversion
10B2. Occupiers' liability	10F2. Trespass to goods
10C. Nuisance	10G. Trespass to the person
10D. Strict liability	10H. False imprisonment
10D1. The rule in Rylands v. Fletcher	10I. Defamation
10D2. Dangerous chattels	10J. Malicious falsehood

This chapter gives a broad outline of the main torts; a detailed knowledge of specific torts is not required.

10A. Negligence

The most important tort today, in terms of the number of cases which come before the courts (and the very much larger number which are settled out of court), is negligence. The growth of the tort of negligence is largely, although by no means wholly, the result of the growth in the number of factory and motor vehicle accidents, and also the greater realisation by people of their legal rights when they suffer personal injury, or their property is damaged, through the fault of another.

The classic definition of negligence is contained in the judgment in *Blyth* v. *Birmingham Waterworks Co.* (1856):

> the omission to do something which a reasonable man, guided upon those considerations which ordinarily regulate the conduct of human affairs, would do, or doing something which a prudent and reasonable man would not do.

The test of negligence is objective; the court considers what a reasonable man would or would not do in given circumstances, and does not consider any special characteristics which may attach to a particular tortfeasor. Thus, a learner driver may drive as carefully as he possibly can, but if, because of his inexperience, he does something which a reasonably competent driver would not do, he is liable if, say, a pedestrian is injured as a result of his action.

Such a case was *Nettleship* v. *Weston* (1971) in which a driving instructor was injured when the defendant learner driver crashed his car into a lamp standard. It was held that the defendant was liable in negligence, and that the standard of care to be applied was that of a reasonably experienced and competent driver. It was stressed by the court that it was necessary to avoid a doctrine of 'varying standards'.

In order to succeed in an action for negligence, the plaintiff must prove:

— that in the circumstances the defendant owed a duty to the plaintiff to take care;
— that the defendant was in breach of that duty;
— that the breach of duty resulted from lack of reasonable care on the part of the defendant;
— that as a result of the breach of duty the plaintiff suffered damage.

The question whether in any particular case the defendant owed a duty to the plaintiff is for the court to decide as a matter of law. The question was discussed at some length in *Donoghue* v. *Stevenson* (1932). The brief facts of the case were that the plaintiff had been given a bottle of ginger beer in an opaque bottle. She drank some of the contents, and when she poured the rest into a glass discovered that it contained the decomposed remains of a snail. She was taken seriously ill as a result of having drunk the liquid.

It was not possible for the plaintiff to bring an action for breach of contract against the manufacturers or the retailer, as she had not herself bought the ginger beer, and it was accepted that there was no negligence on the part of the retailer because, the bottle being opaque, there was no way he could have known that the contents were contaminated. She therefore sued the manufacturers alleging:

— that they owed her a duty of care; and
— that they were in breach of that duty in that a reasonable system of bottle-washing would have ensured the removal of the snail.

The manufacturers' main defence was that they did not owe a duty of care in the circumstances; their only duty, they claimed, was a duty in contract to persons who bought their product.

In giving judgment Lord Atkin said:

> In English law there must be, and is, some general conception of relations giving rise to a duty of care, of which the particular cases found in the books are instances. The liability for negligence, whether you style it such or treat it as in other systems as a species of *culpa* (fault), is no doubt based upon a general public sentiment of moral wrongdoing for which the offender must pay. But acts or omissions which any moral code would censure cannot in a practical world be treated so as to give a right to every person injured by them to demand relief. In this way rules of law arise which limit the range of complainants and the extent of their remedy. The rule that you are to love your neighbour becomes, in law, you must not injure your neighbour; and the lawyer's question, Who is my neighbour? receives

a restricted reply. You must take reasonable care to avoid acts or omissions which you can reasonably foresee would be likely to injure your neighbour. Who, then, in law is my neighbour? The answer seems to be: persons who are so closely and directly affected by my act that I ought reasonably to have them in contemplation as being so affected when I am directing my mind to the acts or omissions which are called in question.

On this general principle, the courts have decided, in particular cases, whether or not a duty exists and have not hesitated in novel circumstances to hold that there is a duty. 'The categories of negligence,' said Lord Macmillan in the *Donoghue* case, 'are never closed.'

Stansbie v. *Troman* (1948) illustrates how far-reaching is the duty to take care. The plaintiff was a painter and decorator engaged under contract to do work at the defendant's house. He left the house unoccupied while he went to obtain material and, in order that he might be able to secure re-entry, pulled back the catch of the Yale lock on the front door. He was away from the premises for two hours and, during his absence, a thief entered the premises by the front door and stole a quantity of jewellery. The plaintiff claimed for the work which he had done and the defendant counter-claimed for damages for negligence. It was held that, in the circumstances, the plaintiff owed a duty to the defendant to take care of the premises and that there had been a breach of that duty because the entry of the thief which caused the loss was the direct result of the plaintiff's negligence.

In deciding whether there is a duty, the courts have, especially in recent years, taken into account the implications which a decision may have for the operation of law in society. In *Home Office* v. *Dorset Yacht Co. Ltd* (1970), for example, a situation arose for which there was no precedent. The Home Office was sued in respect of negligence by Borstal officers who were supervising a group of Borstal trainees working on an island in Poole Harbour. The trainees escaped during the night as a consequence, it was alleged, of the negligence of the officers and boarded a yacht, causing considerable damage. The Home Office argued that the officers' duty was owed to the Crown and not to individual members of the public, and also that it would not be in the public interest for a duty to the public to be imposed upon them, as it would inhibit them in carrying out their main duty, which was to provide suitable training for Borstal trainees, which was often better carried out in public places rather than in Borstal institutions themselves. The House of Lords rejected these arguments and held that a duty of care towards the plaintiffs did exist.

Another important case which can be said to have extended the boundaries of the duty of care was *Anns and Ors.* v. *Merton London Borough Council* (1977). In this case, the local authority had power (not a duty) to make bye-laws regarding the erection of buildings within its area, and this power it indeed exercised. The plaintiffs, lessees of flats, alleged that the block had been built on inadequate foundations and that structural movements had caused cracks in the walls. Further, they alleged that the defendants had been negligent in having failed to carry out an adequate inspection of the foundations to ensure that they complied with the bye-laws. The House of Lords held that these allegations, if proved, constituted negligence on the part of the defendants. The law appears to be that, if a local authority or similar body takes such powers and exercises them negligently, it is liable; but if, as a matter of policy, it decides not to take the powers, then there is no liability.

In *East Suffolk Rivers Catchment Board* v. *Kent* (1941), the Board had power to repair sea walls but were under no duty to do so. A high tide broke the sea wall and flooded the plaintiff's land. The Board sent an inexperienced man with poor equipment to do the repairs, which took 178 days, whereas they could, with reasonable skill, have been done in fourteen days. It was held that the Board were not liable, because, as a matter of policy and exercising their discretion, they had decided not to devote a great deal of resources to the work.

There have been many cases in which liability for nervous shock has been discussed by the courts, and the present position is governed by the decision in *McLoughlin* v. *O'Brian* (1982). For many years it was held that a person who was not directly injured by the negligence of another, but suffered nervous shock, perhaps by being an eye-witness to a particularly distressing road accident, had no right of action. It is now clear that such a right does exist, and that a person is liable in respect of nervous shock if such a shock was reasonably forseeable. In the *McLoughlin* case the plaintiff's husband and three of her children suffered severe bodily injuries in a road accident and were taken to hospital. At the time of the accident the plaintiff herself was at home, some two miles away. She was later taken to the hospital to see her husband and children and was so distressed when she saw the extent of their injuries and was told that one of the children had died that she suffered severe shock, organic depression and a change of personality. It was held that the defendant was liable to her because, although she had not been at the scene of the accident, her illness was a reasonably forseeable consequence of the negligence of the defendant. (Although the term 'nervous shock' is commonly used in such cases, it is an unfortunate choice of words. A person has no right of action just because he is distressed at seeing or hearing an accident, or because he suffers grief or sorrow, and possibly temporary exogenous depression, when he learns that a near relative has been killed, as such feelings are considered to be a part of normal life. To sustain a claim, it must be shown that he had suffered illness or injury, either mental or physical, beyond what a normal person could reasonably be expected to bear.)

The normal rule in an action for negligence is that the onus is on the plaintiff to show, on a balance of probabilities, that the defendant was negligent. There are, however, cases where the facts so strongly suggest that there has been negligence that the burden of disproving negligence is placed on the defendant. In such cases the rule is said to be *res ispa loquitur* – the facts speak for themselves.

For example, in *Ward* v. *Tesco Stores* (1976) yoghourt was spilt on the floor of the shop, as a result of which an accident occurred. The court held that in the circumstances it was for the defendants to show that they had not been negligent, and as they were unable to satisfy the burden of proof, they were held liable.

A successful plea of *res ipsa loquitur* does not necessarily mean that the defendant is liable; it merely requires the defendant to disprove negligence, and this he may be able to do. For example, in *Walsh* v. *Holst and Co. Ltd* (1958) the plaintiff was injured by a brick which fell from a building being worked upon by the defendants. The *res ipsa loquitur* rule applied, but the defendants, although unable to show why the brick had fallen, were able to demonstrate that they had taken all reasonable care to prevent falls; the court held that that was the extent of their duty, and thus they were not liable.

A person may be liable for negligent words which cause the plaintiff financial loss. Before the case of *Hedley Byrne and Co. Ltd* v. *Heller and Partners Ltd* (1963) it was thought that there could be no liability for negligent misrepresentation unless there was a contractual duty of care. In that case, however, it was established that a duty of care might arise if it was reasonably foreseeable that a person to whom a negligent mis-representation is made might act on the misrepresentation and suffer financial loss as a result. Thus, where a person is asked for a loan and takes up bank references as to the borrower's credit-worthiness, if the bank confirms that the borrower is credit-worthy when in fact it knows or ought to know that he is not, the bank may be liable if the lender suffers financial loss consequent on giving a loan to the borrower. In *Hedley Byrne* Lord Morris said:

> . . . if in a sphere in which a person is so placed that others could reasonably rely on his judgment or his skill or on his ability to make careful enquiry, a person takes it on himself to give information or advice to, or allows his information or advice to be passed on to, another person who, as he knows or should know, will place reliance on it, then a duty of care will arise.

If, however, as was the case in *Hedley Byrne,* the person making the negligent mis-representation disclaims responsibility for the advice, then he will not be liable.

In *Woods* v. *Martins Bank Ltd* (1958) a bank advertised investment advice, saying 'the very best advice is available through our managers'. Through a manager of the bank the plaintiff invested £14,800 in a company which the manager knew had a large overdraft and was in need of funds. The plaintiff eventually lost all the money which he had invested and sued the bank. The court rejected the defence that the giving of invest-ment advice was not part of a banker's business, as the advertisement had indicated that investment advice was available: the bank was therefore vicariously liable for the act of its manager. The court also indicated that the duty not to give negligent advice extended to potential customers as well as to existing customers.

Having established that a duty of care exists, the plaintiff must show that there has been a breach of that duty, in that the defendant has failed to take reasonable care. What is reasonable depends on the fact of the particular case. As Lord Justice Salmon said in *Herrington* v. *British Railways Board* (1970): 'What is reasonable care is only such as is reasonable in all the circumstances of the case. The circumstances vary infinitely from case to case'. Although, as stated earlier, the test of reasonableness is always objective, what is reasonable in one situation may differ in another. A few examples may be given:

— In general, the greater the risk, the greater is the standard of care which is expected. In *Saunders (Mayfair) Furs* v. *Davies* (1965) the plaintiff delivered a valuable fur coat to the defendant's shop on a sale-or-return basis. The coat was displayed in the defendant's shop window without any special precautions and was stolen one night in a smash-and-grab raid. It was held that the defendant had taken an unnecessary risk in leaving the coat on display in the window all night, and was therefore liable in damages to the plaintiffs.

— A person exercising a particular profession is judged by what could be expected of a competent person in that profession. Thus, a high degree of skill is expected of an insurance broker when he gives advice on insurance matters, but he is not expected to display any special expertise if asked for advice on matters related to investments other than investment-type insurance policies.

— If harm is reasonably forseeable, a person is expected to take all reasonable care to prevent its occurrence, but if a danger is very remote, less care need be taken, and some risks may be so remote as to justify ignoring them altogether.

— There may be special circumstances which justify the taking of abnormal risks. As Lord Justice Asquith said in *Daborn* v. *Bath Tramways* (1946): 'The purpose behind the defendant's conduct, if sufficiently important, justifies the assumption of abnormal risk'. A typical example is the driver of an ambulance who is taking a seriously-ill patient to hospital; he is justified in travelling at such a speed and in such a manner as would normally constitute negligence.

— What is expected of a person depends on how burdensome it would be on him to remove a risk. If, for example, a considerable risk can be removed at little cost, he will be expected to remove it; but if a remote risk can be removed only at great cost, it may well be held that he need take no steps to remove it.

— A person may in some circumstances owe a duty not only to normal people, but also to those suffering from certain disabilities. For example, it was held in *Haley* v. *London Electricity Board* (1964) that a person ought reasonably to foresee that blind men walk the steeets, and that therefore pavements ought not to be left in such a condition, for example, as a result of excavation work, that they amount to traps for the blind.

Having established the existence of a duty of care, and a breach of that duty, it remains for the plaintiff to show that he suffered damage or injury as a result of the breach, as negligence is not actionable *per se*. In *Burnett* v. *Chelsea and Kensington Hospital Management Committee* (1968) the plaintiff's husband unknowingly drank tea which had been contaminated with arsenic. He was taken to hospital where a doctor failed to examine him, but said that he should consult his own doctor. He died some hours later, and his widow sued the hospital management committee alleging that the hospital doctor had been negligent in not examining her husband. It was held that the doctor had indeed been negligent, but that the husband would have died from the poisoning in any event, so that the doctor's negligence was not the cause of his death.

Where there has been a negligent act or omission, as distinct from a negligent mis-representation, it has always been accepted that the defendant is liable for personal injury and damage to property caused by negligence, but until recently it was thought that there was no liability for economic or financial loss unless it directly resulted from physical damage. However, in *Junior Books Ltd* v. *The Veitchi Co. Ltd* (1982), the House of Lords held that pure economic loss can be recovered. As specialist floor-layers, Veitchi were employed as sub-contractors to a building company who were erecting a factory for Junior Books Limited. There was no contractual relationship between the parties to the action. Building was completed in 1970 but, within two years, defects manifested themselves in the floors and it was alleged that these were the result of negligent workmanship or defective materials or both. Junior Books Limited sought to recover the cost of making good the defective floors and, in addition, pecuniary loss arising out of the removal of machinery so that repairs could be effected. There was no suggestion that the defective floors constituted a risk to persons or property and the only economic loss which had arisen was in the context of disturbance of normal operations by the necessary remedial work. By a majority, the House of Lords decided that there was no reason in logic why 'damage to the pocket' should be rejected as an item of claim while pecuniary loss coupled with physical damage should be allowed.

10B. Breach of statutory duty

Akin to, but distinct from, the tort of negligence, is breach of statutory duty. The two main categories under which liability may arise are employers' liability and occupiers' liability.

10B1. Employers' liability

An employer (master) has a common law duty towards his employees (servants) to provide:
— competent fellow-servants;
— safe and adequate equipment;
— a safe system of work;
— a safe place of work and access to that place.

These duties are simply a specific application of the general law of negligence. Thus, to succeed in a common law action for negligence, an employee would have to show that his employer was negligent in not providing safe and adequate equipment etc., and that damage had been caused as a result of that failure.

In practice, the common law action is rarely brought alone in respect of injuries at work sustained by an employee, as it is generally easier to succeed by bringing an action for breach of statutory duty, so that commonly actions are brought for negligence and/or breach of statutory duty.

In some cases, depending on the interpretation of the statutory provision, the employer's duty is strict, and if this is the case the advantage, from the plaintiff's point of view, of the action for breach of statutory duty, as compared with negligence, is that it is necessary only to prove the breach and damage resulting from the breach. For example, it is generally a breach of strict statutory duty to leave a machine in a factory unguarded, and if such a breach occurs, it is easy for the plaintiff to prove, as it is a simple matter of fact; he need not prove that the employer was negligent. In other cases, the employer is liable for breach of statutory duty only if there has been fault on his part, and in such cases an injured employee has much the same burden as he would have in proving negligence at common law.

The distinction is shown by the case of *Millard* v. *Serck Tubes Ltd* (1969). The plaintiff operated a power drill which was inadequately guarded in breach of Section 14 of the Factories Act 1961. While the plaintiff's hand was resting on the guard a piece of swarf thrown out from the drill wound itself around his hand and drew it into the drill, causing him injury. The defendants argued that they were not liable because, although they were in breach of statutory duty, the accident itself was not foreseeable. It was held that this argument might have succeeded in a common law action for negligence, but could not succeed where the action was for breach of statutory duty: there had been a breach, and the defendants were liable for the consequences, whether reasonably foreseeable or not.

Whether the employer's duty is strict or depends on fault, the defence of contributory negligence on the part of the employee is open to him.

10B2. Occupiers' liability

Until 1957, the liability of the occupier of premises towards people who entered his premises was governed by common law rules, but these had become so complicated that Parliament intervened by passing the Occupiers' Liability Act 1957 which has made the law comparatively simple. The Act lays down that an occupier owes to all visitors to his premises (that is, all persons except trespassers who enter his premises) a common duty of care, with the exception that where people enter the premises under the terms of a contract, the contract may modify the duty. For this purpose premises include land and buildings and also 'any fixed or moveable structure, including any vessel, vehicles or aircraft'.

The common duty of care is defined in the Act as '. . . a duty to take such care as in all the circumstances of the case is reasonable to see that the visitor will be reasonably safe in using the premises for the purposes for which he is invited or permitted by the occupier to be there'. The Act also specifically provides that an occupier must be prepared for children to be less careful than adults. For example a gap in a fence leading to a railway may constitute a warning of danger to an adult, but can be expected to be an attraction to a child.

On the other hand, the Act provides that 'an occupier may expect that a person in the exercise of his calling will appreciate and guard against any special risks ordinarily incident to it so far as the occupier leaves him free to do so'. So, for example, if an electrician is called in to repair defective electrical wiring, he knows of the defect and is expected to take all necessary precautions.

An occupier can contract out of his duty of care to those who enter his premises under the terms of a contract, subject to the provisions of the Unfair Contract Terms Act 1977. Under this Act, *inter alia*, he cannot exclude or restrict his liability for death or personal injury, and any other conditions which he imposes are subject to a test of reasonableness.

The significance of warning notices has been the subject of much litigation in the past. The Act attempts to clarify the position by providing that an occupier discharges his duty by a mere warning of danger only if that by itself enables the visitor to be reasonably safe. So, a notice on a railway platform exhorting passengers to 'mind the gap' is adequate only if a person can reasonably take precautions to 'mind the gap' and be safe in so doing.

An occupier is not liable for the negligence of an independent contractor provided that he has taken reasonable steps to satisfy himself that the contractor is reasonably competent and that the work has been competently executed.

The common duty of care laid down by the Act does not apply to trespassers, but this does not mean that an occupier owes no duty at all to trespassers. The leading modern case on this point is *British Railways Board* v. *Herrington* (1972). Alongside a railway in an area where children were accustomed to play was a fence which at one point was only ten inches high. A child climbed over the fence at this point, came into contact with a live electrified rail, and was severely injured. It was held that although the child was a trespasser, he was entitled to succeed in his action.

Among the points made in judgment were the following:

— An occupier does not owe any duty to a trespasser unless his presence is either known or ought reasonably to have been anticipated.

— If the presence of the trespasser is known or ought reasonably to have been anticipated, some duty towards him is owed.

— The duty owed towards him is not the common duty of care, but merely 'a lower and less onerous duty, which has been described as a duty to treat him with ordinary humanity'.

— The occupier must take reasonable steps to carry out his duty of ordinary humanity, but what is reasonable depends on the circumstances of the occupier: 'An impecunious occupier with little assistance at hand would often be excused from doing something which a large organisation with ample staff would be expected to do'.

— An occupier need not go to great lengths to seek out dangers against which trespassers should be protected. He has no obligation to 'make his land fit for trespassers to trespass in'. It remains the general rule that he who trespasses does so at his peril.

It should perhaps be added that *Herrington* was decided on its own facts, particularly the fact that the trespasser was a child. It is unlikely that the plaintiff would have succeeded had he been an adult. In *Penny* v. *Northampton Borough Council* (1974), however, it was held that the defendants were not liable to a child trespasser. In this case there was a discarded rubbish tip some 50 acres in area, and children had often been warned off by Council workmen. Nevertheless a child was injured by the explosion of an aerosol can which had been thrown on to a fire by another child. The court decided that the authority had behaved with common sense and humanity and could not reasonably be expected to know of the danger on its land. It must also be noted that an occupier is entitled to expect that very young children will be accompanied by adults, so that, for example, in *Phipps* v. *Rochester Corporation* (1955) the defendants were not liable where the plaintiff, a child aged five accompanied only by his sister aged seven, fell into a hole and broke his leg.

10C. Nuisance

Although in some ways having a superficial resemblance to negligence, the tort of nuisance is a quite separate and much older tort. It developed several hundred years ago, compared with negligence's emergence only in the nineteenth century. Nuisances may be either public or private.

A public nuisance is a carrying on of an activity which is likely to cause inconvenience or annoyance to the public or a section of the public, or interference with a right common to all. Thus, it is a public nuisance for an abattoir to release unpleasant smells, and it is equally a public nuisance to block or seriously restrict the passage of a highway, or for a dance-hall to create excessive noise at unreasonable hours.

In general, public nuisances are crimes, but if a person, as the result of a public nuisance, suffers special damage over and above that suffered by the public he may have an action for damages for private nuisance. In *Attorney-General* v. *Gastonia Coaches* (1976) coach operators owned 22 coaches, 16 of which were parked in roads adjoining their offices in such a way that they interfered with the free passage of other traffic. It was held that the coaches constituted a public nuisance, and that damages would be awarded to residents who had suffered from the emission of exhaust gases, excessive noise and obstruction of drives.

A private nuisance exists when a person's right to the use and enjoyment of his land is interfered with. This interference must consist of damage to the land itself or to things on the land, or personal inconvenience, discomfort, or even personal injury to the occupier. Noise and vibration are common instances, but, for example, it is also nuisance if the roots of trees in the garden of the defendant spread and damage the foundations of the plaintiff's property. It is to be noted that negligence is not an essential element of nuisance, and it is therefore no defence that the defendant has taken all necessary care.

The interference must usually be a state of affairs, and not merely an isolated act. This can be shown by a comparison of the following two cases. In *Castle* v. *St. Augustine's Links* (1922) a taxi-driver was injured when a golf ball was sliced from a tee on the defendant's course. It was held that he was entitled to succeed in an action for nuisance, because there was evidence to show that it was a common occurrence for balls to be hit on to the highway, and therefore the tee was a continuing nuisance. In *Bolton* v. *Stone* (1950), however, a woman on a public highway alongside a cricket ground was injured when a batsman hit a cricket ball out of the ground. It was held that she was not entitled to succeed as it was a very rare occurrence for a ball to be hit out of the ground, and it was not therefore something against which the defendants should have guarded.

In some circumstances, an act may constitute a nuisance although it is only temporary. In *British Celanese Ltd* v. *A. H. Hunt (Capacitors) Ltd* (1969) the defendants allowed metal foil to escape from their land and to foul the bus bars of over-head electric cables, with the result that the plaintiffs lost power and their machines were clogged up and time and materials were wasted. It was held that the defendants were liable in nuisance, that an isolated happening could create a nuisance, and that the plaintiffs were directly and foreseeably affected.

Fire, or the danger of it, is something which commonly constitutes a nuisance. For example, in *Spicer* v. *Smee* (1946) defective electrical wiring in the defendant's prem-ises caused a fire which destroyed the plaintiff's bungalow. The defendant was held liable because, although the fire could be looked upon as an isolated incident, the defec-tive electrical wiring had been a continuing source of danger.

The interference must be unreasonable. What is reasonable depends on the circumstances of each case. In *Christie* v. *Davie* (1893) the plaintiff, the owner of a semi-detached house, and her daughter gave piano, violin and singing lessons in the house, practised music and singing themselves, and held occasional musical evenings. The defendant, their neighbour, retaliated by playing concertinas, horns, flutes and pianos, blowing whistles, banging on trays and boards and shrieking and shouting in order to annoy the plaintiff. It was held that the plaintiff was not making an unreasonable use of the house, and that her neighbour would be restrained from carrying on his annoying activities. The nature of a particular locality may be relevant in deciding whether some-thing constitutes a nuisance. It has been said that 'what would be a nuisance in Belgrave Square would not necessarily be so in Bermondsey'. This means, for example, that opening a fish-and-chip shop in a quiet, completely residential area would con-stitute a nuisance, whereas it would not if it were opened in an area where there were already a large number of shops.

The fact that an alleged nuisance serves a useful purpose, or that it confers a benefit on the public is, however, no defence. In *Denton* v. *Dover District Council* (1977) the Council provided a play area at the rear of the plaintiff's hotel for the use of local children. The children caused noise and inconvenience. It was held that the play area constituted a nuisance, and the plaintiff was awarded damages and an injunction that the play area should be open only between 10.00 am and 6.30 pm, and then only to children under 12 years of age.

The law of nuisance provides for a good deal of 'give and take'; everybody from time to time acts in such a way as may cause inconvenience to his neighbour, but where the conduct is likely to be reciprocal no action for nuisance will lie. For example, it is a common practice for people to light fires in their gardens to dispose of waste, and provided that this practice is kept within reason and the fire is not likely to spread, a neighbour cannot object as he is entitled to do the same.

It is only a person who has an interest in the land affected who may have a right to bring an action for private nuisance. He will normally be the occupier at the relevant time, or he may be a reversioner. (A reversioner is a person who is not in possession at a particular time, but has a right to possession at some time in the future, such as a landlord who will be entitled to possession of land when a lease comes to an end.)

It has been held that not even the wife of an occupier can bring an action for nuisance, although in many cases, depending on the exact circumstances, she may on the same facts be able to bring an action for negligence.

In *Malone* v. *Laskey* (1907) the wife of a tenant of property was injured when a bracket on a lavatory cistern fell on her. She sued the defendant, who leased the property, in nuisance, but it was held that she had no remedy as she had no interest in the land.

A person can be sued in nuisance if he has created the nuisance, or if it is caused by neglect of a specific duty on his part, if he has continued an already existing nuisance, or if he is the landlord of the person in possession.

A person creates a nuisance if it arises from his own act, as where he continually operates machinery which causes vibrations.

The most common case of neglect of a specific duty is where a landlord fails to carry out his contractual obligations to repair premises, and a person is injured as a result of such failure.

Where a person occupies land on which a nuisance already exists, he must take all reasonable steps to remove it as soon as he knows, or ought reasonably to know, of it. Thus, in *Sedleigh-Denfield* v. *O'Callaghan* (1940) there was a ditch on the defendant's land which trespassers replaced with a pipe. The defendant did not know of this at the time but later discovered it and did nothing about it. The pipe was defective and during a storm became obstructed, so that water overflowed on to the plaintiff's land causing damage. The defendant was held liable for the damage because, although he had not created the nuisance, he knew of it and had taken no steps to remedy it.

A landlord is liable if he permits a tenant to commit a nuisance (in which case landlord and tenant are joint tortfeasors), or if he lets premises in the knowledge that a nuisance originates from them.

Nuisance is not actionable *per se*; the plaintiff must show that he has suffered some injury, damage or discomfort.

The general defences mentioned in chapter 9 apply to nuisance, but there is also the special defence of prescription. Under the Prescription Act 1832 an occupier acquires a right to continue a nuisance after it has been in existence openly and continuously for a period of twenty years. The right is not acquired, however, unless an actionable nuisance has existed for the full period.

For example, in *Sturges* v. *Bridgman* (1879) the defendant had used noisy machinery in his premises for more than twenty years. After that period the plaintiff, a doctor, built a consulting room on adjoining land and found that the noise of the machinery seriously interfered with his use of the room. It was held that he was entitled to succeed in an action for nuisance; the defendant's plea that he had used the machinery for more than twenty years was not accepted, as the noise had not created an actionable nuisance before the consulting room had been built.

Damages or an injunction, or both, are the usual remedies for nuisance, but there is also the special remedy of abatement. An occupier of land is entitled to take steps to abate a nuisance, that is, to remove its cause by, for example, cutting the roots or branches of a neighbour's tree which encroach upon his property. In some circumstances he is even entitled to enter his neighbour's land to abate a nuisance, as for example, in the case of a fire on his neighbour's land which threatens to spread and cause damage to his own property. An abatement must not involve any unnecessary damage, and prior notice of entry on another's land must be given, except in the case of emergency.

The right to 'ancient lights' does not strictly fall under the heading of nuisance, but it is convenient to deal with it here. A person who has, for upwards of twenty years, enjoyed the benefit of daylight coming from his neighbour's land, has the right not to have that benefit substantially interfered with. The neighbour is not prohibited from building on his land, but if he does he must not reduce the light to any significant extent; the extent to which he may reduce the amount of light is a question of reasonableness, to be determined on the facts of each particular case.

10D. Strict liability

It has been seen that the law of negligence is based on fault. There are, however, cases where liability is strict, that is, where a person may be liable even although he has been in no way at fault. But even where liability is strict, as will be seen later, the defendant has certain defences open to him.

10D1. The rule in Rylands v. Fletcher

By far the most important area of strict liability is that covered by what is known as the rule in *Rylands* v. *Fletcher* (1868). In that case, the plaintiff's coalmine was flooded. The cause of the disaster was that the defendant had caused a reservoir to be constructed to supply water to his mill. In the course of the work, the contractor employed by the defendant had come across shafts under the land. They were part of old mine workings which had been abandoned several years before. After the work was completed, one of the shafts gave way and water burst through into the old workings. Through them it flooded into the plaintiff's colliery. The defendant was personally unaware of the existence of the old workings beneath his reservoir, and when the plaintiff sued him for damages there arose the argument that in law a man should not be held liable for consequences which he could not reasonably foresee. Counsel for the defendant maintained that, as his client had not been proved negligent in the way he had caused the reservoir to be constructed, and as no reasonable person could have foreseen the damage which resulted, he could not be held liable. Against this, counsel for the plaintiff relied on the law relating to the detention of wild animals. In *May* v. *Burdett* (1846) it had been ruled that 'a person who keeps a wild animal, with knowledge of its propensities, is bound to keep it secure at his peril', and he argued that an artificial accumulation of water came into the same category as 'mischievous animals'.

It was held that the defendant was liable. In giving judgment, Blackburn L.J. expressed the law in this way: 'We think that the true rule of law is that a person who for his own purposes brings on to his land and collects and keeps there anything likely to cause mischief if it escapes, must keep it in at his peril, and if he does not do so, is *prima facie* answerable for all the damage which is the natural consequences of its escape.' This is what has since become known as the rule in *Rylands* v. *Fletcher*.

The amplification of the rule in the judgment of Blackburn L.J. is also of importance. He said: 'He (the defendant) can excuse himself by showing that the escape was owing to the plaintiff's default; or perhaps that the escape was the consequence of *vis major*, or the Act of God; but as nothing of this sort exists here, it is unnecessary to enquire what excuse would be sufficient. The general rule, as above stated, seems on principle just.'

Before *Rylands* v. *Fletcher*, there had been liability in certain specified cases, for example, for the escape of fire or cattle, but the rule extended liability to cover mischievous or dangerous things generally. Furthermore, it established that the occupier of land from which such things escape is liable not only for his own acts and those of his servants, but also for the acts of his independent contractor.

It is not, however, sufficient that the defendant has dangerous things on his land. The rule does not apply unless there is also an escape. So, in *Read* v. *Lyons & Co. Ltd* (1947) the plaintiff was an inspector in the defendants' munitions factory and was injured by the explosion of a shell within the factory in the course of her employment. Unquestionably, high-explosive shells are dangerous things, but it was held that the defendants were not liable because there had been no escape from their premises. Escape for the purposes of the rule was defined as 'escape from a place where the defendant has occupation or control over land to a place which is outside his occupation or control'.

Although recent cases indicate that the matter is not entirely free from doubt, the better opinion appears to be that the rule extends to both damage to property and personal injury, and that it is irrelevant whether or not the plaintiff has a proprietary interest in the land to which the dangerous thing escapes.

For liability under the rule to arise, there must be 'non-natural' user of the land. In *Rylands* v. *Fletcher* itself, the defendant had brought the water on to his land, but the rule would not have applied if the escape of water had been from, say, a natural lake on his land: something must have been brought on to the land which was not naturally there. 'Non-natural user' was defined in *Rickards* v. *Lothian* (1913) as 'some special use bringing with it increased danger to others and must not merely be the ordinary use of the land or such a use as is proper for the general benefit of the community.' This definition restricts the scope of the rule considerably: for example, a cricket ball is potentially dangerous if it is hit out of a cricket ground, and is not 'naturally' on land, but in the absence of negligence or nuisance the proprietors of a cricket ground are not liable for the escape of a ball, as the use of a ground for cricket has been held to be for the general benefit of the community.

The following have been held to be natural user and so outside the scope of the rule:
(*a*) water installed in residential premises;
(*b*) a fire in a domestic grate;
(*c*) electrical wiring and gas pipes in houses and shops;
(*d*) the erection or demolition of houses; and
(*e*) the generating of steam in a steamship.

On the other hand, the following have been held to be non-natural and so within the scope of the rule:
(*a*) storage of industrial water under pressure;
(*b*) storage of gas and electricity in bulk;
(*c*) the keeping in a garage of a car with petrol in its tank; and
(*d*) the keeping of a motor-coach in a car park, although there was no fuel in its tank.

Apart altogether from the question of user of land, difficulty arises in determining what things are 'mischievous' or 'dangerous', as the distinction is one of degree rather than of kind. Water, for example, which was the substance in issue in *Rylands* v. *Fletcher,* is not usually considered to be dangerous, but may be so in certain circumstances. A gun, on the other hand, is usually considered to be dangerous, but this is not the case if it is not loaded. The test which must be applied is whether, in the circumstances of the particular case, the 'thing' in question is likely to do damage if it escapes. In a number of cases, there have been references to 'things dangerous in themselves', but this is of little help in determining liability: a bull, for example, is likely to do damage if it escapes, but not because it is dangerous in itself, as it will do no harm if it is kept under proper control so that it cannot escape.

Although liability under the rule in *Rylands* v. *Fletcher* is strict, there are a number of defences available:

Consent. When the plaintiff, either expressly or by implication, consents to the presence of the danger, there is a valid defence. This defence is a particular application of the general defence of *volenti non fit injuria*. Where there is express consent, no problem arises, but it is not always easy to say whether there has been implied consent. Where a number of persons occupy the same building, for example, it is assumed that they consent to the use of water by the others, so that there is no liability under the rule if water escapes from an upper floor and causes damage to property on lower floors. Where persons occupy adjoining premises, however, the position is less clear. It has been held that the rule does not apply where the respective occupiers are landlord and tenant, but it is not certain whether it applies if the landlord/tenant relationship does not exist.

Common benefit. A similar defence is that of common benefit, that is, that the danger is maintained for the common benefit of both the plaintiff and the defendant. For example, in *Peters* v. *Prince of Wales Theatres (Birmingham) Ltd* (1943) the plaintiff was the tenant of a shop in a building which was otherwise occupied as a theatre, and which was protected by a sprinkler installation. Water escaped from the sprinkler system in the theatre and spread to the plaintiff's shop, where it damaged his stock. It was held that the defendant was not liable for the damage under the rule in *Rylands* v. *Fletcher,* as the sprinkler system had been installed for the common benefit of the plaintiff and the defendants. (On the facts, it was also held that the defendant had not been negligent.)

Act of a stranger. The rule does not apply when the damage has been done by the act of a stranger. In *Rickards* v. *Lothian* (1913), for example, a third party deliberately blocked the waste pipe in the lavatory on the defendant's premises, as a result of which the plaintiff's premises were flooded. It was held that the defendant was not liable. In the present context, a person is not a stranger to the defendant if he is a servant acting in the course of his employment; an independent contractor acting in the normal course of his business; or a member of the defendant's family.

If the act of the stranger could have been anticipated or its consequences prevented, the defendant will be liable. In *Northwestern Utilities Ltd* v. *London Guarantee and Accident Co. Ltd* (1936) a gas main owned by the defendants was fractured during the construction by a third party of a storm sewer, and gas percolated beneath the plaintiff's hotel; the gas ignited and the hotel was destroyed. It was held that, notwithstanding the fact that the damage was caused in the course of work carried out by a third party, the defendants were liable, as they knew of the construction of the sewer and ought to have anticipated and guarded against the possibility that their mains would be damaged in the course of the work.

Statutory authority. Statutory authority may or may not be a defence to an action brought under the rule in *Rylands* v. *Fletcher*: it is a question in all cases of the particular statute. In general, if the defendant is under a statutory obligation to perform a particular act, he is not, unless the statute otherwise provides, liable for any consequence which may result. But if he has merely statutory permission, rather than an obligation, to perform the act, then the defence of statutory authority is not available to him.

Act of God. The defence of Act of God has been considered in chapter 9.

Act or default of the plaintiff. The rule does not apply when the damage has been caused by the act or default of the plaintiff himself. If he knows of the danger, he should take reasonable steps to see that it does not occur. For example, in *Ponting* v. *Noakes* (1894) the plaintiff's horse died when it reached over the boundary of the defendant's land and ate some leaves from a poisonous tree. It was held that the defendant was not liable, as the horse ought not to have been allowed to encroach on the defendant's land.

10D2. Dangerous chattels
Before the decision in *Donoghue* v. *Stevenson* (1932) there was no recognised general duty of care with regard to chattels, but a duty existed in respect of a chattel which was in a category recognised by law as dangerous, or which was dangerous for some reason known to the defendant. In *Dominion Natural Gas Co.* v. *Collins & Perkins* (1909) Lord Dunedin said: 'It has . . . again and again been said that in the case of articles dangerous in themselves, such as loaded firearms, poisons, explosives, and other things *ejusdem generis,* there is a peculiar duty to take precaution imposed upon those who send forth or instal such articles when it is necessarily the case that other parties will come within their proximity.'

However, as has been seen in discussing the rule in *Rylands* v. *Fletcher,* the concept of things which are dangerous in themselves has never been satisfactory, and *Donoghue* v. *Stevenson* laid down the rule that a person may be liable in respect of a thing (in that case a bottle of ginger beer) which could not be said to be dangerous in itself. It is now more true to say, not that there is liability in respect of things dangerous in themselves (with no liability in respect of things which are not dangerous), but that the more dangerous a chattel is, the greater is the degree of care which should be exercised in respect of it.

Liability in respect of chattels may arise either in contract or in tort, and in contract particularly under certain sections of the Sale of Goods Act 1979. It may here be noted that, if goods do not comply with certain implied undertakings under the Act, the seller is liable to the buyer notwithstanding that he has taken all possible care and is in no way to blame for the defect. Furthermore, the seller's duties are made more onerous by the terms of the Unfair Contract Terms Act 1977, which severely restricts the seller's ability to contract out of his liability under the Sale of Goods Act. Although, therefore, the buyer has a right of action in tort against the seller as well as a right in contract, the right in tort is of very little practical importance, as he is better protected by his right under contract, where liability is strict.

Where there is no contractual link between the plaintiff and the defendant, however, the plaintiff must rely on his right in tort as laid down in *Donoghue* v. *Stevenson*. This case clearly laid down that a consumer who is not in contractual relationship with the defendant may have a right of action, and such right is not dependent on any special rule regarding dangerous chattels. *Donoghue* v. *Stevenson* was concerned with the liability of a manufacturer to the ultimate consumer, but later cases show that liability may also fall on persons such as repairers, fitters, erectors and assemblers who may create a danger, and persons such as second-hand car dealers who, although they may not have created a danger, know that there are potential dangers in the products which they sell, and are under a duty of care to the buyer. As McNair J. said in *Andrews* v. *Hopkinson* (1957): 'Having regard to the extreme peril involved in allowing an old car with a defective steering mechanism to be used on the road, I have no hesitation in holding that the defendant was guilty of negligence in failing to make the necessary examination, or at least in failing to warn the plaintiff that no such examination had been carried out.'

A supplier, however, need only do what is reasonable by way of checking the possibility of defects. A grocer, for example, has generally no means of knowing of defects in tinned goods which he sells, provided that he is satisfied that they have been supplied to him by a reputable supplier. Neither will it necessarily be assumed that a supplier is liable for injury or damage caused by something which he has supplied: it must be shown that he has in some way been at fault.

10E. Trespass to land

Trespass to land is an unlawful interference with another person's possession of land; it differs from nuisance in that it involves direct rather than indirect interference. It may be committed by unlawfully, albeit perhaps innocently, entering the land; or by abusing a right of entry; or by remaining on the land after authority to be there has expired or has been withdrawn. Motive is immaterial, and so the defendant is liable even if he thinks that he has a right of entry or does not know that he has been trespassing. Trespass to land is one of the torts which are actionable *per se* but if no damage has been done the plaintiff will receive only nominal damages.

Trespass to land is not usually a crime, and therefore the familiar notice 'Trespassers will be prosecuted' generally has no legal significance; an aggrieved landowner's right is limited to the bringing of civil proceedings. There are, however, certain exceptions where trespass is made a criminal offence by a statute or by bye-laws issued under the authority of a statute. It is, for example, an offence for unauthorised persons to go on to land owned by British Rail.

A rather special form of trespass to land is trespass *ab initio*, which occurs when a person lawfully enters land but while there performs some unlawful act; he is then considered to have been a trespasser from the moment he entered the land. The unlawful act must have been something positive and not a mere omission. Thus, in the *Six Carpenters' Case* (1610) six carpenters entered an inn and consumed some bread and wine for which they refused to pay. It was held that they were not trespassers *ab initio*, as their refusal to pay was an omission rather than a positive act.

The occupier of land has rights, not only to the land itself, but also to the subsoil and the airspace above. Thus, it is trespass to excavate material from below land belonging to another, and also to erect an advertising sign in such a way that it projects above the land belonging to another. At common law an aircraft flying over land would be committing trespass, but the Civil Aviation Act 1949 provides that no action shall lie in respect of trespass or nuisance for flights over any property at a reasonable height. On the other hand, the aircraft owner is liable for all damage caused by it, or by anything falling from it, while it is taking off, flying or landing. This liability is strict; it is not necessary to show that the owner acted intentionally or negligently.

In addition to the general remedies in tort, the following remedies are also available in respect of trespass to land:

— Mesne profits. Where a person has been prevented from enjoying possession of his land, he may bring an action for 'mesne profits' to recover his loss.

— Recovery of land. A person wrongfully dispossessed of land may bring an action for its recovery. If he is successful, and the defendant refuses to hand over possession, the defendant may be forcibly removed by officers of the court.

— Ejection of a trespasser. Where a trespasser has peaceably entered land, the person in possession may ask him to leave and give a reasonable time to go. If he refuses to go, the person in possession may forcibly eject him, but he must use no more force than is reasonably necessary.

—Forcible entry. A person who has been wrongfully dispossessed of his land is entitled to use force to regain possession and eject the trespasser, but again he must use no more force than is reasonably necessary. In respect of tenants of private houses who remain in possession after the expiry of a lease, however, a landlord can regain possession only by means of court proceedings.

The following are special defences to an action for trespass to land:

—that the entry was legally justified, for example, where bailiffs, acting in accordance with a court order, enter land for the purpose of seizing goods. The law on this matter has been considerably extended in recent years, culminating with the case of *Chic Fashions (West Wales)* v. *Jones* (1968). In that case, the police had a warrant to search the plaintiff's premises for particular goods, which it was suspected might be on the premises and which had been stolen. The goods were not in fact on the premises, but the police seized other goods which they suspected had been stolen. The plaintiffs sued the police for trespass to land, but it was held that the police were not liable. Although the police had a warrant only in respect of certain goods, they could also seize other goods which they reasonably suspected had been stolen. The justification for this decision was stated by Lord Denning to be that 'in these present times, with the ever-increasing wickedness there is about, honest citizens must help the police and not hinder them in their efforts to track down criminals'. This may be so, but it comes near to giving the police unfettered powers to enter people's business and domestic premises;

—that neither the person in possession nor the alleged trespasser had a good title to the land; this is known as the defence of *jus tertii*. Thus, if A is in actual possession of land but has no legal right to be there, and he is ejected by B, who also has no legal title, A has no legal right of action against B, although the person having the legal title will of course have such a right;

—that the alleged trespasser is a licensee. A licensee is somebody who cannot be described as an occupier but who has a legal right, contractual or otherwise, to enter land or premises. Examples are persons holding tickets for a particular theatre performance, or potential customers in a shop. A licensee must leave the land or premises when the licence has terminated, for example, within a reasonable time after a theatre performance has finished.

10F. Wrongful interference with goods

Until 1977 there were three main torts which prohibited interference with the goods of another – conversion, trespass to goods, and detinue. The Torts (Interference with Goods) Act 1977 abolished the action of detinue, and thus only conversion and trespass to goods need to be dealt with.

10F1. Conversion

Conversion consists of any unauthorised dealing with the goods or chattels of another which amounts to a denial of the owner's title, or is inconsistent with his rights to immediate possession of them. Examples of conversion of goods include wrongful taking of goods with the intention of exercising rights of ownership over them, wrongful detention of goods in defiance of the plaintiff's rights, wrongful delivery, wrongful disposition, and wrongful destruction. Conversion may, but does not always, amount to a crime as well as a tort.

It is not necessary to show that the defendant had any wrongful motive in acting as he did; provided that his action amounted to a denial of the plaintiff's title, he is liable. For example, in *Hollins* v. *Fowler* (1875) a cotton broker innocently purchased cotton from a person who had fraudulently obtained possession of it from the plaintiff and later sold it to a manufacturer, receiving a commission on the transaction. It was held that the broker was liable to the true owner, the plaintiff, for the full value of the cotton. In such a case, however, the innocent purchaser has a right of action against the person who sold the goods to him to be indemnified against his loss and expenses. Where the vendor has acted fraudulently it is likely that he cannot be traced and the right is therefore worthless, but if there has been a chain of sales and purchases it may be possible to refer a particular claim back to some other vendor.

There have been several cases dealing with the rights and obligations of a person who finds goods. The true owner of the goods is always entitled to recover them, but if the true owner cannot be traced, the general rule is that the finder is entitled as against any other person. For example, in *Armory* v. *Delamirie* (1721) a boy chimney-sweep found a jewel and offered it for valuation to a jeweller, who refused to return it to him. It was held that, in the absence of any knowledge as to who the true owner was, the boy was entitled to the jewel.

There is, however, an exception to this rule based on the principle that possession of land carries with it possession of everything attached to or under the land. This is illustrated by *South Staffordshire Water Co.* v. *Sharman* (1896) where workmen employed to clear a pond found two gold rings at the bottom of the pond. It was held that the owners of the pond, and not the workmen, were entitled to them.

This does not mean, however, that the owner is always entitled as against the finder, as the owner may not have possession. In *Hannah* v. *Peel* (1945) the defendant owned, but had never occupied, a house. The plaintiff, while living in the house, found a brooch which he handed to the police. The owner was never traced, and the brooch was eventually handed back to the defendant, who sold it for £66. The plaintiff sued for the brooch or its value, and it was held that he was entitled to do so, as the defendant had not been in possession of the house and had no knowledge of the brooch until the plaintiff found it.

In some cases statutory regulations or by-laws deal with the procedure for dealing with lost property; for example, a passenger who finds property on a bus must hand it to the conductor and is not entitled to the property if the owner is not traced nor to any reward for finding it. Similarly, the conductor is not entitled to retain the property nor to receive any reward.

10F2. Trespass to goods

Trespass to goods consists of any unlawful act of direct physical interference with a chattel which is in the possession of another person. An action for trespass to goods is nowadays rare, for what constitutes a trespass to goods usually also constitutes a conversion.

Although, generally, only conversion and trespass to goods are treated in textbooks under the heading of unlawful interference with goods, there are also other torts in part concerned with interference with goods. Examples are negligence and nuisance.

10G. Trespass to the person

Trespass to the person usually takes the form of an assault and battery, which is also a crime. Although assault and battery are usually spoken of together, it is possible for there to be assault without battery and *vice versa*.

An assault is merely an attempt or threat to do bodily harm to another in such a way that the other reasonably fears that the harm will be done. Thus, the mere brandishing of a knife may by itself constitute an assault. Battery consists of the actual infliction of harm on another. So to brandish a knife is an assault, and then to stab another person with it is a battery. To brandish the knife and then put it away is an assault without a battery; to stab a person in the back is a battery without an assault. If people assent to be assaulted and battered in a legal 'sport' such as a boxing-match under Queensberry rules, no right of action, either civil or criminal arises; but the law stops short of allowing such activities as prize-fighting.

Trespass to the person was until 1959 always considered to be actionable *per se*, but in *Fowler* v. *Lanning* (1959) A unintentionally shot B, and the court held that B could not recover damages unless he could prove that A had acted intentionally or negligently. Later cases suggest that if there is intent rather than negligence, an action for trespass to the person will lie, and nominal damages can be claimed even though no harm has been suffered; but if negligence is alleged, the case must be treated as in the tort of negligence, and damages can be claimed only if it can be shown that harm has been suffered.

10H. False imprisonment

Where one person physically restricts the freedom of another he is liable for the tort of false (which in this context means unlawful) imprisonment. Imprisonment does not in this context have its usual meaning; if the defendant, without lawful excuse, completely restricts the physical freedom of the plaintiff, for example by confining him to his house, he is liable for false imprisonment. But the restriction must be complete. If a line of pickets prevents a worker from entering a factory they are not liable for false imprisonment; the worker is still at liberty to go anywhere he wants to go – except into the factory.

In the normal case assault accompanies false imprisonment and two distinct rights of action arise. But there may be false imprisonment without assault, as where A locks the door of a room in which he knows B to be and there is no escape route.

The right to bring an action for false imprisonment is useful once the incarceration has ceased, but does not directly help a person during his confinement, or guarantee that he will in fact be freed. It is for this reason that the writ of *habeas corpus* is so important; it is the only means by which a person, acting on behalf of another who has been unlawfully detained, can enlist the services of the court to ensure the release of the person detained.

Closely associated with false imprisonment is the question of powers of arrest. This is a complicated topic, but two points may be made. The first is that where an 'arrestable offence' as defined by the Criminal Law Act 1967 has been committed (in broad terms an arrestable offence is one carrying a maximum penalty of five years' imprisonment or more), anybody may arrest a person caught in the act of committing the offence or a person who may reasonably be suspected of having committed the offence. The person making the arrest is usually a policeman.

The second is that any person, in this case invariably a policeman, who has a lawful warrant usually issued and signed by a magistrate may arrest the person named in the warrant.

There are two special defences to an action for false imprisonment:

Firstly, that the defendant has been acting in self-defence. For example, a person is entitled to lock an intruder in a room if he has reasonable grounds for fearing that the intruder intends to cause him personal injury or to interfere with his property.

Secondly, that the defendant is a parent or schoolteacher, to whom English law gives the right to detain a child by way of punishment, for example, by locking him in his bedroom. It is to be presumed, in the absence of any authority on the matter, that the length of detention must be reasonable.

10I. Defamation

The tort of defamation includes both libel and slander. Libel consists of publishing to a third party, without lawful excuse, an untrue and defamatory statement regarding the plaintiff, by means of printing, writing, painting or sculpting, public broadcasting (either radio or television) or other permanent means. A slander is a similar statement by word of mouth (not broadcast), gesture, or other transient means. The speaking of defamatory words in the course of the performance of a play is, by the Theatres Act 1968, deemed to be libel rather than slander. Whether a defamatory statement on a gramophone record is libel or slander is open to doubt, but it is probably libel. It has been held that the sound track of a film can be libel.

A statement is defamatory if it exposes the plaintiff to hatred, ridicule, or contempt so that his reputation suffers, or if it prejudices him in his office, profession, or trade. Generally, the statement concerned is defamatory in its ordinary and natural meaning, but it is open to the plaintiff to show that what is an apparently harmless statement is, in the particular circumstances in which, or among the persons to whom, it was published, in fact defamatory; this is what is known as proving the innuendo. For example, in *Tolley* v. *J. S. Fry and Sons Ltd* (1931) the defendants published, by way of an advertisement, a caricature of the plaintiff and words which made it appear that he was extolling the virtues of their chocolate. The plaintiff was an amateur golfer, who argued that the advertisement had a secondary meaning, namely, that he had accepted money to lend his name to the advertisement, in conflict with his amateur status. The court accepted that such an innuendo did exist, and the plaintiff was awarded damages. It may be noted that the innuendo must be untrue; if it is true the defendant is not liable.

Insults or abuse are not defamatory; they may hurt a person's feelings but not his reputation.

In general, a statement which is true cannot be defamatory; to say that a man has been in prison for seven years is not defamatory if in fact that has been the case. And if the reviewer of a play condemns it and says: 'It will no doubt flop like the author's last three flops', the statement will not be deemed defamatory if the court decides that the author's three previous plays could justifiably be called 'flops', but if the court is not satisfied that they were failures the statement would be defamatory.

It is not possible to defame a class of people. 'All politicians are liars' is vulgar abuse but not defamation.

In *Schloimovitz* v. *Clarendon Press* (1973) the plaintiff claimed that the definition of the word 'Jew' in three dictionaries published by the defendants was defamatory. It was held that the question of whether the definition was correct did not arise. The word 'Jews' related to a group of people, and the plaintiff had no cause of action simply because he was a member of that group: he could bring an action only if he could show that the definition referred to him personally.

There are three main differences between libel and slander:

— a libel is in a permanent form, whereas a slander is in a transient form;

— a libel is actionable *per se*, that is, it is not necessary to show that any damage has been suffered, but, except in four cases (see below) the plaintiff in slander must prove damage;

— a libel may in some circumstances be a crime as well as a tort, but a slander is never a crime. Libel is a crime if it is calculated to cause a breach of the peace.

The four cases in which slander is actionable *per se* are where the slander consists of:

— an accusation of crime punishable with imprisonment;

— an accusation of unchastity or adultery against a woman (but not against a man);

— an accusation that the plaintiff suffers from a contagious or infectious disease, which is likely to make others avoid him socially;

— an imputation against the plaintiff in respect of a business, office, or profession carried on by him at the time of the publication.

In *Lumley* v. *Allday* (1831) it was held that a statement that a man, employed by a gas company as a clerk, associated with prostitutes was not *per se* defamatory, as it cast no reflection on his business, office or profession: a man could associate with prostitutes and still be a good clerk. But the decision would probably have been otherwise if it had been said of a clergyman.

To succeed in an action for defamation, the plaintiff must show that the defamatory statement was published to a third party other than the defendant's spouse (and even handing it to a secretary to be typed constitutes publication) and that the person or persons to whom it was published understood it as referring to the plaintiff. The publication may be intentional or negligent, or indeed quite innocent.

In *Hulton (E) & Co.* v. *Jones* (1910) a newspaper published an article in which derogatory remarks were made about a person referred to as Artemus Jones. The writer of the article contended that he had invented the name, which he thought to be fictitious, but there was in fact a barrister and journalist of that name, and evidence was called to show that there were people who, on reading the article, thought that it referred to him. It was held that the newspaper was liable for the libel.

There is always a presumption that a postcard has been published, that is, that Post Office employees read what is written on postcards, but this does not apply to letters.

The following special defences are available in an action for defamation:

Justification. This defence will succeed if the allegation is substantially true; it is not necessary for the defendant to show that each and every detail was true.

In *Alexander* v. *The North Eastern Railway Co.* (1865) the defendants published a notice saying that the plaintiff had been fined £9. 1s. including costs for refusing to pay the proper fare for a railway journey, with the alternative of three weeks' imprisonment. In fact, the alternative was fourteen days' imprisonment, but it was held that the statement was substantially true, and a plea of justification therefore succeeded.

Under Section 8 of the Rehabilitation of Offenders Act 1974, a plaintiff who can prove that the defendant has maliciously published details of a spent conviction can recover damages, and in that case the defence of justification will not succeed. (The section does not, however, affect the defences of absolute or qualified privilege or fair comment.)

Privilege. A statement made on a privileged occasion is in general not actionable. Privilege may be absolute or qualified; absolute privilege carries with it complete immunity, but statements made in circumstances of qualified privilege are actionable if made with a malicious motive.

Absolute privilege attaches to:

(i)   statements made in judicial proceedings;
(ii) statements made by a member in either House of Parliament;
(iii) communications made between officers of state in the course of their duty;
(iv) communications made between officials of the European Communities in the course of their official duties;
(v)   fair, accurate, and contemporaneous reports in newspapers of judicial proceedings in the United Kingdom, provided that they do not include any blasphemous or indecent matter;
(vi) papers published by order of either House of Parliament;
(vii) any statements made between husband and wife, as such statements are not considered to constitute publication.

There is qualified privilege only 'where the person who makes a communication has an interest or a duty, legal, social or moral, to make it to the person to whom it is made, and the person to whom it is so made has a corresponding interest or duty to receive it. This reciprocity is essential'. (*Adam* v. *Ward* (1917))

Qualified privilege attaches to:

(i)   references given by one employer to another in respect of a former employee;
(ii) communications between solicitor and client;
(iii) fair and accurate reports of the proceedings of either House of Parliament, or of judicial proceedings, even if the report is not contemporaneous;
(iv) reports of public meetings or of local authority meetings in a newspaper;
(v)   reports of foreign judicial proceedings in newspapers;
(vi) statements made in his own defence by a person whose reputation has been attacked in public.

The defence of qualified privilege may be defeated if the plaintiff can show malice on the part of the defendant. Thus, a bad reference by an employer may give rise to an action for defamation if the former employee can show that his employer was actuated by malice in giving the reference, for example, in order to prevent the employee from obtaining a job in which he would compete with his original employer.

Fair comment. It is possible for an opinion to be defamatory, but it is a defence if the defendant can show that his statement was an opinion, not an assertion of fact, that it was substantially fair comment on a matter of public interest, that it was based on facts which were either true or privileged, and that, however strongly expressed, it was not malicious. This defence is often used in connection with comments on the sayings and doings of people in public life, and also in connection with reviews of books and films. A writer, for example, puts himself in the public eye by writing and publishing books, and it is in the public interest that his books should be criticised, but this does not extend to his private life.

Innocent intent. Section 4 of the Defamation Act 1952 provides that where words were not intended to be defamatory, the person who has innocently published them may offer to publish a suitable correction and apology and, as far as practicable, for example, by a notice in a newspaper, to notify persons who have received copies of the defamatory statement. On doing this, he is relieved from liability in an action for damages.

Most cases of defamation are tried by judge and jury. Normally, it is for the jury to decide whether or not a statement is defamatory, but a judge may withdraw a case from the jury if he feels that no reasonable jury could find the statement to be defamatory.

The usual remedies for defamation are damages and possibly an injunction to prevent repetition. Defamation is unusual, however, in that exemplary damages may be awarded where normal damages would still leave the defendant, perhaps the publisher of a book, better off than if he had not published the defamatory matter.

10J. Malicious falsehood

Similar to, but quite distinct from, the tort of defamation, is that of malicious falsehood, which may take a number of forms, and thus is a group of torts rather than a single tort.

The essence of malicious falsehood is that a person makes false, malicious imputations which damage an interest, usually a business interest, of a person without harming his reputation (if his reputation is harmed his redress lies, as has been seen, in an action for defamation). The imputations may be made either in writing or orally.

A good example of malicious falsehood is to be found in *Ratcliffe* v. *Evans* (1892) where the defendant, falsely and maliciously, made a statement in a newspaper to the effect that the plaintiff had closed his business. Only in very exceptional circumstances could such a statement be said to constitute a libel, but clearly it could harm the plaintiff's business interests, and so was held to be a malicious falsehood.

Malice is of the essence of this tort; mere falsehood without more is not a tort. But malice is not synonymous with spite; it signifies any improper intention.

Like libel, but unlike slander, malicious falsehood is actionable *per se.*

Two special forms of malicious falsehood are slander of goods and slander of title.

Slander of goods occurs when the defendant falsely and maliciously denigrates goods manufactured or sold by the plaintiff. This is why manufacturers and retailers have to exercise a degree of care in advertising their wares. To use meaningless phraseology such as 'Brand X washes whiter than white' can incur no penalty, but to state in an advertisement that, say, a drug manufactured by a named competitor is less safe than one's own may be actionable if the competitor can prove the statement to be false and also show that it was intended to harm his business interests.

There is slander of title when the defendant denigrates the plaintiff's title to property. For example, if A were to allege that the only reason why B could sell goods cheaply was that he had evaded payment of customs duty on them, B would have a right of action, assuming that the statement was false and was intended to harm B's business interests.

Appendix A

HOTEL PROPRIETORS ACT 1956

Chapter 62

An Act to amend the law relating to inns and innkeepers (2 August 1956).

Be it enacted by the Queen's most Excellent Majesty, by and with the advice and consent of the Lords Spiritual and Temporal, and Commons, in this present Parliament assembled, and by the authority of the same, as follows:–

Inns and innkeepers.

1. (1) An hotel within the meaning of this Act shall, and any other establishment shall not, be deemed to be an inn; and the duties, liabilities and rights which immediately before the commencement of this Act by law attached to an innkeeper as such shall, subject to the provisions of this Act, attach to the proprietor of such an hotel and shall not attach to any other person.

(2) The proprietor of an hotel shall, as an innkeeper, be under the like liability, if any, to make good to any guest of his any damage to property brought to the hotel as he would be under to make good the loss thereof.

(3) In this Act, the expression 'hotel' means an establishment held out by the proprietor as offering food, drink and, if so required, sleeping accommodation, without special contract, to any traveller presenting himself who appears able and willing to pay a reasonable sum for the services and facilities provided and who is in a fit state to be received.

Modifications of liabilities and rights of innkeepers as such.

2. (1) Without prejudice to any other liability incurred by him with respect to any property brought to the hotel, the proprietor of an hotel shall not be liable as an innkeeper to make good to any traveller any loss of or damage to such property except where—

(a) at the time of the loss or damage sleeping accommodation at the hotel had been engaged for the traveller;

(b) the loss or damage occurred during the period commencing with the midnight immediately preceding, and ending with the midnight immediately following, a period for which the traveller was a guest at the hotel and entitled to use the accommodation so engaged.

(2) Without prejudice to any other liability or right of his with respect thereto, the proprietor of an hotel shall not as an innkeeper be liable to make good to any guest of his any loss of or damage to, or have any lien on, any vehicle or any property left therein, or any horse or other live animal or its harness or other equipment.

(3) Where the proprietor of an hotel is liable as an innkeeper to make good the loss of or any damage to property brought to the hotel, his liability to any one guest shall not exceed fifty pounds in respect of any one article, or one hundred pounds in the aggregate, except where—

(a) the property was stolen, lost or damaged through the default, neglect or wilful act of the proprietor or some servant of his; or

(b) the property was deposited by or on behalf of the guest expressly for safe custody with the proprietor to some servant of his authorised, or appearing to be authorised, for the purpose, and, if so required by the proprietor or that servant, in a container fastened or sealed by the depositor; or

(c) at a time after the guest had arrived at the hotel, either the property in question was offered for deposit as aforesaid and the proprietor or his servant refused to receive it, or the guest or some other guest acting on his behalf wished so to offer the property in question but, through the default of the proprietor or a servant of his, was unable to do so:

Provided that the proprietor shall not be entitled to the protection of this subsection unless, at the time when the property in question was brought to the hotel, a copy of the notice set out in the Schedule to this Act printed in plain type was conspicuously displayed in a place where it could conveniently be read by his guests at or near the reception office or desk or, where there is no reception office or desk, at or near the main entrance to the hotel.

Short title, repeal, extent and commencement.

3. (1) This Act may be cited as the Hotel Proprietors Act, 1956

(2) The Innkeepers' Liability Act, 1863, is hereby repealed.

(3) This Act shall not extend to Northern Ireland.

(4) This Act shall come into operation on the first day of January, nineteen hundred and fifty-seven.

SCHEDULE

NOTICE

Loss of or Damage of Guests' Property

Under the Hotel Proprietors Act, 1956, an hotel proprietor may in certain circumstances be liable to make good any loss of or damage to a guest's property even though it was not due to any fault of the proprietor or staff of the hotel.

This liability however—
(a) extends only to the property of guests who have engaged sleeping accommodation at the hotel;
(b) is limited to £50 for any one article and a total of £100 in the case of one guest, except in the case of property which has been deposited, or offered for deposit, for safe custody;
(c) does not cover motor-cars or other vehicles of any kind or any property left in them, or horses or other live animals.

This notice does not constitute an admission either that the Act applies to this hotel or that the liability thereunder attaches to the proprietor of this hotel in any particular case.

Appendix B

A.C.T. CONSTRUCTION LIMITED
(RESPONDENTS)
v.
COMMISSIONERS OF CUSTOMS AND EXCISE
(APPELLANTS)

Lord Diplock
MY LORDS,
I have had the advantage of reading in draft the speech prepared by my noble and learned friend, Lord Roskill. For the reasons he has given, I too would dismiss the appeal.

Lord Elwyn-Jones
MY LORDS,
I have had the advantage of reading in draft the speech of my noble and learned friend, Lord Roskill. For the reasons he has given I would dismiss the appeal.

Lord Keith Of Kinkel
MY LORDS,
I agree with the speech of my noble and learned friend, Lord Roskill, which I have had the benefit of reading in draft. Accordingly, I too would dismiss the appeal.

Lord Scarman
MY LORDS,
I have had the advantage of reading in draft the speech to be delivered by my noble and learned friend, Lord Roskill. For the reasons he gives I also would dismiss the appeal.

Lord Roskill
My Lords, this appeal by the Commissioners of Customs and Excise against an order of the Court of Appeal (Lord Denning M.R., Brandon L.J., as he then was, and Ackner L.J.) dated 9th October 1980, whereby that court affirmed an order of Drake J. dated 16th March 1979, raises directly one short point of construction of Group 8 in Schedule 4 to the Finance Act 1972 ('the 1972 Act') as amended by paragraph 3 of the Value Added Tax (Consolidation) Order 1976 ('the 1976 Order') S.I. 1976 No. 128. But, as will later emerge, the appeal also raises, albeit indirectly, a second point of construction of that group upon which two members of the Court of Appeal, Lord Denning M.R. and Ackner L.J. expressed their views, albeit *obiter*.

My Lords, I should explain that section 12(4), together with section 43(2), of the 1972 Act authorised the Treasury to amend Schedule 4 by Statutory Instrument by adding to, or deleting from that Schedule, any description or by varying any description for the time being specified in it, subject to the parliamentary safeguard specified in section 43(4); the 1976 Order was made pursuant to those powers on the 29th January 1976. It was duly laid before the House of Commons on the 10th February 1976, and came into operation on the 2nd March 1976.

My Lords, the provisions of Schedule 4 both before and after amendment by the 1976 Order, was concerned with zero-rating for the purposes of Value Added Tax. Group 8 of that Schedule makes certain provisions for zero-rating in connection with 'Construction of Buildings etc.'. Group 8 specifies three items, each numbered, which qualify for zero-rating. Those three numbered items are followed by what are described as 'Notes', four in number, each numbered. Section 46(2) of the 1972 Act enjoins, *inter alia*, that Schedule 4 'shall be interpreted in accordance with the notes contained therein', power also being given by that subsection to amend those notes along with the substantive provisions of that Schedule.

My Lords, since everything in this appeal turns upon the construction of item 2 of Schedule 4 and of Note (2)(a) of the 'Notes' I set out the relevant wording for ease of reference:

'2. The supply, in the course of the construction, alteration or demolition "of any building or of any civil engineering work, of any services. . . ."

'Notes:
. . .
'(2) Item 2 does not include –
'(a) any work of repair or maintenance; . . .'

My Lords, the facts which give rise to this dispute are set out in detail in the carefully reasoned decision of the Value Added Tax Tribunal sitting in London, presided over by Mr. Neil Elles. Suffice it to say that the respondents are a construction company, and were employed to carry out certain underpinning operations to a number of houses of which the original foundations, which were laid in the 1930's and were acceptable under the then current building regulations but no longer acceptable under those regulations in force when the work, which led to the present dispute, was done, had been found seriously wanting as a result of the drought which took place in 1976. The respondents had developed a new method of underpinning to avoid the subsidence which would otherwise have occurred. This new method consisted of the construction of an additional foundation to the affected building in danger of subsidence, that additional foundation being not only additional to but also entirely separate from whatever original foundations still existed. It follows that whatever remained of those original foundations, and however defective they were or had become, was left unaltered. Your Lordships were shown a rough sketch of the underpinning in question which illustrated this brief description.

My Lords, the appellants assessed certain underpinning work done by the respondents to Value Added Tax in the sum of £1,072.44. This assessment followed certain correspondence. It related to four underpinning jobs carried out by the respondents – see the appellants' letter of 9th January 1978, Appendix pp. 17 and 18. The respondents appealed against that assessment but the Value Added Tax Tribunal in London, to which I have already referred, dismissed this appeal on the 8th August 1978. The respondents then appealed to the High Court. Drake J. allowed the appeal. His judgment is reported in (1979) 1 W.L.R. 870. An appeal by the appellants to the Court of Appeal was, as already mentioned, dismissed but your Lordships' House later gave leave to appeal against that decision.

My Lords, I said earlier that this appeal directly raised a single short point of construction, namely, whether the underpinning work which I have described was 'repair or maintenance' within Note (2). If it were, it is not zero-rated but positive-rated. But Mr. Simon Brown, for the appellants, urged your Lordships also to consider, when approaching this question of construction, the second question I have mentioned, namely, the meaning of the word 'alteration' in Item 2 in the context in which that word there appears, namely, 'in the course of the construction, alteration or demolition of any building. . . .' His contention was that in that context the word alteration meant 'structural alteration' and he urged that if that contention, which had been rejected both by the learned Master of the Rolls and Ackner L.J., were right, it not only supported his submission as to the true construction of the phrase 'any work of repair or maintenance' in Note (2)(a) but vitiated much of the reasoning of the learned Master of the Rolls in the latter part of his judgment (1981) 1 W.L.R. 49 at page 55.

My Lords, in one sense it may be said that this second point does not arise, since Mr. Brown rightly conceded that the underpinning work which I have described was, in any event, a 'structural alteration', and therefore even if the construction of the word for which he contended were correct, that pre-requisite to zero-rating required by the relevant wording of Item 2 was in any event satisfied. But since he urged that the determination of that true construction was essential to the proper interpretation of Note (2), and that the views of the majority of the Court of Appeal, albeit *obiter*, could have far reaching and perhaps unintended effects, I understand all your Lordships to agree that this House should now determine this matter as well as the other.

My Lords, the meaning of 'alteration' in this context had arisen in a previous Value Added Tax case, *Customs and Excise Commissioners* v. *Morrison Dunbar Ltd* (1979) STC 406, a decision by Neill J. about a fortnight before the hearing of the instant case before the Value Added Tax Tribunal, but not mentioned in their decision. The tribunal held that this underpinning work was an alteration, see page 8 of their decision.

At page 413 of the report of his judgment, Neill J. said:

'In dealing with a case to which item 2 of Group 8 is said to apply, I consider that one should first look to see whether the supply of the services in question is a supply in the course of the construction, alteration or demolition of a building. Each of these words is important and should be given its proper weight. The word "alteration", it is to be noted, is found between "construction" and "demolition" and it follows, in my view, that the alteration to which item 2 applies is an alteration *of the building* and therefore one which involves some structural alteration . . .'

In the Court of Appeal in the present case, Lord Denning M.R., at page 53, after quoting this passage said that he could not agree with it and that the adjective 'structural' should not be inserted. Ackner L.J. at page 57 agreed. Brandon L.J. expressed no opinion. Neither the learned Master of the Rolls nor Ackner L.J. gave any reasons for their disapproval of what Neill J. had said. My Lords, with profound respect, I agree with the view of Neill J., whose reasoning seems to me impeccable. If the contrary view were right, the repainting of a house in a different colour from that previously used would be an 'alteration', a conclusion which in this context, I venture to think, cannot be sustained.

My Lords, I therefore accept Mr. Brown's contention on this issue, and turn to the question of construction of Note (2) upon that basis. It seems to me clear that for the relevant work to qualify for zero-rating two requirements must be satisfied. It must be a 'structural alteration', and it must not be 'any work of repair or maintenance'. As already stated, the first requirement is by concession satisfied; I therefore turn to the second.

My Lords, the argument in the courts below appears to have proceeded upon the basis that the words 'repair or maintenance' are used in antithesis to one another. Indeed, it was conceded in the Court of Appeal that this underpinning could not be said to be a 'repair' and therefore the only question was whether it was maintenance. See the judgment of Brandon L.J. at page 56 and Ackner L.J. at page 58. My Lords, I think, as indeed Mr. Brown accepted in argument before your Lordships' House, that this concession was wrongly made by him in the Court of Appeal. The two words are not used in antithesis to one another. The phrase is a single composite phrase 'repair or maintenance' and in many cases there may well be an overlap between them, as indeed there may also be between 'structural alteration' on the one hand, and 'repair or maintenance' on the other.

My Lords, Mr. Brown contended that this underpinning was 'repair or maintenance' because it was done to stop these buildings falling down. He went so far as to submit that any work done to stop a building collapsing was 'pure maintenance' since it was maintenance to promote the essential safety of that structure.

My Lords, in the courts below there was much reference to well-known decisions in disputes between landlords and tenants arising from repairing covenants in leases where contractual obligations to repair and maintain had been assumed by tenants towards their landlords. These decisions are referred to in several of the judgments below and require no further mention, but in my opinion they shed little or no light upon the construction of the Statutory Instrument now in question.

My Lords, on the central question I find the reasoning in the judgment of Brandon L.J. compelling. The learned Lord Justice said at page 57 of his judgment:

'In the present case the work done was not done to any existing part of a building; it was entirely new work. It involved a radical and fundamental alteration to the construction of the building as it had been before. It involved an extension of the existing building in a downward direction. Such work in my view is not capable of coming within the expression "maintenance" in the ordinary and natural meaning of that word. It is conceded that, if that is right, then the work was work of alteration within the meaning of that expression in Item 2 of Group 8 and is accordingly zero-rated.'

My Lords, I stress, like the learned Lord Justice, that this was new work which converted buildings which, apart from this work, would have had a short life, into buildings which as a consequence of this work became endowed with a long life. This consequence was achieved only by the installation of a new structure upon which the buildings thereafter rested. My Lords, I decline to attempt to define 'repair or maintenance' when the 1972 Act and the 1972 Order do not do so, but leave those ordinary words which are in common use to be given their ordinary meaning. In some cases, there may be room for dispute which side of the line particular work falls. If so, that would be a question of fact or degree for the tribunal of fact concerned to determine. The problem should not prove difficult of solution if their task is approached by applying the facts as that tribunal finds them to the relevant statutory provisions interpreted as I have endeavoured to state.

My Lords, in common with the courts below, I am unable to see how this underpinning work can possibly be classed as 'repair or maintenance' within the ordinary meaning of those words. I would, therefore, dismiss this appeal with costs.

Cases cited

Adam v. Ward [1917], A.C. 309, 1L, 10I
Alexander v. The North Eastern Railway Co (1865), 6B. & S. 340, 10I
Allcard v. Skinner (1887), 36 Ch.D. 145, 6I6, 9C10
Allen v. Rescous [1676], 1 Freem. (K.B.) 433, 6G
Andrews v. Hopkinson [1957], 1 Q.B. 229, 10D2
Anglia Television Ltd v. Reed [1971], 3 All E.R. 690, 7B1D
Anns & Ors v. Merton London Borough Council [1971], 2 All E.R. 492, 10A
Ansell v. Thomas, The Times, 23 May, 1973, 5D1B
Armory v. Delamirie (1721), 1 Stra. 505, 10F1
Ashbury Railway Carriage & Iron Co Ltd v. Riche [1875], L.R. 7 H.L. 653, 6F3
Ashton v. Turner [1980], 3 All E.R. 870, 9C9
Attorney General for Northern Ireland v. Gallagher [1963], A.C. 349, 5C
Attorney General v. Gastonia Coaches, The Times, 12 November, 1976, 10C

Baily v. de Crespigny (1869), L.R.4 Q.B. 180, 7A3
Baker v. Willoughby [1969], New L.J. 1197, 9C1
Balfour v. Balfour [1919], 2 K.B. 571, 6/Intro.
Bates (Thos.) & Son v. Wyndhams (Lingerie) [1981], 1 All E.R. 1077, 6I2
Beach v. Reed Corrugated Cases Ltd [1956], 2 All E.R. 652, 1L, 7B1A
Beard v. London General Omnibus Co. (1900), 2 Q.B. 530, 9F
Bebee v. Sales (1916), 32 T.L.R. 413, 9D3
Behn v. Burgess [1863], 3 B&S 751, 7A2A
Bettini v. Gye (1876), 1 Q.B.D. 183, 7A2B
Bird v. Brown [1850], 4 Exch. 786, 8A4
Blyth v. Birmingham Waterworks Co (1856), 11 Ex. 781, 10A
Bolton v. Stone [1950], A.C. 650, 10C
Brace v. Calder [1895], 2 Q.B. 253, 7B1B
Bradford Corporation v. Pickles [1895], A.C. 587, 9B
Branca v. Cobarro [1947], 2 All E.R. 101 6C
Brinkibon Ltd. v. Stahag und Stalhwarenhandelsgesellschaft mbH [1982], 4 C.L. 31, 6C
British Car Auctions v. Wright [1972], 3 All E.R. 462, 1C
British Celanese Ltd v. A.H. Hunt (Capacitors) Ltd [1969], 2 All E.R. 1252, 10C
British Railways Board v. Herrington [1972], 1 All E.R. 749, 10B2
British Russian Gazette & Trade Outlook Ltd v. Assoc. Newspapers Ltd [1933], 2 K.B. 616, 7A4
British Wagon Co v. Lee (1880), 5 Q.B.D. 149, 6J2
Burnard v. Haggis (1863), 14 C.B.N.S. 45, 9D3
Bushell's Case [1670], Freem. K.B. 1, 3F1, 3F2

Carlill v. Carbolic Smoke Ball Co [1893], 1 Q.B. 256, IL, 6C
Carpenters Estates Ltd v. Davies [1940], 1 All E.R., 7B3
Cassell & Co Ltd v. Broome [1972], 1 All E.R. 801, 5D1C
Castellain v. Preston (1883), 11 Q.B.D. 380, 1K3
Castle v. St Augustine's Links (1922), 38 T.L.R. 615, 10C
Cellulose Acetate Silk Co Ltd v. Widnes Foundry Ltd [1933], A.C. 20, 7B1F
Central London Property Trust Ltd v. High Trees House Ltd (1947), K.B. 130, 6E
Chadwick v. British Railways Board [1967], 1 W.L.R. 912, 9C3
Chic Fashions (West Wales) v. Jones [1968], 2 Q.B. 299, 10D2
Christie v. Davie [1893], 1 Ch. 316, 10C
Clifford Davies Management v. W.E.A. Records [1975], 1 All E.R. 237, 6I6
Clubb v. Hutson (1865), 18 C.B. (H.S.) 414, 6G
Clyde Cycle Co v. Hargreaves (1898), 78 L.T. 296, 6F1
Cooden Engineering Co Ltd v. Stanford [1952], 2 T.L.R. 822, 7B1F
Cooper v. Phibbs [1867], L.R. 2 H.L. 149, 6I1E
Cope v. Sharp [1912], 1 K.B. 496, 9C6
Cox v. Philips Industries Ltd [1976], 3 All E.R. 161, 7B1C
Craven-Ellis v. Canon Ltd [1936], 1 K.B. 403, 7B2
Cresswell v. Potter [1978], 1 W.L.R. 255, 6I6
Cundy v. Le Cocq (1884), 13 Q.B.D. 207, 5B
Cundy v. Lindsay [1878], 3 App. Cas. 459, 6I1B
Currie v. Misa [1875], L.R. 10 Ex. 153, 6D
Cutler v. United Dairies Ltd [1933], 2 K.B. 297, 9C3

Daborn v. Bath Tramways [1946], 2 All E.R. 333, 10A
Davies v. Beynon-Harris (1931), 47 T.L.R. 424, 6F1
Davies v. Liverpool Corporation [1949], 2 All E.R. 175, 9H1
Dickinson v. Del Solar [1930], 1 K.B. 376, 9D1
Dimes v. Grand Junction Canal Proprietors [1852], 3 H.L.C. 759, 2B3C
Dominion Natural Gas Co v. Collins & Perkins [1909], A.C. 640, 10D2
Donaldson v. McNiven [1952], 2 All E.R. 691, 9D3
Donoghue v. Stevenson [1932], A.C. 562, 10A, 10D2
Doyle v. White City Stadium Ltd [1935], 1 K.B. 110, 6F1
Dunmore v. Alexander (1830), 9 Sh. (Ct. of Sess.) 190, 6C

Eastes *v.* Russ (1914), 30 T.L.R. 237, 6H1
East Suffolk Rivers Catchment Board *v.* Kent [1941], A.C. 74, 10A
Edgington *v.* Fitzmaurice (1885), 29 Ch. D. 459, 6I3
Edwards *v.* Newlands & Co [1950], 2 All E.R. 1072, 6J2
Ellis *v.* Sheffield Gas Consumers Co (1853), 2 El. & Bl. 767, 9F
Emanuel (H. & N.) Ltd *v.* Greater London Council [1971], 1 All E.R. 853, 9F
English Hop Growers Ltd *v.* Dering [1928], 2 K.B. 174, 7B1F
Entores Ltd *v.* Miles Far East Corporation [1955], 2 Q.B. 327, 6C
E.P. Nelson Ltd *v.* Rolfe]1950], K.B. 139, 8C2
Esso Petroleum Co Ltd *v.* Harper's Garage Ltd [1967], 1 All E.R. 699, 6H1

Fagan *v.* Metropolitan Police Commissioner [1968], 3 All E.R. 442, 5B
Felthouse *v.* Bindley (1862), 11 C.B. (N.S.) 869, 6C
Fisher *v.* Bell [1961], 1 Q.B. 394, 6C
Foakes *v.* Beer (1884), 9 App. Cas. 605, 6D2
Foster *v.* Mackinnon [1869], L.R. 4 C.P. 704, 6I1A
Fowler *v.* Lanning [1959], 1 All E.R. 290, 10G

Gilford Motor Co *v.* Horne [1933], Ch. 935, 4B2B
Greenock Corp *v.* Caledonian Railway Co [1917], A.C. 556, 9C5
Griffiths *v.* Studebakers Ltd [1924], 1 K.B. 102, 4B2B

Hadley *v.* Baxendale (1854), 9 Exch. 341, 7B1C
Haley *v.* London Electricity Board [1964], 3 All E.R. 185, 10A
Hannah *v.* Peel [1945], K.B. 509, 10F1
Hargreaves *v.* Bretherton [1958], 3 W.L.R. 463, 9B
Haynes *v.* Harwood [1935], 1 K.B. 146, 9C3
Hedley Byrne & Co Ltd *v.* Heller & Ptnrs Ltd [1963], 2 All E.R. 575, 10A
Henderson *v.* Stevenson [1875], L.R. 2 H.L. Sc. 470, 6C
Henthorn *v.* Fraser [1892], All E.R. 908, 6C
Herbert Morris Ltd *v.* Saxelby, [1916], 1 A.C. 688, 6H1
Hermann *v.* Charlesworth [1905], 2 K.B. 123, 6H1
Herne Bay Steamboat Co *v.* Hutton [1903], 2 K.B. 683, 7A3
Herrington *v.* British Railways Board [1970], 2 W.L.R. 477, 10A
Hill *v.* Aldershot Corporation [1933], 1 K.B. 259, 1K5
Hogan *v.* Bentinck Collieries Ltd [1948], 1 All E.R. 129, 9H1
Hollins *v.* Fowler [1875], L.R. 7 H.L. 757, 10F1
Hollywood Silver Fox Farm Ltd *v.* Emmett, [1936], 2 K.B. 468, 9B
Holwell Securities *v.* Hughes [1974], 1 W.L.R. 155, 6C
Home Office *v.* Dorset Yacht Co Ltd [1970], 2 All E.R. 294, 10A
Houghton Main Colliery Ltd (*re*) [1956], 1 W.L.R. 1219, 7B1A
Howatson *v.* Webb [1908], 1 Ch. 537, 6I1A
Hulton (E.) & Co *v.* Jones [1910], A.C. 20, 10I
Humble *v.* Hunter (1848), 12 Q.B. 310, 8E
Hutton *v.* Esher Urban District Council [1973], 2 W.L.R. 917, 1I
Hutton *v.* Warren (1836), 150 E.R. 517, 1E
Hyde *v.* Wrench (1840), 3 Beav. 334, 6C

Ingram *v.* Little [1960], 1 Q.B. 31, 6I1B
Interoffice Telephones Ltd *v.* Robert Freeman & Co Ltd [1957], 3 W.L.R. 971, 7B1

Jackson *v.* Horizon Holidays [1975], 3 All E.R. 92, 6A
Jenkin *v.* Pharmaceutical Society [1921], 1 Ch. 392, 6F3
Jennings *v.* Rundall (1799), 8 Term Rep. 335, 9D3
Jones *v.* Vernon's Pools Ltd [1938], 2 All E.R. 626, 6/Intro.
Junior Books Ltd *v.* The Veitchi Co Ltd, The Times, 17 July 1982, 10A

Kemp *v.* Baerselman [1906], 2 K.B. 604, 6J1
Krell *v.* Henry [1903], 2 K.B. 740, 7A3

Leaf *v.* International Galleries [1950], 2 K.B. 86, 7C
Legal and General Assurance Society *v.* General Metal Agencies (1969), 113 S.J. 876, 6I1F
Leigh *v.* Gladstone (1909), 26 T.L.R. 139, 9C6
Lewis *v.* Averay [1971], 3 W.L.R. 603, 6I1B
Limpus *v.* London General Omnibus Co [1862], 1 H&C 526, 9F
Lloyd *v.* Grace Smith & Co [1912], A.C. 716, 9F
London Street Tramways Co *v.* L.C.C. [1898], A.C. 375, 1K2A
Luker *v.* Chapman (1970), 114 Sol. J. 788, 7B1B
Lumley *v.* Allday (1831), 1 Cr. & J. 301, 10I
Lumley *v.* Wagner (1852), 1 De G.M. & G. 604, 7B3, 7B4
Lynn *v.* Bamber [1930], 2 K.B. 72, 7C

McArdle (re) [1951], Ch. 669, 6D3
McLoughlin v. O'Brian [1982], 1 All E.R. 809, 10A
Malone v. Laskey [1907], 2 K.B. 141, 10B2
Marriage v. East Norfolk Rivers Catchment Board [1950], 1 K.B. 284, 9C7
Marzetti v. Williams (1830), 109 E.R. 842, 7B1
Matthey v. Curling [1922], 2 A.C. 180, 7A3
May v. Burdett (1846), 9 Q.B. 101, 10D1
Meah v. Roberts [1977], 1 W.L.R. 1187, D.C., 5B
Mercantile Union Guarantee Corporation v. Ball [1937], 2 K.B. 498, 6F1
Mercer v. Denne [1905], 2 Ch. 534, 1E
Merritt v. Merritt [1970], 2 All E.R. 760, 6/Intro.
Mersey Docks & Harbour Board v. Coggins & Griffiths (Liverpool) Ltd (1946), A.C. 1, 9F
Metropolitan Rail Co v. Jackson (1877), 3 App. Cas. 193 H.L., 3F1
Metropolitan Water Board v. Dick, Kerr & Co Ltd (1918), A.C. 119, 7A3
Millard v. Serck Tubes Ltd [1969], 1 All E.R. 598, 10B1
Miller v. Jackson [1977], 3 W.L.R. 20, 9H3
Miller v. Race (1758), 1 Burn. 452, 6J4
Morris v. C.W. Martin & Sons Ltd [1965], 1 All E.R. 725, 9F
Morriss v. Marsden [1952], 1 All E.R. 1213, 9D5
Mountford v. Scott [1974], 1 All E.R. 248, 6C

Napier v. National Business Agency Ltd [1951], 2 All E.R. 264, 6G
Nash v. Inman [1908], 2 K.B. 1, 6F1
Nettleship v. Weston [1971], 3 All E.R. 581, 10A
New Windsor Corporation v. Mellor [1975], Ch. 380, 1E
Nichols v. Marsland [1876], 2 Ex. D. 1, 9C5
Nordenfelt v. Maxim Nordenfelt Guns & Ammunition Co Ltd [1894], A.C. 535, 6H1
Northwestern Utilities Ltd v. London Guarantee & Accident Co Ltd [1936], A.C. 108, 10D1

Omnium D'Enterprises v. Sutherland [1919], 1 K.B. 618, 7A2B
Overseas Tankship (UK) Ltd v. Morts Dock & Eng Co Ltd [1961], A.C. 388, 9H1
Owens v. Brimmel [1976], 3 All E.R. 765, 9C1

Padbury v. Holliday & Greenwood Ltd (1912), 28 T.L.R. 494, 9F
Parsons (H) Livestock Ltd v. Uttley Ingham & Co Ltd, The Times, 19 May 1977, 7B1C
Pasternack v. Poulton [1973], 2 All E.R. 74, 9C1
Pearce v. Brooks [1866], L.R. 1 Exch 213, 6G
Penny v. Northampton Borough Council, The Times, 20 July 1974, 10B2
Penton v. Southern Railway Co [1931], 2 K.B. 103, 6C
Peters v. Prince of Wales Theatres (Birmingham) Ltd [1943], K.B. 73, 10D1
Pharmaceutical Soc. of Gr. Britain v. Boots Cash Chemists [1953], 1 Q.B. 401, 6C
Pharmaceutical Soc. of Gr. Britain v. Dickson [1968], 2 All E.R. 686, 6H1
Phipps v. Rochester Corporation [1955], 1 Q.B. 450, 10B2
Pilkington v. Wood [1955], Ch 770, 7B1
Pinnel's Case (1602), 5 Co Rep 117a, 7A4
Ponting v. Noakes [1894], 2 Q.B. 281, 10D1
Poussard v. Spiers & Pond (1876), 1 Q.B.D. 410, 7A2B
Powell v. Kempton Park Racecourse Co [1899], A.C. 143, 1I
Price v. Moulton (1851), 10 C.B. 561, 7A6
Provident Clothing & Supply Co Ltd v. Mason [1913], All E.R. Rep 400, 7B4

R. v. Bingham Justices, ex parte Jowitt, The Times, 3 July 1974, 2B3C
R. v. Dudley & Stephens (1844), 14 Q.B.D. 273, 5C
R. v. Gould (1968), 112 Sol. J. 69, 1K2B
R. v. Jordan (1956), 40 Cr. App. R. 152, 5B
R. v. Tolson (1889), 23 Q.B.D. 168, 5C
Raleigh v. Atkinson (1840), 6M & W 870, 8G
Ramsgate Victoria Hotel Co v. Montefiore [1866], L.R. 1 Exch. 109, 6C
Ratcliffe v. Evans [1892], 2 Q.B. 524, 10J
Rawlinson v. Ames [1925], 1 Ch 96, 6B2
Read v. Lyons & Co Ltd [1947], A.C. 156, 10D1
Richard's and Bartlet's Case (1584), 74 E.R. 17, 7A4
Rickards v. Lothian [1913], A.C. 263, 10D1
Ridge v. Baldwin [1963], 2 All E.R. 66, 2B3C
Rimmer v. Webster [1902], 2 Ch 163, 8E
Robinson v. Davison [1871], L.R. 6 Ex 269, 7A3
Robinson v. Harman [1848], 1 Ex. 850, 7B1
Rookes v. Barnard [1964], 1 All E.R. 367, 5D1C
Rose v. Plenty [1976], 1 All E.R. 97, 9F
Rose & Frank Co v. Crompton Bros [1925], A.C. 445, 6/Intro.
Routledge v. Grant (1828), 4 Bing. 653, 6C
Rylands v. Fletcher (1868), L.R. 3 H.L. 330, 9B, 10D1

Salomon v. Salomon & Co [1892], A.C. 22, 4B2B
Sanders v. Parry [1967], 2 All E.R. 803, 6H1
Saunders v. Anglia Building Society [1970], 3 All E.R. 961, 6I1A
Saunders (Mayfair) Furs v. Davies (1965), 109 Sol. J. 922, 10A
Schloimovitz v. Clarendon Press, The Times, 6 July 1973, 10I
Schorsch Meier GmbH v. Hennin [1975], 1 All E.R. 152, 1J
Scriven Bros & Co v. Hindley & Co [1913], 3 K.B. 564, 6I1C
Scruttons Ltd v. Midland Silicones Ltd [1962], A.C. 446, 6D4
Sedleigh-Denfield v. O'Callaghan [1940], A.C. 880, 10B2
Shadwell v. Shadwell (1860), 9 C.B. (N.S.) 159, 6D2
Shaw v. D.P.P. [1961], 2 All E.R. 446, 5B
Simpkins v. Pays [1955], 3 All E.R. 10, 6/Intro.
Six Carpenters' Case (1610), 8 Co Rep 146a, 10D2
Smith v. Baker [1891], A.C. 325, 9C3
Smith v. Hughes [1960], 2 All E.R. 859, 1I
Smith v. Leech Brain & Co Ltd [1961], 2 W.L.R. 148, 9H1
Snelling v. John G. Snelling Ltd [1972], 1 All E.R. 79, 6A
South Staffordshire Water Co v. Sharman [1896], 2 Q.B. 44, 10F1
Spicer v. Smee [1946], 1 All E.R. 498, 9F
Stanley v. Powell [1891], 1 Q.B. 86, 9C4
Stansbie v. Troman [1948], 2 K.B. 48, 10A
Street v. Blay [1831], 2B and Ach 456, 7A2B
Strickland v. Turner (1852), 7 Exch 208, 6I1D
Sturges v. Bridgman (1879), 11 Ch. D. 852, 10B2

Tarry v. Ashton (1876), 1 Q.B.D. 314, 9F
Taylor v. Caldwell (1863), 3 B & S 826, 7A3
Taylor v. Laird (1856), 156 E.R. 1203, 6C
Thomas v. Thomas (1842), 2 Q.B. 851, 6D1
Tolley v. J. S. Fry & Sons Ltd [1931], A.C. 333, 10I
Tomlin v. Standard Telephone & Cables Ltd [1969], 3 All E.R. 201, 6C
Towle & Co Ltd v. White (1873), 29 L.T. 78, 8/Intro.
Tsakiraglou & Co v. Noblee-Thorl [1961], 2 W.L.R. 633, 7A3

Victoria Laundries (Windsor) Ltd v. Newman Industries Ltd [1949], 1 All E.R. 997, 7B1C

Wagon Mound (The) [1961], A.C. 388, 9H1
Waldron-Kelly v. British Railways Board [1981], 3 Current Law, para 33, 6/Intro.
Walsh v. Holst & Co Ltd [1958], 1 W.L.R. 800, 10A
Walton Harvey Ltd v. Walker & Homfrays Ltd [1931], 1 Ch 274, 7A3
Ward v. Tesco Stores [1976], All E.R. 219, 10A
Warner Bros Pictures Inc v. Nelson [1936], 1 K.B. 209, 7B4
Warren v. Henley's Ltd [1948], 2 All E.R. 935, 9F
Watteau v. Fenwick [1893], 1 Q.B. 346, 8D3
Weiland v. Cyril Lord Carpets [1969], 3 All E.R. 1006, 9H1
Welby v. Drake (1825), 1 C & P 557, 7A4
Welch v. Cheesman (1974), 229 Est. Gaz. 99, 6I6
White v. Bluett (1853), 23 L.J. Ex 36, 6D1
Whiteley v. Chappel (1868–9), 4 L.R.Q.B. 147, 1I
Woodman v. Dixons Photographic, The Times, 20 June 1981, 6/Intro.
Woods v. Martins Bank Ltd [1958], 3 All E.R. 166, 10A
Woolmington v. D.P.P. [1935], A.C. 462, 5B
W.T. Lamb & Sons v. Goring Brick Co Ltd (1932), 1 K.B. 170, 8/Intro.

Yonge v. Toynbee [1910], 1 H.B. 215, 8G
Young v. Bristol Aeroplane Co Ltd [1944], 2 All E.R. 293, 1K2A
Young v. Kitchen [1878], 3 Ex D 127, 6J1

List of statutes

Administration of Justice Act 1969, 2B4, 9H1
Administration of Justice Act 1970, 2A
Appellate Jurisdiction Act 1876, 1K1, 3A1
Arbitration Acts 1950–79, 2H
Assize of Clarendon 1166, 3F2
Assize of Northampton 1176, 3F2

Betting Act 1853, 1I
Bills of Exchange Act 1882, 1F, 6J4

Chancery Amendment Act 1858, 1D
Chancery Regulation Act 1833, 1D
Civil Aviation Act 1949, 10E
Civil Liability (Contribution) Act 1978, 9E
Codifying Acts, 1F3
Companies Acts, 1G2, 4B2B, 6F3
Congenital Disabilities (Civil Liability) Act 1976, 9D2
Courts Act 1970, 2A
Criminal Justice Act 1967, 5D2B
Criminal Law Act 1967, 5B, 10H
Crown Proceedings Act 1947, 4B

Defamation Act 1952, 9C8, 10I

Employment Protection Act 1975, 4B
Employment Protection Act 1978, 2F4
European Communities Act 1972, 1I, 1J, 6F3

Factories Act 1961, 1G3, 10B1
Family Law Reform Act 1969, 6F1
Fatal Accidents Acts 1846–1976, 9G
Food and Drugs Act 1955, 5B
Furnished Houses (Rent Control) Act 1946, 2F2

Gaming Act 1845, 6H1

Health and Safety at Work etc. Act 1974, 4B2B
Hotel Proprietors Act 1956, 1I, 1M

Infants Relief Act 1874, 6F1
Insurance Companies Act 1958, 1G3
Insurance Companies Act 1982, 1G3, 1H
Interpretation Act 1889, 1I

Judicature Acts 1873–75, 1D, 1K1, 6J1
Justices' Protection Act 1848, 3E

Law Commission Act 1965, 1G3
Law of Property Act 1925, 6J1, 8E, 8G
Law Reform (Contributory Negligence) Act 1945, 9C1, 9E
Law Reform (Frustrated Contracts) Act 1943, 7A3
Law Reform (Miscellaneous Provisions) Act 1934, 9G
Law Reform (Miscellaneous Provisions) Act 1970, 6/Intro
Law Reform (Miscellaneous Provisions) Act 1971, 6/Intro
Legal Aid Act 1974, 3H
Limitation Act 1980, 6B3, 7C, 9C10
Limited Partnership Act 1907, 4B3A
Lloyd's Act 1982, 1G2

Marine Insurance Act 1906, 1A, 1F, 1G3
Mental Health Act 1959, 4A2
Misrepresentation Act 1967, 6I3
Moneylenders Act 1927, 6H1

National Insurance Act 1965, 1G3

Occupiers' Liability Act 1957, 10B2
Offences against the Person Act 1861, 1I, 5A3

Partnership Act 1890, 4B3A
Post Office Act 1969, 4B1
Powers of Criminal Courts Act 1973, 5A3, 5D2H
Prescription Act 1832, 10C
Prevention of Corruption Acts 1889–1916, 8B4
Provisions of Oxford 1258, 1C1

Rehabilitation of Offenders Act 1974, 5D2M, 10I
Rent Act 1977, 2F2
Resale Prices Act 1976, 2E4, 6H
Restrictive Trade Practices Act 1956, 2E4
Restrictive Trade Practices Act 1976, 2E4
Road Traffic Act 1972, 5A3

Sale of Goods Act 1979, 1F, 1G3, 7A2A, 7A2B, 7A3
Statute of Westminster II 1285, 1C1
Street Offences Act 1959, 1I
Supreme Court Act 1981, 1D, 3A2

Theatres Act 1968, 10I
Torts (Interference with Goods) Act 1977, 10F
Trade Descriptions Act 1968, 6I3
Trade Union and Labour Relations Acts 1974–76, 4B3C, 4B3D
Tribunals and Enquiries Act 1971, 2F5

Unfair Contract Terms Act 1977, 6/Intro, 10B2

Index

Act of God, 9C5
Acts of Parliament 1G
actus reus, 5B
administrative tribunals, 2F
    advantages of, 2F5
    disadvantages of, 2F5
Admiralty Court, 2B3C
agency, 8
    apparent authority, 8A2, 8D4
    authority of agent, 8D
    consent, 8A1
    creation of agency, 8A
    duties of agent, 8B
    express authority, 8D1
    implied authority, 8D2
    Lien, 8C3
    necessity, 8A3
    ratification, 8A4
    relationship between agent and third
      party, 8F
    remedies for breach by agent, 8B6
    rights of agent, 8C
    termination, 8G
    undisclosed principal, 8A5
    usual authority, 8D3
arbitration, 2H
Arches Court of Canterbury, 2E2
attachment of earnings, 2B2
Attorney-General, 3D2

Bankruptcy Court, 2B2
bankruptcy proceedings, 2B2
barristers, 3G2
bills, 1G2
breach of statutory duty, 10B
bye-laws, 1H

case law, 1K, 1M
Central Criminal Court, 2C2
certiorari, 2B3C
Chancery Court of York, 2E2
charging order, 2B2
circuit judges, 3A4
codification, 1G3
Commercial Court, 2B3C
common law, 1C
    deficiencies of, 1C1
    history of, 1C1
companies, 4B2B
    dissolution of, 4B2B
    formation of, 4B2B
    private, 4B2B
    public, 4B2B
Companies Court, 2B3A
compensation for criminal injuries, 5D
consistory courts, 2D2
contracts, 6, 7
    acceptance, 6C
    accord and satisfaction, 7A5
    assignment, 6J
    breach, 7A2
    capacity, 6F
    conditions, 7A2A
    consensus ad idem, 6I
    consideration, 6D
    damages, 7B1
    definition of, 6/Intro
    discharge of, 7A
    duress, 6I5
    estoppel, 6E
    evidenced by writing, 6B2
    frustration, 7A3
    in restraint of trade, 6B3
    in writing, 6B2

injunctions, 7B4
interpretation of, 7D
invitation to treat, 6C
legality, 6G
merger, 6B3, 7A6
misrepresentation, 6I3
mistake, 6I1
negotiability, 6J4
novation, 7A5
of guarantee, 6B2
of indemnity, 6B2
of record, 6B1
offer, 6C
penalties, 7B1F
performance, 7A1
rectification, 6I2
release, 7A4
remedies, 7B
simple, 6B2
specific performance, 7B3
under seal, 6B3
undue influence, 6I6
void, 6H1
warranties, 7A2B
contributory negligence, 9C1
conventional custom, 1E
conversion, 10F1
coroners' courts, 2E3
corporations, 4B2, 6F3
    aggregate, 4B2B
    sole, 4B2A
county court, 1K2B, 2B2
county court registrars, 3D1
Court of Appeal – Civil Division, 1K2A,
    2B4
Court of Appeal – Criminal Division,
    1K2A, 2C3
Court of Chancery, 2A3A
Court of Ecclesiastical Cases Reserved,
    2E2
Court of Protection, 2A3A
courts-martial, 2E1
criminal liability, 5B
Crown, 4B1
custom, 1E

damages, 5D, 9H1
    aggravated, 5D1B
    contemptuous, 5D1A
    exemplary, 5D1C
    general, 9H1
    in contract, 7B1
    in tort, 9H1
    liquidated, 7B1F
    remoteness, 9H1
    special, 9H1
damnum sine injuria, 9B
defamation, 10I
delegated legislation, 1H
diminished responsibility, 4A2
diplomatic immunity, 9D1
Director of Public Prosecutions, 3D3
drunkenness, 5C, 6F2

Ecclesiastical Courts, 2E2
EEC legislation, 1J
ejection of trespassers, 10E
employers' liability, 10B1
Employment Appeal Tribunal, 2F4
enforcement of judgments, 2B2
English law, characteristics of, 1A
equity, 1D
    defects of, 1D
estoppel, 6E

European Court, 2D, 3B
execution, warrant of, 2B2

fair comment, 10I
false imprisonment, 10H
forcible entry, 10E

garnishee proceedings, 2B2
guardian *ad litem*, 4A1
guardianship,

habeas corpus, 2B3C
High Court, 1K2A, 2B3
    Chancery division, 2B3A
    Family division, 2B3B
    Queen's Bench division, 2B3C
High Court judges, 3A3
House of Commons, 1G
House of Lords, 1K2A, 2B5, 2C4
husband and wife, 4A4, 9D4

illegality, 9C9
inevitable accident, 9C4
inferior courts, 2A
injunctions, 7B4, 9H3
    interlocutory, 9H3
    mandatory, 9H3
    perpetual, 9H3
    prohibitory, 9H3
injuria sine damnum, 9B
insanity, 4A2, 6F2, 9D5

joint torts, 9E
judgment summons, 2B2
Judicial Committee of the Privy Council,
    1K2C
judicial immunity, 3E
judicial independence, 3E
judicial precedent, 1K
juries, 3F
    civil, 3F1
    criminal, 3F2
jus tertii, 10E
justification, 10I
juvenile courts, 2C1

laches, 9C10
lands tribunals, 2F2
law, 1A
    nature of, 1A
    sources of, 1B
    unwritten, 1C
Law Commission, 1G3
law merchant, 1F
law officers of the crown, 3D2
Law Society, 3G1A
'leapfrog' procedure, 2B4
legal aid and advice, 3H
legal executives, 3G1C
legal personality, 4B
legal profession, 3G
legal tender, 7A1
libel, 10I
limitation, 7C, 9C10
Lloyd's underwriters, 4B3B
Lord Chancellor, 3A
Lord Chief Justice, 3A2
Lords of Appeal in Ordinary, 3A1
Lords Justices of Appeal, 3A2

magistrates, 3C
    lay, 3C
    stipendiary, 3C
magistrates' courts, 1K2B, 2B1, 2C1

malice, 10J
malicious falsehood, 10J
mandamus, 2B3C
Master of the Rolls, 3A2
mens rea, 5B
mental patients, 4A2, 9D5
mesne profits, 10E
minors, 4A1, 6F1, 9D3
mistake, 9C8

natural justice, rules of, 2B3C
necessity, 5C, 9C6
negligence, 10A
negotiability, 6J4
'next friend', 9D3
nuisance, 10C
    private, 10C
    public, 10C

obiter dictum, 1K3
occupiers' liability, 10B2
Orders in Council, 1H

Parliament, 1G1
partnership, 4B3A
    limited, 4B3A
penalties, 5D2
Post Office, 4B1
precedent, 1K
    advantages, 1K5
    disadvantages, 1K5
privilege, 10I
prohibition, 2B3C
punishments, 5D2
    absolute discharge, 5D2K
    community service order, 5D2H
    conditional discharge, 5D2K
    death, 5D2A
    deprivation of property, 5D2I
    disqualification of driving, 5D2J
    fines, 5D2E
    imprisonment, 5D2B
    probation, 5D2F
    purposes of, 5D2
    recognizance, 5D2G
    Youth Custody, 5D2C

quantum meruit, 7B2
Queen, the, 4B1
Queen's Counsel, 3G2

ratio decidendi, 1K3
receiver, appointment of, 2B2
recorders, 3A5
recovery of land, 10E
registrars, 3D1
rehabilitation of offenders, 5D2M
rent tribunals, 2F2
res ipsa loquitur, 10A
Restrictive Practices Court, 2E4
retroactive legislation, 1G3
Roman law, 1A
rules and regulations, 1H

self-defence, 9C2
slander, 10I
Solicitor-General, 3D2
solicitors, 3G1, 3G1C
Solicitors' Disciplinary Tribunal, 3G1B
sources of English law, 1B
specific performance, 7B3
specific restitution, 9H2
status, 4A
statute law, 1G, 1M

statutory authority, 9C7
statutory instruments, 1H
statutory interpretation, 1I
    golden rule, 1I
    literal rule, 1I
    mischief rule, 1I
strict liability, 10D
superior courts, 2A
survival of actions, 9G

tortious liability, principles of, 9A
torts, 9
    definition of, 9A
trade unions, 4B3C
treasure trove, 2E3

trespass, 10E
    to goods, 10F2
    to land, 10E
    to the person, 10G
trespassers, 10E

unborn children, 9D2
unincorporated associations, 4B3
utmost good faith, 6I3

vicarious liability, 9F
volenti non fit injuria, 9C3

wrongful interference with goods, 10F